A
Historical Approach
to
Evangelical Worship

A

Historical Approach

TO

Evangelical Worship

Ilion T. Jones

ABINGDON PRESS
New York • Nashville

To MY WIFE

Who enthusiastically shares the evangelical beliefs herein expressed, whose life has been a radiant exemplification of those beliefs, and whose assistance in the preparation of the manuscript has been of inestimable value

FOREWORD

THE liturgical movement is one of the significant movements of our times. It is affecting all the major communions. It not only is creating a revival of interest in worship but is bringing about changes in church architecture, in the arrangement of sanctuaries, in the use of symbols, in the attire of ministers, and in the elements of the order of worship. It is thus beginning to modify both the conceptions and the practices that have hitherto characterized evangelical Protestantism. Conceivably, in time it could change the course and even alter the nature of that Protestantism.

Unfortunately there has not been on the part of a sufficient number of ministers and laymen enough discriminating thought about the long-range results of the movement. Instead there has been a hasty, almost blind acceptance of the current trends as the things that ought to be done because everybody else is doing them. The time has come for a thorough study to be made to determine what ought to be done about worship and why it ought to be done in the light of the basic principles of evangelical Christianity and of the direction we want that Christianity to go in the next few centuries. I hope this book will make a contribution toward these ends and will provoke thought in the same directions on the part of others. It undertakes to discover the nature of evangelical worship in the light of its history, to lay down a broad basis for formulating a doctrine of worship in harmony with that nature, and to implement the doctrine in respect to the various elements that go to make up a suitable cultus.

Throughout the book the words "Protestant" and "evangelical" are used interchangeably to denote all those non–Roman Catholics who regard themselves as the representatives and the custodians of the spiritual *Christianity of the New Testament.*

ILION T. JONES

CONTENTS

Part I

The Historical
Background of Evangelical Worship

1

Old Testament Background

IT should be emphasized from the outset that evangelical worship has its roots far back in the Old Testament days when men first began to think critically about the nature of God and of God's purpose for humanity. In fact it is found, in principle and in germ, wherever men maintain a spiritual instead of a formal approach to God.

Paul said: "The law was our schoolmaster to bring us unto Christ" (Gal. 3:24). It may be said with equal truth that the whole Old Testament is a schoolmaster to bring us to New Testament worship. For that worship cannot be understood properly except as it is thought of as emerging at the forward end of the complex religious experiences of the Hebrews lasting for some fifteen centuries more or less. In the Old Testament both the spiritual and the formal approaches to God are found and will be referred to throughout this book respectively as the "prophetic" and the "priestly" elements of the Hebrew religion.

By "priestly" is meant the approach to God through priests and the ceremonials, or rituals, and the "holy" places over which they were supposed to be the custodians. To the priests obedience to God meant primarily the meticulous conformity to traditional rites. To them "holiness" meant ritualistic perfection. Their chief concern was the outward and the external in worship. Their major energies were consumed in detailed rites, rules, and rubrics pertaining to the sacred places, the observance of holy days and seasons, the handling of holy objects, the variety of practices such as sacrifices, ablutions, anointings, investitures, the altar and its sacred vessels, the incense, the fires, and so on, which accompanied their conduct of worship. By "prophetic" is meant the individual, direct, per-

13

sonal approach to God. To the prophets obedience to God meant conformity to God's moral laws. To them "holiness" meant moral perfection, or righteous living. They were concerned primarily with inward or spiritual matters. Their major energies were devoted to aspects of worship which are designed to appeal to the moral judgment and move the will of the worshipers and lead to ethical living.

To say that both elements are "found" in the Old Testament does not describe the situation adequately. They existed together almost from the beginning, not merely in the sense of being side by side, but also in the sense of being intertwined, so that it is often difficult to unravel them. I shall now proceed to trace the two types through the Old Testament, hoping the reader will recognize the difficulties involved in the effort to do justice to the one type while the other is under consideration.

A. THE PRE-MOSAIC AGE

One of the problems of Old Testament study emerges at this point. Owing to the nature of Old Testament documents, it is difficult to ferret out the exact facts about any particular period. These documents were compiled and edited many years—even centuries—later than some of the events they record, and often for purposes other than the mere listing of facts chronologically. The several strands of data of different dates are woven together in the same document without any indication that the process of weaving is going on. This makes it difficult, if not almost impossible, to determine the exact worship procedures of any period as compared to those of preceding and succeeding periods. The scant information we have about the pre-Mosaic period is found in the book of Genesis, which in its present form appeared during the Babylonian exile as a part of the Pentateuch compiled at that time by the priestly scholars. But by a study of Semitic worship in general and by comparing this with the records in the book of Genesis, the scholars believe they can arrive at a fairly true indication of the nature of the worship of the Israelites in this age.

It seems clear that both the prophetic and the priestly elements are found in this period. The prophetic element appears in the direct, personal approach of the individual patriarchs to God. God *appeared* to them, *spoke* to them, *revealed* to them his purposes, gave them insights into his character. The priestly element appears in the worship

14

practices, in so far as they can be ascertained approximately. The earliest group worship may have been family or tribal in nature, the heads of households or the tribal chiefs acting in the capacity of priests. The records indicate that quite early worship took place at certain spots made sacred by some unusual experience with God (by scholars called a "theophany"), the spots being marked by some natural object such as a stone or a tree or a fountain. It has been observed that in the book of Genesis, Abraham's acts of worship are represented as being usually connected with trees, those of Isaac and Ishmael with wells or fountains, and those of Jacob with stones. These places became the sanctuaries or traditional "holy" places of worship.

R. L. Ottley gives a description of what he believes to have been the prevailing mode of worship in these times, stating frankly that his conclusions were arrived at from a study of Semitic religion and from the developed practices of the Hebrews in later times. He is convinced that sacrifices were first presented in the form of food or vegetables and later in the form of animal sacrifices, and in some instances of human sacrifices offered by fire. As to sacred seasons he says it is "not improbable that the later *Passover* represented an ancient solar or astronomical feast, connected with the sacrifice of the firstlings of the flock or herd," that the feast of the *New Moon* and the *Sabbath* were probably features of the ancient religion, and that the occasion of *Sheep-shearing* was celebrated as a festival. As to sacred customs he says:

There can be little doubt that the chief sacred customs of later times already existed in germinal form in the prehistoric age, for example, abstinence from blood, and repugnance to the use of certain animals for food. . . . The practice of circumcision was certainly common among the Semites but not until postexilic times did it become an indispensable requirement for every son of Israel.[1]

It would appear, therefore, that some of the basic principles and practices of both the prophetic and priestly religion of the Old Testament were present from the start, though in elementary form.

B. The Mosaic Age

The records for this period are found in the books of Exodus, Leviticus, Numbers, and Deuteronomy, which, together with Genesis, constitute

[1] *The Religion of Israel*, pp. 15-22.

the Pentateuch compiled during the exile. As indicated above, the nature of these documents makes it difficult to decide what were the actual events of Moses' day and what must be attributed to the later compilers who ascribed to him the institutions and ordinances which reached their advanced form in later generations. In the records as they now stand God is represented as revealing to Moses both a cultus and a moral law. Moses is presented as a priest. It is possible, though not certain, that a regular priesthood of some description was instituted by him and made responsible for the worship procedures. The worship centered in the primitive sanctuary called the "Tabernacle" or the "Tent of Meeting." This housed the ark and was the scene of sacrifices in some form. But the scholars feel sure the elaborate priestly practices and procedures found in the records cannot be attributed to Moses.

The postexilic priests who compiled the Pentateuch specifically represented their work to be, not a new code of laws, but a carefully codified account of ancient practices and customs connected with the worship of Yahweh. It is, therefore, supposed that some of the institutions and ceremonies there recorded existed in germinal form in the days of Moses. Specifically what institutions and ceremonies, however, it is not possible to say with certainty. As we read in these ancient books the many details concerning the Tabernacle and its furniture, the priests and their apparel and other paraphernalia, the anointing and the incense, the sacrifices and the offerings, ceremonial cleanness and uncleanness, and the religious festivals of a variety of kinds, we must think of these practices as having existed only in some simple and primitive, or in an incipient, form in the days of Moses. Certain passages (for example, Exod. 33:7 ff.) seem to indicate that the sanctuary was not only a place of worship but the seat of justice and the place for instruction in the "law." If this was true, the priests undoubtedly assisted Moses in such matters. In which case at this early date the two functions of teaching the law and leading in the ceremonial worship were combined in one office. But there is no indication that the teaching was an integral part of the worship.

But the main emphasis in the record is upon the work of Moses as lawgiver and prophet. To him alone was assigned the role of prophet, or man of God, chosen by the Spirit of God to be the "organ of the divine purpose," the revealer of the character, purpose, and requirements of God. In Deuteronomy it is said: "There hath not arisen a prophet since in Israel like unto Moses, whom Jehovah knew face to face" (34:10 A.S.V.). The later prophets regarded him as the first of the prophets and themselves as being responsible for carrying on his prophetic functions and practices. He presented God to the Israelites under the new name "Yahweh" (Jehovah), as one who had adopted them as his chosen people, purchased them to himself by delivering them from the bondage of Egypt, led them through the vicissitudes of the wilderness, manifesting himself the while as the God of righteousness, compassion, and grace to whom they were obligated to give loyal and moral obedience. The Ten Commandments, in the form of ten simple statements easy to be remembered, certainly came from Moses and from the outset were the very foundation of the life of Israel.

The "Book of the Covenant" (Exod. 20:22–23:33) is likewise believed to contain at least a nucleus of moral laws enacted by Moses. In addition to the fundamental principles of group living found in the Ten Commandments there were laws to protect the poor and slaves; laws requiring compensation for damages done to beasts or by beasts, or to property and to people; laws requiring restitution for the loss of or injury to property of others entrusted to one's care; laws against afflicting widows and orphans and against wresting justice; and even laws to protect the land by permitting it to lie fallow at regular intervals. Here are found the rudiments of social justice and humane dealings characteristic of all future law codes. Moses thus enunciated, at least in some elemental way, the ethical principles and revealed in some primitive manner the conception of God as a moral being which became the foundation upon which the later prophets carried on the development of the religion of Israel.

Thus both priestly and prophetic religion was incorporated officially and institutionally into the stream of Hebrew religious thought in the period that was regarded as its fountain source. But the manner in which these two phases of their religion were to function in conjunction with each other had yet to be wrought out under the guidance of the Spirit of God through their maturing historical processes.

C. From Moses to the Eighth-Century Prophets

When the tribes of Israel undertook the conquest of Canaan, they found there a worship of nature deities known as "Baalim." This worship was rather quickly absorbed into their worship of Jehovah. They took over the local sanctuaries known as "high places," identified their

17

God with the local "Baal," and transferred to the worship of their God the rituals, ceremonies, and practices of the popular shrines. Solomon erected the Temple in Jerusalem not so much for a national sanctuary as to provide a regular and stately "high place" for his own purposes. To satisfy his heathen wives, he tolerated the erection in Jerusalem of shrines of foreign deities. Later a new type of "Baal" worship appeared in the northern kingdom in the form of the Tyrian "Baal" imported through Jezebel, the daughter of the King of Tyre, who became King Ahab's wife. The state of worship became more and more corrupt as the years went by. God was worshiped under the form of a metal bull. The Israelites borrowed other emblems from the heathenism about them, which they used beside the altar. Sacred prostitutes were in attendance at the sanctuaries. The practice of magic, necromancy, and other superstitious rites became common. The priests, the common people, the political leaders, and many of the prophets themselves, labeled "false prophets" by the few sincere prophets, continued to think of Jehovah as a Semitic deity who was "jealous" for the exactness of the worship ritual and the amount and number of the sacrifices offered.

The earliest group to attack this situation were the judges, who were not only the deliverers of their people politically but champions of Israel's religion which traced its origin back to Moses. Endued with the Spirit of God they came forth again and again to fight their enemies without and the pagan religion within. Later Samuel, according to tradition, not only appealed to the people to give up their strange gods and censured the rulers for their misdeeds, but organized the prophets into a school known as the "sons of the prophets." This school undertook to train men in the prophetic gifts, to give systematic instruction in the Mosaic religion, and to fan the flame of patriotism. In the early days these prophets exercised the functions of priests, but later they became a recognized order, along with the priests, in the religious life of the nation.

They undertook to root out the false notions of Jehovah and to call the people to national repentance and to a renewal of their allegiance to the moral precepts of the original Israelitist covenant with their God. It is believed that the earliest literary efforts of Israel originated in these schools. Biblical scholars agree that in all probability the two "connected versions of Israel's past history," labeled by them "Jehovistic" (J) and "Elohistic" (E), may in their original form be traced to these schools.

These documents are usually dated sometime during the ninth and eighth centuries B.C. By the time of the eighth-century prophets, therefore, there existed a considerable amount of literary materials, which were being used by the prophets to "construct an authoritative national history."

In this period we see exhibited quite forcefully one of the distinctive characteristics of the prophets: their direct, individual approach to God. Apparently they approached God each for himself, wholly apart from the Temple, and without intermediaries of any sort. Out of their "mystical" communion with God, involving not only the emotions but the mind and the conscience and the moral judgment, they came forth to proclaim that God had spoken to them and revealed to them his nature and his purposes. So we hear them saying to the people over and over, "The Word of Jehovah came unto me saying . . ." and, "Thus saith Jehovah." God spoke to them in solitude apart from the sanctuary. Moses communed "face to face" with God and emerged with the law of God. His successors came forth from a similar communion to rebuke the unrighteousness even of the kings themselves. Samuel reproved the willfulness of Saul. Nathan rebuked the foul deed of David. Elijah took Ahab to task for "stealing" Naboth's vineyard. Ahijah denounced the sins of Jeroboam. Amos, who was not a member of the school of prophets, brooding over the ills of his people as he herded his sheep, claimed the right, as the result of his call from God, to champion Israel's ancient faith and to judge the conduct of priests, kings, businessmen, and common folk alike.

The work of these prophets was most vividly and forcefully manifested in the great prophets of the eighth century B.C. In these days zeal for ritualistic worship was high. Sacrifices were offered in mounting numbers and with regularity. But pagan practices accompanied these acts of worship. And what was still worse, the moral laws of God were forgotten or ignored by the priests, who were supposed to teach them to the people. The religious festivals attracted throngs of worshipers, but in society without there were brutish luxury in one group and extreme poverty in another, avarice, dishonest traders, harsh creditors, venal judges, shameless sensuality, and other sorts of iniquity carried on, at times under the very cloak of religion. Into this situation stepped Amos and Hosea to speak to the northern kingdom and Isaiah and Micah to speak to the southern kingdom in the name of God. They regarded themselves as the spiritual successors of Moses and hurled their invectives against what to them was a perversion of their ancient religion.

They rebuked the people chiefly for what Hosea called a lack of "knowledge of God in the land" (4:1). Isaiah represented God as saying, "Israel doth not know, my people doth not consider" (1:3). That is, the people simply were not thinking straight about the nature of God and of God's requirements. They undertook to correct this situation. They found their key to the understanding of God in the moral law of Moses which, by some means not indicated, had been bred into their souls. God came to them meaningfully in their ethical passions and desires, in their deepest humane and humanitarian impulses. To them God was essentially a moral personality like themselves. They opposed all material representations of God, all images and emblems of all kinds, because, as Isaiah said, these representations were "idols" (19:1, 3), which in the original Hebrew means literally "nothings." Since these idols were not living personalities, like real men, they could not be labeled deities.

So the prophets insisted that this moral Being, this God of righteousness, expects righteousness and is pleased only with righteousness—yea, is actually displeased with all acts of worship which are mere formalities unrelated to ethical living. Such acts, they said, constituted sins of the most grievous nature. Isaiah told them God was weary with their numerous sacrifices and offerings, that their oblations were nothing but vanity, that their weekly assemblies were iniquities before God. He said God "hated" their appointed feasts and was completely indifferent to their pious prayers. He called them back to the moral law and pleaded with them to cease their evil ways and to practice simple justice (1:10-17). Amos severely reproved their formal worship practices and exhorted them to "let judgment roll down as waters, and righteousness as a mighty stream" (5:24). Micah reached one of the high-water marks of spiritual religion when he said God did not want them to come before him with material sacrifices, however numerous, but rather required them "to do justly, and to love mercy, and to walk humbly with [their] God" (6:8).

Hosea's language was somewhat more restrained, but his judgments were equally incisive. He represented God as saying, "I desire goodness, and not sacrifice; and the knowledge of God more than burnt offerings" (6:6). He laid the blame specifically upon the priests for neglecting the teaching of the law and threatened them with the loss of their priesthood (4:6). And he was the first to hint at a purely prayer worship as distinct from a sacrifice worship. He urged them to come before God with "words," to bring him the "fruit of [their] lips" (14:2 R.S.V.), implying that God prefers the offering of prayers to the offering of material sacrifices.

This prophetic movement was one of the most significant spiritual movements in the history of mankind, but its immediate results were scant indeed. The prophets were unable to bring about the reformation they hoped for. Let us pause a moment to inquire why this was so. Their failure may be attributed in part to the moral and spiritual corruption of the times, in large part even to the corruption of the priests and the false prophets. It may also be attributed partly to the difficulty of educating any large number of people to any large degree in high, spiritual religion for any great length of time. But it must be attributed in some—perhaps in large—measure to the fact that the prophets failed to bring about the constructive step necessary to insure larger results from their labors. From our long perspective we can see that in order to succeed, ethical religion needed to be incorporated in a type of worship which would provide a suitable medium for its cultivation and transmission.

It has long been debated whether the prophets attacked the abuses of the sacrificial system only and not the system itself. Those who believe the former, claim that the prophets thought of the Temple ceremonies and the moral law as complementary, not as essentially opposed to each other. But that is regarded by others as a superficial evaluation of the prophetic movement which fails to take account sufficiently of God's unfolding revelation through the history of the Hebrews. It is difficult to resist the impression that the prophets were raising grave questions concerning the desirability and necessity of the sacrificial cult, that they were engaged in the preliminary stages of a divine reappraisal of the function both of the cultus in their religion and of sacrifice in the cultus.

The popular belief was that God was pleased with ceremonies. The prophets insisted, on the contrary, that God himself regarded ceremonies as unimportant in comparison with morality. They definitely subordinated the cultus to morality as a means of pleasing God. In their minds the two were not co-ordinate in rank. Yet they did not follow their own teachings through to logical conclusions. Why? Because as yet, under the tutelage of God, they were not prepared to do so. All they did, apparently, was to preach in the hope this would provoke a reformed priest-

21

hood to supplement the cultus with proper instruction in the law. It was left to others in future generations to take the radical step needed when God had fully prepared them for it. The net results were that the old worship practices continued unchanged and the moral law was largely neglected for another hundred years.

D. FROM THE EIGHTH-CENTURY PROPHETS TO THE EXILE

The Reformation under King Josiah. The next effort of any proportion to reform Hebrew religion took place under King Josiah in 621 B.C., at which time a serious effort was made to reform popular religion along the lines laid down by the prophets. In that year the book of the law, regarded by the scholars as being at least the essence of the present book of Deuteronomy, was found in the temple by Hilkiah the chief priest. This book clearly reflects the impact of the prophetic movement. In it sacrifice and ritual have been subordinated to the prophetic requirement of social righteousness. There are some eighty laws in the code. While these reflect the primitive cultus, many of them are advanced laws against idolatry and other forms of paganism. They also exhibit deep human sympathies and contain a noble appeal for humanitarianism and to righteous living. The latter are evidenced in the legislation concerning property and the rights and welfare of women and children, of domestic slaves and aliens, and even of animals, which are in advance of similar laws found in the Book of the Covenant (Exod. 22 ff.). The book teaches that God alone is to be worshiped without any material representations of him, that he is a moral being who governs the world on moral principles, that he demands of Israel a wholehearted love for him and requires that men should deal with one another righteously.

As a result of the discovery of this book a sincere reformation was undertaken under the leadership of King Josiah. The local sanctuaries and the objects connected with the worship of Baal were abolished. The worst of the pagan cults and the altars dedicated to the worship of foreign gods were destroyed. The prophets seemed to realize this time they would succeed only if the Temple priests and their worship rituals were enlisted in favor of the reforms. Some scholars believe that, in fact, the reformation was actually an alliance between the prophetic group and the Zadokite priesthood. At any rate, the idolatrous priests and the heathen emblems were removed from the Temple and the Zadokite priesthood was made official. The priests who had been officiating at the "rural" high places were brought to Jerusalem as assistants to the official priests. The Temple was made the central altar of the nation. There and there alone could animal sacrifices be offered and then only on the occasion of the three great annual feasts. At long last idolatry was practically abolished, and the ethical monotheism of the prophets was established as the official national faith. Also by taking the sacrifices away from the local communities and centering them in the national sanctuary they actually said that sacrifices were no longer an indispensable element in worship. This struck a telling blow at the whole institution of sacrifice, but the reformers either were not willing or in the providence of God were not prepared to abolish the system at one stroke.

As a partial compensation for the loss of the popular institution of sacrifice, they undertook to place the written law at the center of the people's interest. Regular study of and instruction in the law were enjoined upon all members of the community (Deut. 6:4-9). It was definitely expected that this study of the law together with prayer would substitute for the loss of animal sacrifices in the popular worship of the people. Yet no provision was made for a local institution, comparable to the high places, where this could take place. In fact the people were left without corporate local worship, which had hitherto taken the form of sacrifices offered by individuals or families at the shrines in their own neighborhoods or communities. This deficiency was made up in part later by the organization of synagogues. But at this time the reformers did not seem to realize this step was necessary if the prophetic teachings were to become incorporated in the common life of the people.

The final outcome was that the Temple cultus gained in importance, the rituals not only were not altered but were greatly elaborated, and the prophetic faith was still left without a worship procedure suitable to its nature. The hope of the reformers that their teaching would be followed was soon forgotten, and Deuteronomy soon came to be regarded not as a moral code but as a law book of worship. The failure of the movement is usually attributed to the overemphasis upon the law. In fact the legalistic movement which came to have such a prominent place in later Judaism is regarded by some as having originated at this time. So it is said that the effort failed because the leaders attempted a legal reformation instead of a moral one, because they hoped to produce better men by reforming an institution rather than by reforming the men. There is much to be said for this explanation. But again the question is raised as to whether

23

or not the failure is due in large part to the lack of a proper "body" through which the prophetic teachings could function in the life of the people, a proper worship vesture in which to clothe itself.

The Reformation Under Jeremiah. Jeremiah, whose public ministry began shortly before the finding of the Book of the Law, did not denounce the new code and the reformation undertaken under its influence. But apparently he came to feel that the newly kindled zeal of the priests was somewhat misdirected and that the people had not grasped the true nature of God's requirements. He seemed not to share the popular hopes for permanent results either from a mere written law code or from the elaboration of the Temple worship. Instead he looked forward to a spiritual religion apart from the Temple and the ark: "And it shall come to pass, when ye are multiplied and increased in the land, in those days, saith Jehovah, they shall say no more, The ark of the covenant of Jehovah; neither shall it come to mind; neither shall they remember it; neither shall they miss it; neither shall it be made any more." (Jere. 3:16.)

He also failed to share the prevailing effort to save the nation as a whole by reforming its institutions without at the same time having a regard for the regeneration of individuals. The burden of much of the prophetic message of Israel hitherto had been, "Produce social righteousness in order to save the state from ruin." The destiny of the nation is the recurring note in Deuteronomy (Cf. 4:37; 7:7-8; 9:5; 10:15). Indeed not a few scholars believe the idea of a national covenant, a covenant binding the nation to their God, entered the stream of Hebrew thought through Deuteronomy. Be that as it may, Jeremiah, as the state began to disintegrate before his eyes, was forced to think of what was to become of the individual, what responsibility the individual had in the total situation, what part he would play in the eventual recovery. It has been supposed that his concern at this point grew out of his own bitter experience of standing alone against the popular opinion. In his great agony of heart, with a deep sense of personal sin and of need of repentance, he found solace and strength in his own personal communion with God. This provoked him to inject the individual into the center of his nation's ills.

He undertook to get at the root of their troubles by emphasizing the responsibility of individuals and the necessity of changing their hearts. The former he set forth in this manner: "In those days they shall say no more, The fathers have eaten sour grapes, and the children's teeth are set

24

on edge. But every one shall die for his own iniquity; every man that eateth the sour grapes, his teeth shall be set on edge." (31:29-30.) This was followed immediately by his well-known doctrine of spiritual regeneration: "But this is the covenant that I will make with the house of Israel after those days, saith Jehovah: I will put my law in their inward parts, and in their heart will I write it; and I will be their God, and they shall be my people. And they shall teach no more every man his neighbor, and every man his brother, saying, Know Jehovah; for they shall all know me, from the least of them unto the greatest of them, saith Jehovah" (31:33-34). It should be observed that although Jeremiah had little faith in the Temple ceremonies as such, or in the promulgation of a written code, and although he saw the necessity of the regeneration of the hearts of individuals, he seems not to have made an effort—perhaps felt no need of making an effort—to devise any other method by which the change of heart could be achieved, other than the Temple cultus.

The Reformation Under Ezekiel. Ezekiel, whose labors took place during the exile, also tried to correct the weaknesses of the Deuteronomic reformation. He joined Jeremiah in teaching individual responsibility for sin. (Cf. 18:3-4.) He even went beyond Jeremiah in teaching that there must be a change of heart. That change, he said, must come about as the result of the workings of the Spirit of God. That divine experience and that alone would provide the resources necessary to walk in the ways of God. (Cf. 36:26-27.) In this doctrine that religion is an inward thing and that the Spirit of God may be given to every faithful soul, something traditionally regarded as reserved for the prophets only, prophetic religion approached its consummation. The spiritualization of religion was almost complete. Religion was at last carried to its center and source— God in the heart of man. It became an inner experience, within humble human souls.

Yet in spite of having attained this high position, Ezekiel did not dissociate himself as did Jeremiah from the legalistic tendencies nor to any degree from the priestly practices. This may have been due in part to the fact that he was himself in all probability a Temple priest of Zadokite descent, and in part to his confidence in the worship cultus. As he looked forward to a new Israel, he envisioned at its center a visible sanctuary in which worship would be organized under a restored Zadokite priesthood who would be accorded the highest place of honor. A whole section of his book (chapters 40–48) was given over to an elaborate program for

25

reconstructing Israel, a program which rested squarely upon the ancient priestly usages. In the ideal community he dreamed of, every detail of the social and religious life of the people was to be regulated by the ideas of "holiness" which had characterized the priestly teaching for centuries. He shared the popular belief that holiness was as much ritual as moral in nature.

He also shared the priestly teaching that God must be approached by means of carefully restricted ceremonial techniques, and, like the priests, regarded the cultus as the best way to prevent idolatry and to insure the continued favor of God upon the nation. Thus he combined in his thinking both the prophetic and the priestly elements of religion and seemed never to have felt any contradiction between the two. Certainly there is no indication that he questioned the inability of the priestly system to produce the fruits of the prophetic faith. Precisely how he expected it to do so, he never explained. Ezekiel was carried to Babylonia along with his people in 597 B.C. There he had a notable ministry as pastor to his people and as prophet. He certainly influenced and encouraged, and may have actually participated in, the literary activity that took place during the captivity. As will be observed later, Israel's community life was reconstructed after the exile along the general lines he laid down in his prophecies.

The Holiness Code. Incorporated in the present book of Leviticus is a section (chapters 17–26), known as the "Holiness Code" because of its recurring theme of holiness, and sharply distinguished from the rest of the priestly legislation of the book. This code is supposed to have been the first results of the labors of that group of scholars who collected, revised, and edited the sacred writings and traditions of the Hebrews while they were in exile. It is dated by some scholars shortly before and by others shortly after the beginning of the exile. Like the book of Deuteronomy it reflects the impact of the prophetic movement, and like that book it contains advanced legislation embodying the principles of social morality. There are, for example, laws concerning the gleanings (19:9-10) and concerning the year of Jubilee (25) designed to alleviate the condition of the poor, laws against dealing falsely (19:11), laws requiring that wages be paid hired servants at the end of each day, laws against abusing the deaf or putting stumbling blocks before the blind (19:13-14), laws against unrighteousness in judgment or respect for either the person of the poor or for the honor of the mighty (19:15), and laws enjoining the use of just balances, weights, and measures (19:35, 36).

Included in the code is the second commandment of the two quoted by Jesus as being those on which hang both the law and the prophets (Matt. 22:39), "Thou shalt love thy neighbor as thyself." This is in fact quoted twice, once in connection with the treatment of their own people and the other in connection with the treatment of sojourners or aliens (Lev. 19:17, 18, 33, 34). These laws are regarded as another high-water mark of Old Testament religion and ethics because they deal with the attitude and disposition of the heart, rather than with the mere outward deed. The code also contains laws concerning the cultus, its personnel, its furniture, its sacred feasts, and the like, indicating that the worship practices were to continue substantially as they had been in times past. Again there is no question raised as to the necessity of modifying the cultus in order better to achieve righteous living.

E. Post-Exilic Judaism

The Priestly Code. The second result of the labors of the exile scholars is known by biblical scholars as the "Priestly Code" (P). It was compiled sometime between the death of Ezekiel (ca. 572 B.C.) and the return of the exiles to Jerusalem under Nehemiah in 444 B.C. Sometime during the exile it was combined with the Deuteronomic Code. It is believed that the Pentateuch as we now have it was completed before Ezra's visit to Jerusalem in 458 B.C. and that most of the work of compiling and editing the present books of Joshua, Judges, Samuel, and Kings was completed not long afterward. Both Ezra and Nehemiah brought portions, or possibly all, of this code with them; and it became the basis of the restored Temple and of the New Israel that resulted. At this point in the history of the Hebrews the scholars date a new era. They no longer speak of the Hebrew religion but of "Judaism." During this period the Judaism dealt with by Jesus and the early Christians began to take final form. The thing happened here that happened in all previous reformations: the law, containing the prophetic traditions, was attached to the priestly cultus. And the priestly cultus was not only not reformed but greatly elaborated.

The New Israel was no longer a state. It became a religious community, a "holy" community, with the rebuilt Temple at its center. The rituals, in the elaborated form in which they are now found in

27

the Pentateuch, were practiced in the Temple. The maintenance of this sanctuary with its priests became the first and the principal duty of the community. For this purpose they were obligated to pay heavy taxes and dues and present abundant free-will offerings. As may be discovered by reading the latter part of the book of Exodus, the book of Leviticus, and the nonnarrative portions of Numbers, the largest part of the space in the Priestly Code was given to the "regulation of the cultus." In general there were two features to the code: a system of atonement for sin and a system of purification. The ancient idea of "holiness" as something outward and physical was still retained, and the holiness of the community culminated in the holiness of the priests, of whom the highest representative was the "High Priest." Circumcision was required of all males and was the "sign" of membership in the community. The priests became powerful and influential, partly because of their "hereditary privileges," and partly because of their "unique prerogatives."[1] One of their most important functions was to offer the daily sacrifice in behalf of the whole of Israel and of each individual therein. Since they alone had this right, as well as the privilege of performing many other "rites" of importance to every person and every family, their authority and prestige became high indeed. Incidentally they also acquired considerable wealth, which accumulated in the Temple in colossal amounts from the offerings and dues of the people.

When fully developed, the priesthood became a hierarchy with three grades: (1) Levites, or Temple servers; (2) the priests proper, who were descendants of Zadok, whose functions were almost exclusively ritual and ceremonial in nature, and who alone had the right of entry into the "Holy Place"; and (3) the "High" or "Great" Priest, who alone had the right to enter into the "Holy of Holies." Very quickly— probably shortly after the time of Ezra—the priesthood proper and the Levites who assisted them were divided into twenty-four courses who took their turn in the various forms of ministration in the Temple. As we shall see later, the ancient duty of teaching the "Torah," or law, so long that of the priests, was now transferred to the scribes and the schools they established, leaving the priests with the sole duty of carrying on the worship practices in the Temple. To be an acceptable member of the religious community, the individual had to approach

---

[1] R. L. Ottley, *The Religion of Israel*, p. 187.

God through the prescribed rituals of the Temple. That is, the individual's relation to God was not immediate and personal, but was a community or group relation mediated by the Temple ordinances.

Sacrificial worship—not by the people in their local communities as of old, but at the central altar as a national act—became now the culminating, almost the chief, function of Israel. To obey the Temple ordinances exactly and punctiliously became the outward symbol—for the great masses of the people the actual essence—of obedience to God's laws. Everything pertaining to the sacrifices and the victims to be used was set forth in the minutest detail: burnt offerings, peace offerings, trespass offerings, and the Day of Atonement where the whole sacrificial system came to its climax. Likewise there were minute details concerning the various rites of purification and the holy seasons and feasts. The whole scheme became one vast system of external, formal, ritualistic religion from which almost every vestige of the prophetic principles had been squeezed out; certainly in it prophetic religion had been radically subordinated. This was the reverse of what the eighth century prophets did. They subordinated ritual to morality.

Emphasis upon Personal Religion. The teachings of Jeremiah and of Ezekiel upon the importance of the individual and of his inner life, the separation of the people from their central place of worship during the Exile, and the lack of provision in the restored Israel for personal communion with God all undoubtedly played their part in an emphasis on personal devotion during and following the Exile. When the Jews were taken into captivity, not only was their central place of worship destroyed, but they were too far removed from it to worship according to the traditional methods. Indeed they may have been forbidden to worship in large groups, particularly during the early period of their captivity. Furthermore they were without the equipment long considered necessary to do so. Many of the captives began to feel that their religion itself had been destroyed, reasoning that if there is only one place and one way to worship God, as they had been taught, then their religion had come to an end, yea, their God himself had failed or yielded his jurisdiction to other gods. To counteract this discouraged, fatalistic attitude, there arose a body of literature of which the exilic psalms constitute a major portion. In this literature the individual worshiper addressed himself directly to God and found the spiritual resources for his daily life.

The Book of Psalms in its present form was undoubtedly compiled during and after the Exile. It is often called the "hymnbook of the second Temple." There can be no doubt that many of the psalms have to do with the national worship in Jerusalem—at least the longing for it (for example, Ps. 42). The contents of certain psalms would indicate that they were used expressly for public worship on special occasions or for the celebration of particular events. By their very form some of them give evidence, for example, of having been used for antiphonal singing, others of having been sung by the pilgrims as they journeyed toward Jerusalem for their festive celebrations. All the psalms are lyric poetry and were ultimately set to music. But the scholars are not agreed that the book was intended solely or primarily for use in the liturgy of the Temple.

Because a number of them were manifestly written by those who found a fresh channel of devotion in the study of the Law, it seems certain they were used in the synagogue worship (for example, Ps. 119). Rabbi Solomon B. Freehof in his study of the synagogue entitled *The Small Sanctuary*[2] says that one of the outstanding contributions of this institution to worship was the manner in which it utilized the psalms to provide a service of prayer and personal devotion for the people. It may be held with some assurance therefore that the psalms were compiled partly for use in public worship, either in the Temple or in the synagogue.

But the tone of numerous psalms is so personal as to make it certain they were intended for individual devotions. In psalm after psalm we find such an outpouring of the individual's soul to God in all sorts of moods and for a variety of moral and spiritual needs that they must be classified unmistakably as personal in nature. It is this aspect of the Book of Psalms that has made it the prayer book for individual worshipers over the centuries.

The importance of the psalms for the history of Protestant worship therefore cannot be exaggerated. They brought into the main stream of Hebrew thought and life the individual, personal element of religion which is characteristic of all mature, living religion. And since it seems certain that at least some of them were used in public worship, both in the Temple and in the synagogue, the book is responsible for bringing into corporate worship, which as we have seen had hitherto

[2] Pp. 33-34.

been so prevailingly formal and ritualistic, that note of individual communion with God which prepared the way for the New Testament doctrine of the priesthood of individual believers.

It should also be emphasized that the conceptions of God and of his moral nature in the psalms are clearly those held by the prophets. The psalmists had discovered that God is indeed the God of the individual soul, that he is everywhere present and available for his children, and that they may have spiritual fellowship with him anywhere wholly apart from a place of worship and its rituals (cf. Ps. 139, a magnificent utterance concerning the omnipresence of God). Many times in the psalms may also be found the prophetic teaching that God is pleased only with righteousness (cf. Pss. 15 and 84). They also reflect the prophetic teaching about sacrifices. For example, Ps. 51 says God is delighted not with material sacrifices but with the "sacrifice" of a humble and contrite heart. There is little need of a sacrificial system if men are privileged to present humble and repentant hearts to God directly and without intermediaries, and to know at once that they are forgiven, cleansed, and accepted. Further evidence of the prophetic nature of the later Old Testament writings may be found in Proverbs: "The sacrifice of the wicked is an abomination to Jehovah; but the prayer of the upright is his delight" (15:8. Cf. also 21:3, 27).

The Scribes and the Synagogue. The scribes as an official group emerged as a result of the developments of postexilic Judaism. Ezra seems to have had the honor of being the first to whom the title was applied. At least it was applied to him both in the book of Ezra and in the book of Nehemiah (Cf. Ezra 7:6; Neh. 8:1). Ezra was a priest, a member of the group that compiled the priestly documents (P) during the exile. In spite of the ritualistic interests characteristic of his class he had a passion to teach the law ("Torah"). It was said of him that he "had set his heart to seek the law of Jehovah, and to do it, and to teach in Israel statutes and ordinances" (Ezra 7:10). One of the purposes of Ezra and his associates was to organize Jewish life afresh around loyalty to the law once they were restored to their homeland. When the returned captives had rebuilt the walls of Jerusalem, Ezra read to them the book of the law. After it had been duly explained, they covenanted together to keep it, as more than once before in their history they had done. Thus the scribal movement was transplanted from Babylonia and began to take root in the Jewish homeland.

Originally the scribes were from among the priests and the Levites. But later pious laymen devoted their lives to the study of the law. In time they came to be a class, relatively independent, who were the official interpreters of the law. As the priests were considered the custodians of the Temple and its rituals, the scribes considered themselves the custodians of the law. The elaboration of the Temple worship after the exile absorbed all the energies, the interests, and the time of the priests, making inevitable a group of some sort to take over from them this responsibility for the law. Their expert "exegesis" of the law, designed to discover for the common folk the sense of the law and provide guidance for every separate situation in life, was handed down in the form of decisions, like court precedents. The number of these decisions, which in time came to be enormous, became known as "traditions" or the "oral law." The "traditions" were regarded as supplemental to the written law and in the process of time acquired an authority of even greater importance than the written law. Thus in addition to being students, teachers, judges, and interpreters of the law the scribes became legislators. In time the "law" came to mean the written law, or "Torah," plus the "traditions." It is not necessary to go further into these details until we come to study the New Testament, since this study is not concerned primarily with this aspect of the scribal movement.

The significant thing for our study is that the scribes were responsible for the creation of the institution known as the synagogue. It was unknown previous to the Exile. Its origin is obscure, but it probably originated and developed in its early stages during the Babylonian exile, when the Jews were cut off from the Temple and its services and in part to compensate for that loss. It is doubtful whether the religion of the Hebrews could or would have survived the double shock of losing their fatherland and their organized national worship as a result of the Exile had it not been for the synagogue. In several ways the synagogue worship became a substitute for the Temple worship.

It is believed that other public gatherings similar to the one called by Ezra to hear the scriptures read and expounded were held occasionally and for the same purposes. In time these meetings became worship services and the places of meetings became known as synagogues. The heart of the worship was the reading and expounding of the scriptures. It became a part of the ritual of worship to take the scrolls out of the ark and return them thereto after they had been used. Then blessings and prayers for use before and after the use of the scriptures arose and later became a permanent part of the Jewish prayer book. It is supposed that here originated the custom of the people and the reader standing while the scriptures were read. (Cf. Neh. 8:4-6, where it is stated that when Ezra read the law, he "stood upon a pulpit of wood" and "when he opened [the book], all the people stood up.") This emphasis upon the scriptures in public worship made the animal sacrifices seem less and less necessary. This attitude was increased by the use of the psalms as a means of direct approach to God. Here according to Freehof for the "first time in human history the sacred books of a faith ceased to be secret books. Learning was no longer confined to the professional priestly élite. All the people were taught to listen, to understand, to discuss, and to reason." Thus emerged the "first evidence of democratic education in the story of man's mental growth." [3]

In a similar fashion "prayer" became a substitute for sacrifices. Members of the congregation qualified to do so were invited to lead the congregation in prayer, the invitation being given by the use of the phrase "come and offer" instead of "come and pray." The idea was that prayer in the form of praise, adoration, and thanksgiving was an offering, equivalent to the offering of material sacrifices. In fact a definite effort was made to develop in the synagogue a cultus to take the place of the Temple cultus. Regular hours of prayer (evening, morning, and noon) were arranged to take the place of the daily services in the Temple. Here according to Freehof emerged for the first time in history "prayer worship" as distinct from "sacrifice worship."

In effect the synagogue became the local church, conveniently located in each community, where people could worship God both personally and corporately, weekly and even daily if desired, without the necessity of long trips to the Temple and without the necessity of sacrifices. The Pharisees emphasized the importance of the synagogue and took it as their objective "to make Judaism the practice of every man until every home became a temple and every father a priest." Freehof says the Pharisees became the representatives of the rights of the people as over against the prerogatives of the hereditary priesthood and that they de-

---

[3] *The Small Sanctuary*, pp. 31-32.

liberately strengthened the synagogue "as a counterpoise to the Temple at Jerusalem." [4]

The result was that by the time of Jesus the synagogue had become a keen competitor with the Temple for the allegiance of the people. Its worship became the major religious activity of the community. The rabbis, as the interpreters of the law and the traditions, overshadowed the priests in popular esteem. The acts of worship in the synagogue were thought of as fulfilling a function similar to that of Temple sacrifices and at the same time as belonging to a higher order and as being of a more mature nature.

Here also laymen began to take an active part in the service for the first time, thus adding another democratic feature to worship. There were rulers of the synagogue, but they did not themselves conduct the service. Rather they designated those members of the congregation who were expected to do so. The members could be called upon to assist in the service in several ways, such as reading the scripture lessons, interpreting and translating[5] the same, leading in prayer, giving the address, and handling the scroll of the scriptures. While women were not considered members of the synagogue congregation, they were zealous attendants and were often permitted to take part in the reading of the Sabbath lesson in spite of the fact that it was considered inappropriate for women to read from the Torah in public. In time there developed an etiquette pertaining to everything connected with the worship, not unlike, at least in principle, the etiquette governing the Temple practices. But opportunities for spontaneity and freedom were provided in the selections of the scripture to be read, in the spontaneous prayers, in the sermon and in the questions about it which the congregation was permitted to raise.

It is not possible to overestimate the influence of the synagogue upon the future course of worship. Its importance for our study may be said to lie in two directions. (1) It furnished the prophetic religion the beginnings of what it had not had before, a type of worship befitting its basic beliefs. Its service blended the study and preaching of the word of God with those elements of prophetic religion having to do with direct, spontaneous, personal worship in contrast to the purely cere-

[4] *Ibid.*, p. 34.

[5] When the Hebrew language was no longer understood even in Palestine, it was the function of the interpreter to translate the lessons in the vernacular.

monial worship of the Temple. In short it was, as Freehof expressed it, "the world's first democratic, purely spiritual worship of God." [6] (2) It became the cradle of the Christian Church and the forebear of Protestantism. Until this day the services of a synagogue are similar in general outline to a Protestant preaching service.

At the time of the early Christian Church every Jewish community in Palestine and in the Roman world—and this meant hundreds—had its synagogue. There was a saying in the early centuries of the Christian era that a synagogue was one of the qualifications of a city in which a scribe may settle down. The synagogue service had attracted the Gentiles in considerable numbers, because they were dissatisfied with the contemporary paganism about them and at the same time attracted by the simplicity and purity of Judaism. These Gentiles, called "The Devout" or the "Godfearers," are mentioned several times in the book of Acts. Most of the early Christians were recruited from this group. Paul found synagogues everywhere he went on his journeys. The synagogue set the pattern in general for the worship of the new Christian communities, as we shall see later.

F. Conclusion

As we look back upon this study of the Old Testament worship and endeavor to view it as a whole, it is difficult to escape the impression that the prophetic tradition contains the true interpretation of the history of the Jews and that the records themselves intend to convey this impression. The inescapable feeling is that the prophetic teaching is the controlling and shaping force through it all, that the history is written to record the story of the unfolding revelation of the prophetic teaching in Israel. That teaching kept breaking into the process, as though God himself was trying patiently to say something to them about his nature and purposes that could be said only through the limitations of their experiences and thought processes. He met resistance, but kept trying to persuade them not only to grasp the meaning of the truths uttered by the prophets, but to create the institutions and devise the forms through which these could operate effectively for the redemption of the world.

Even when their institutions were rudimentary and their ideas crude,

[6] *Op. cit.*, p. 35.

childish, and pagan, beneath them all, imbedded in them, overshadowing and shaping them, were the spiritual ideas which gave them a meaning far beyond what appeared on the surface or was consciously being enacted at the moment. The prophetic faith was grasped and presented to each age afresh in ways the leaders themselves did not fully comprehend, while they kept pointing to a future time when those ideas would find their complete fulfillment. So the record from the beginning, and as a whole, finds its meaning in what ultimately emerged in the gospel of Christ and in the Christian Church, thus verifying the old principle that the "beginning finds true interpretation in the end."

2

New Testament Background: Jesus

BEFORE undertaking the specific study of what Jesus taught about worship, let us take brief notice of the fact that he emphasized and embodied in his gospel the teachings of the prophets and considered it his divine function to bring the work of the prophets to their completion. The intention of Jesus in the matter of worship, as in all other important phases of his gospel, can be rightly understood only as it is thought of as growing out of this larger purpose.

Jesus, like so many of the prophets before him, was a layman. He carried on a large portion of his public ministry in the open places, apart from either the synagogue or the Temple, the two established religious institutions of his day. He believed himself chosen, called, and set aside by God for his task. With authority direct from God he passed judgment upon the religious beliefs, practices, and institutions of the times. Like the prophets he taught that God is essentially a spiritual and moral being, whose character can best be described as righteousness, or moral perfection. This righteous God expects righteousness in the moral character of his children and in the moral quality of their dealings with one another. He said, "Ye therefore shall be perfect, as your heavenly Father is perfect" (Matt. 5:48). This statement concluded the section of the Sermon on the Mount in which he set forth a number of the moral qualities human beings should embody in order to fulfill the demands of God. Upon another occasion he said that the whole teaching of both the law and the prophets can be put into two

37

commandments: love God and love your neighbor as yourself (Matt. 22:37-40). Thus in his gospel religion and ethics merge.

He was essentially and primarily a preacher and teacher who endeavored to bring individuals face to face with God in their minds, moral judgments, and consciences. He did not seek their blind acceptance of the truth. He waited for his hearers to think things through for themselves, to respond to the truth with their own judgments, and to follow it of their own volition and inner compulsion. He never attempted to command or coerce their wills. He wanted them to attain what Ernest F. Scott once called "moral autonomy," or independence of outward compulsion. That is, he taught what has come to be called the "doctrine of the responsible person."

He drove straight for the hearts of men, calling people one by one to repentance (Mark 1:14-15); probing deeply into their motives, thoughts, and desires; and tracing both good and evil deeds to their roots in the inner man (cf. Matt. 7:16 ff. and Luke 6:45). He took the scribes and Pharisees to task for giving more attention to external matters than to the state of the heart (Matt. 23:25-28). His criticism of the law amounted in effect to saying that obedience to God's laws means little unless it grows out of right motives. Hence he emphasized the necessity of a regenerated will, a vital inner spiritual rebirth capable of generating power to live the moral life God expects. This is implied in the Sermon on the Mount (cf. Matt. 7:16 ff.) and is categorically stated in the third chapter of the Gospel of John.

Here again religion and ethics meet. Scott says the whole teaching of Jesus is grounded in what may be termed "ethical mysticism." [1] John Wick Bowman says the content of the prophetic word can best be described as "ethical theism." [2] That is to say, religion and ethics are inseparable. Religion is defective unless it produces righteous living, and sustained ethical living is impossible unless God is experienced ethically and vitally in the citadel of the soul. So Jesus shared the position of the prophets that the only way to produce righteousness is to change the quality of the human heart. This accounts for the fact that both the prophets and Jesus were evangelistic preachers whose primary method was to appeal through the spoken word directly to the seat of the moral judgments and actions of men.

[1] The Ethical Teaching of Jesus, p. 41.
[2] The Religion of Maturity, p. 75.

Jesus identified himself not only with the teachings of the prophets but with their purpose. He considered himself as bringing the work of the prophets to its divine fulfillment. Biblical scholars tell us that the prophetic teachings of the Old Testament reached their climax in the dream of the peoples of earth being transformed into a people of God who will obey his laws from their hearts, walk in his ways, and incorporate in their dealings with one another his principles of justice, kindness, and love. This dream reached its highest expression in the doctrine of the "remnant" as it was elaborated by the unnamed prophet whose message is found in the last chapters of the book of Isaiah. His message was directed solely to the small remnant who were to be God's "suffering servants" for the redemption of the world. They were called first to kindle new life in the hearts of their own people. Then after the regeneration of Israel had been accomplished, they were to take God's salvation to the ends of the earth.

This dream of a redeemed earth through the ministry of a redeemed group emerged in its final and full form in Jesus' teaching concerning the "kingdom of God." Jesus began his public ministry with the announcement, "The time is fulfilled, and the kingdom of God is at hand: repent ye, and believe in the gospel" (Mark 1:15). From one point of view his ministry may be thought of as an attempt to persuade his people to accept a revised conception of the kind of king that would come and the kind of kingdom that would be established. It is written indelibly in the original gospel records that Jesus represented himself to be God's Messiah. Not as a kingly creature before whom the world would bow in obedience, but as the "Son of Man," the "Suffering Servant" through whose vicarious death mankind would be redeemed. But it is also written indelibly in these same records that he told his followers they too would share his suffering. They were to become the "light of the world," the "salt of the earth," the "leaven" hidden in the world that would at last leaven the whole "lump." To these ends they were summoned to take up their crosses and follow him. Endued with power by the Spirit of God they were to become the Church ("ecclesia," literally "the called out"), the group through whom God's redemptive work would finally be completed.

As our study proceeds, we shall see how all this affects the nature of both the work and the worship of the church. It is within the framework of this larger prophetic setting that the purpose of Jesus with reference to worship must be sought. Let us now turn our attention in that direction.

A. Jesus' Attitude Toward Contemporary Worship Practices

In Jesus' day there were two prevailing types of worship, one represented by the synagogue, the other by the Temple. We shall study each of these in detail.

The Synagogue. Let us consider this under three headings: the scriptures, prayer, and spiritual worship.

The Scriptures. As we saw in the last chapter, the synagogue service was organized around the reading and exposition of the Law. By the time of Jesus the reading of the prophetic books of the Jewish scriptures was also included in the service. The central act of worship, the reading and explaining of the scriptures, was framed with singings, responses, and prayers. The scroll of the scriptures was kept in the ark, which was curtained off at the end of the room. In front of the ark were the seats for the leaders and the platform containing the reading desk. Much was made of the dramatic action of removing the scroll from its case, unwrapping the cloths from around it, bringing it to the reading desk, and returning it later to the ark. A number of selections would be read by several persons in the Hebrew, then translated into the vernacular, after which a sermon or exposition would be delivered, followed by questions from members of the congregation. Every procedure pertaining to this and other parts of the service was carefully prescribed and punctiliously followed.

There is abundant evidence in the Gospels that Jesus was greatly influenced by the synagogue. At the beginning of Jesus' public ministry Luke says, "And he came to Nazareth, where he had been brought up: and he entered, as his custom was, into the synagogue on the sabbath day" (4:16). Repeatedly it is stated that he not only attended services regularly in the synagogue but expounded the scriptures, taught, preached, and healed there. But he was not altogether pleased with what went on there, nor did what he said altogether please his hearers. He announced at the beginning of his ministry in the synagogue at Nazareth (Luke 4) that he came to fulfill their ancient prophetic scriptures. His hearers considered this blasphemy and proceeded to cast him out of the city and attempted unsuccessfully to kill him by throwing him over the brow of the hill.

By the time of Jesus the work of the scribes and Pharisees, which was closely associated with the synagogue, had degenerated into a system of casuistry in the handling of the scriptures, which was bitterly denounced by Jesus. Religion had become a legally correct walk before God instead of spontaneous communion with him and service for him. To all effects the Law was worshiped as another God. Prophetic religion was stifled, almost buried, beneath a mass of burdensome observances. Against this situation and those responsible for it Jesus uttered his most scathing words. His denunciations are recorded at some length in the twenty-third chapter of Matthew, where he chastises the leaders of the synagogue for doing works merely to be seen of men, for seeking chief places at the feasts and chief seats in the synagogue, for giving attention to the minutiae of the Law and being indifferent to its major principles, for their casuistry by which they tried to escape their moral obligations, for emphasizing external matters instead of the state of the heart, for persecuting the prophets and blocking the new truth revealed through them, for misleading the people, thus becoming stumbling blocks in their way, and for hindering the progress of the kingdom of God. He called them "hypocrites," "sons of hell," "fools and blind," "whited sepulchres," "serpents," and "offspring of vipers."

These castigations, together with his other public utterances, created violent opposition among the leaders of the synagogue and prompted their plot to kill him. Upon several occasions he warned his followers that they would face bitter opposition in the synagogues and would be scourged, persecuted, and mayhap killed by its leaders (cf. Matt. 10: 16 ff.; Mark 13:9 ff.; Luke 12:1 ff.). These leaders saw clearly from the very outset that if his gospel was accepted, it would mean the end of both the legalistic system of the scribes and the rabbinical system of conduct. In rejecting these systems Jesus was proclaiming afresh the prophetic teaching of the inwardness of religion, and restating anew the opposition of the prophets to the setting up of any barrier—even the barrier of the Law itself—between God and man. At the same time he was seeking the fulfillment of the purpose of the old law in the higher law of God written in the heart, a prophetic concept which had all but been smothered by the casuistry of the scribes and Pharisees and by their meticulous attention to external matters. He said, "Think not that I came to destroy the law or the prophets: I came not to destroy, but to fulfil. For verily I say unto you, Till heaven and earth pass away, one

41

jot or one tittle shall in no wise pass away from the law, till all things be accomplished." (Matt. 5:17-18.)

That is, he was not opposed to the law as such. He believed in its purposes, but was endeavoring to inaugurate a new era when those purposes would be achieved better by allegiance from within to the higher law of love. When Jeremiah's and Ezekiel's dream of a new order should come true—the time when men would obey God's law from the heart—the system of external laws would no longer be needed. This was exactly what Paul later taught in the thirteenth chapter of Romans. He said if a Christian loves his fellow men, he needs no formal laws; he will obey laws voluntarily and from an inner, instead of from an outer, compulsion. "Love therefore is the fulfilment of the law." (Rom. 13:10.) It can be said then that Jesus' teaching about the use of the scriptures in worship was thoroughly in harmony with the prophetic faith. It is to be quoted, its meaning explained, its truths preached and used to appeal to the moral judgments of the worshipers to stir their consciences, to change the quality of their motives and desires. These uses constitute a vital, not a mechanical, process. It is the spirit not the letter of the scriptures that gives them life. The fact that Jesus both preached and taught in the synagogues shows he approved of the instructional or didactic element in worship.

Prayer. In the time of Jesus the prayers used in the synagogue worship consisted of an invocation, a main prayer recited by the people under the leadership of the officiating member of the congregation, special "free" prayers suitable for the particular day offered by the leaders and interspersed between the parts of the main prayer, short prayers called "ascriptions," and the benediction. Most of the prayers had become fixed, as to both form and content, for liturgical purposes. They were recited from memory or handed down by word of mouth as an "oral tradition." They probably were not reduced to writing until the fourth or fifth century A.D. The rabbis had also developed a set of "rubrics," or directions, for every movement and attitude in prayer, which were meticulously followed. Thus both leaders and people repeated the same prayers and went through the same procedures over and over from Sabbath to Sabbath.

It was this practice Jesus dealt with in the Sermon on the Mount and which provoked him to say:

When ye pray, ye shall not be as the hypocrites: for they love to stand and pray in the synagogues and in the corners of the streets, that they may be seen of men. Verily I say unto you, They have received their reward. But thou, when thou prayest, enter into thine inner chamber, and having shut thy door, pray to thy Father who is in secret, and thy Father who seeth in secret shall recompense thee. And in praying use not vain repetitions, as the Gentiles do: for they think that they shall be heard for their much speaking. (Matt. 6:5-7.)

This does not mean necessarily that Jesus was opposed to public prayer or that, as sometimes has been asserted, the only type of worship he approved was private worship. He is, however, proclaiming a particular doctrine of prayer: that to be of any value, it must be spontaneous, personal, direct, free, sincere; that it should not be merely formal or the repetition of words; and that it may be offered anywhere at any time by the simple procedure of withdrawing into a "closet" of prayer—that is, by shutting out the world and turning inwardly to God.

It was in this connection that Jesus gave what has come to be called the Lord's Prayer (Matt. 6:9 ff.). First and last a great many people seem to think Jesus intended this prayer to be used for liturgical purposes. It was thus used of course sometime later by the Christian Church and is universally used as such in our own day. But it is quite certain this was not the original intention of Jesus in making the statements which we call his prayer. It cannot properly be called "a" prayer at all. At the moment he was talking about "secret" prayer in contrast to the prayers offered in the synagogues and other public places, and about simple, sincere prayers in contrast to the "vain repetitions" of the Gentiles, the latter almost certainly being a reference to the liturgical prayers used over and over again in their worship. After a general commendation of sincere prayer offered in secret he indicated what might wisely be the content of such a prayer. His introductory expression was, "After this manner therefore pray ye." "After this manner" means "like this" or "in some such fashion as this." Manifestly he was not offering the draft of a prayer for continuous repetition in public worship.

The comprehensiveness of his suggestions about prayer has often been noted. He lays down certain principles upon which true prayer is based, such as brevity and simplicity. He describes the spirit in which prayer should be offered, such as trust in and reverence for God and a willingness to forgive. He illustrates some of the types of prayer that might be offered, for example, adoration, intercession, petition, and confession. He lists some of the things for which it is proper to ask in prayer: the coming of the kingdom of God on earth, our daily needs, strength for meeting temptation and overcoming evil. To have censured the use of "vain repetitions" in prayer and then to have proceeded to give a prayer to be repeated in precisely the same way over and over to the end of time would have made him guilty of doing the very thing he was condemning. It needs to be said quiet frankly that it is very difficult to repeat this "prayer" in a formal worship service without doing violence to Christ's purposes in suggesting it. In fact, one wonders how seldom it is the utterance of a humble, sincere, earnest heart and how often it is another "vain repetition" which Jesus condemned. He referred to this conception of prayer again in a brief manner in the parable of the Pharisee and the publican (Luke 18:9-14), which teaches that prayer is acceptable to God only if it comes from a humble and contrite heart.

Spiritual worship. Under this heading we shall look at several other passages which reinforce what has already been made clear, that Jesus was interested primarily in "spiritual" not "formal" worship.

Jesus clearly set forth the doctrine of "spiritual" worship in his conversation with the woman from Samaria at the well of Sychar (cf. John 4:1 ff.). She said to him, "Our fathers worshipped in this mountain; and ye say, that in Jerusalem is the place where men ought to worship." To which Jesus replied, "Woman, believe me, the hour cometh, when neither in this mountain, nor in Jerusalem, shall ye worship the Father. . . . The hour cometh, and now is, when the true worshippers shall worship the Father in spirit and truth: for such doth the Father seek to be his worshippers. God is a spirit: and they that worship him must worship in spirit and truth." This is a straightforward assertion that there is no single, holy place where God is to be worshiped to the exclusion of all others, and no single method of worship that is acceptable to the exclusion of all others; but that to be acceptable worship needs only to be sincere, personal, from the heart. He emphasized within-the-soul, behind-the-scene religion when he said of almsgiving: "When . . . thou doest alms, sound not a trumpet before thee. . . . But . . . let not thy left hand know what thy right hand doeth; that thine alms may be in secret; and thy Father who seeth in secret shall recompense thee" (Matt. 6:2-4); and of fasting: "When ye fast, be not . . . of a sad countenance. . . . But . . . anoint thy head, and wash thy face; that thou be not seen of men to fast, but of thy Father who is in secret; and thy Father, who seeth in secret, shall recompense thee" (Matt. 6:16-18).

In another connection he said worship is real and acceptable only when it leads to righteous action: "Not every one that saith unto me, Lord, Lord, shall enter into the kingdom of heaven; but he that doeth the will of my Father who is in heaven" (Matt. 7:21). This says, what was almost axiomatic with the prophets of Israel, that God desires and is pleased with, not profuse adulation, or many words of praise and adoration, or much servile bowing, but lives that are in accordance with his righteous will. In still another connection he said, "If therefore thou art offering thy gift at the altar, and there rememberest that thy brother hath aught against thee, leave there thy gift before the altar, and go thy way, first be reconciled to thy brother, and then come and offer thy gift" (Matt. 5:23). This repeats the prophetic teaching that sacrifice is worthless and meaningless if there is unrepented sin in the heart, that the true sacrifice is a life that is on proper moral terms with one's fellow men. All these passages taken together point definitely to a particular type of worship, of the sort so often set forth by the prophets, and of the same general type of worship the synagogue was first organized to provide for the people.

The Temple. Let us consider under two headings: the sacrificial system and ritual.

The sacrificial system. Apparently Jesus visited the Temple as often as opportunity afforded. In the Synoptic Gospels only two visits of his to the Temple are mentioned, the first when he was twelve years of age, the second during his last visit to Jerusalem the week before his crucifixion. But the Gospel of John contains references to several other visits to the Temple, two of them seemingly for annual feasts (cf. John 2:13; 5:1; 6:4; 7:2; 10:22). Much of Jesus' most important teaching was given in the Temple, especially during the last week of his earthly ministry, as can be seen by checking Matt. 21-23; Mark 11-12; Luke 19-21. Luke says Jesus not only taught in the Temple but preached the "gospel" there (20:1). Every day during his last week he went early to the Temple, taught all day, and in the evening found lodging outside the city (cf. Luke 21:37-38; Matt. 21:17; Mark 11:11, 19).

It is to be remembered that the Temple was not comparable to the synagogue as a regular place of worship. It was the national sanctuary which the great masses of the Jews attended only upon occasions of annual festivals, or for some special purpose such as the making of an offering for the success of an important enterprise, or to secure the removal of ceremonial uncleanness, or to make a vow, or to consecrate themselves or some "thing" for sacred uses. Sacrifices were offered daily in the Temple, but only the Jews who lived in Jerusalem could attend those with any degree of regularity. In fact, it is presumed that the Jews who lived in Jerusalem went to their own synagogues for the regular weekly worship on the sabbath and to the Temple for special purposes only. According to one tradition there were in Jerusalem shortly before the destruction of the city by Titus 394 synagogues; according to another tradition there were 480. Some scholars of note maintain that there was a synagogue in the Temple itself.

The daily sacrifices in the Temple were for the most part attended by visitors who came to the Temple after the manner of pilgrims in our day to the Vatican at Rome for stated celebrations or for special purposes. The number of such visitors over the period of a year would be sufficient to keep the sacrificial system going. In connection with the Temple sacrifices the psalms were chanted and prescribed prayers were offered. But aside from these the service was entirely sacrificial in nature. That is, it consisted of the preparation of the victim and the symbolic use of the same. It is not certain precisely what an individual worshiper's responsibility was in connection with each service, whether he paid his proportionate share of the expense of the objects offered or whether by paying his Temple tax and making an occasional offering he was privileged to attend these services. Jesus paid his Temple tax (Matt. 17:24-27). He attended services in the Temple when he was in Jerusalem. But there is nothing in the record to indicate whether or not at any time he personally participated in any type of sacrificial offering for any purpose. Like all other Jews his visits to the Temple were upon festive or special occasions, while his regular weekly worship took place in the Synagogue.

It needs to be said at the outset that Jesus did not condemn the Temple and its practices, nor make a direct attack upon its system of worship, as such. At no time did he offer criticism of the Temple system comparable in intensity and bitterness to his scathing criticism of the scribes and Pharisees. His only criticism of the priests, as such, was the unfavorable light in which he put the priest and the Levite in the parable of the good Samaritan. In fact, upon first reading of the Gospels we might easily conclude that Jesus' attitude toward the priestly system was that of the more thoughtful and pious rabbis of his day: namely, he opposed the abuse or misuse of an otherwise necessary, acceptable, and legitimate system. After healing the lepers he urged them to obey the ceremonial laws concerning cleansing (Mark 1:44; Luke 17:14 ff.). When he condemned the scribes and Pharisees for tithing "mint and anise and cummin" and leaving undone the "weightier matters of the law, justice, and mercy, and faith," he added, "These ye ought to have done, and not to have left the other undone" (Matt. 23: 23 ff.).

Upon two occasions he referred to Hos. 6:6, "For I desire goodness, and not sacrifice; and the knowledge of God more than burnt-offerings" (cf. Matt. 9:13; 12:7). The key word in that quotation is the word "more." It could be that Jesus was here, as in other instances, dealing with the problem of relative values, not attacking a system, that he was censuring the practice of emphasizing one thing to the neglect of something else of equal, or of more, importance. But upon closer inspection it appears that he did contemplate the disappearance of the old system of sacrifices when the new order he came to inaugurate had been fully established. This becomes clear when certain incidents are studied in the larger setting of his prophetic concepts and intentions, or in the light of his total ministry or of the whole tenor and trend of his gospel.

Let us look first at the incident of the cleansing of the Temple (cf. Matt. 21:12-17; Mark 11:15-18; Luke 19:45-48; John 2:13-17). The practices he was condemning at the moment took place in the outer court where the "Gentiles," or peoples other than Jews, were supposed to worship. The buying and selling of the victims and of the other materials for the several offerings, the exchange of foreign money into Jewish money, the noise of the beasts to be offered, and the din of the men carrying the vessels through the court made quiet prayer by the Gentiles incongruous in the very place set aside for their use. The Temple had been diverted from its proper spiritual function to a purely secular trade. What was still worse, the secular trade had been turned into an unscrupulous mercenary traffic which in our terminology would be called a "graft" or "racket." Against both of these evils Christ protested. Mark says he would not allow so much as a vessel to be carried through the Temple, a detail peculiar to Mark's Gospel (Mark 11:16). Some insist his action should be interpreted not as a condemnation of the system but only as an objection to its abuse. For example, Percy Dearmer says that Jesus was driving out those who dishonored Temple worship with commercialism, not those who adorned it with ceremonial. Thus he was protecting Temple worship against "profane interruption" of the ceremonial there going on.[3] But let us look more closely at the incident.

Upon this occasion he said, "Is it not written, My house shall be called a house of prayer for all the nations? but ye have made it a den of robbers." (Mark 11:17.) Is there any significance to the use of the expression "a house of prayer"? Did he mean to say the Temple is supposed to be a "house of prayer" rather than a "house of sacrifices"? It is recorded that his conduct upon this and other occasions antagonized the priests to such an extent that they plotted to destroy him. It was charged at his trial that he had threatened to destroy the Temple (cf. Mark 14:58; 15:29; Matt. 26:61; John 2:19). This charge was not proved. It may have been, as was at the time stated, a trumped-up charge due to a misunderstanding of what he had really said. Mark reports Jesus predicted the destruction of the Temple (13:2), which is something quite different from threatening to destroy it.

But the point to be emphasized—and this is significant—is that the priests "sensed" that Jesus' teachings and actions prophesied the ultimate end of the priestly system, just as the scribes and Pharisees "sensed" that his teachings would lead to the destruction of their legalistic system. The priests continued for many years to act as though they believed this, as is evidenced by the fact that when Stephen was on trial before the council, the witnesses charged, "This man ceaseth not to speak words against this holy place, and the law: for we have heard him say, that this Jesus of Nazareth shall destroy this place, and shall change the customs which Moses delivered unto us" (Acts 6:13-14). Again it was stated this testimony was given by "false" witnesses. But it is difficult to resist the impression that this represented what the Temple authorities were thinking in their own minds: namely, that if accepted and put into practice, the gospel of Jesus would bring an end to the priestly system. In the courts the enemies of Jesus tried to lay their hands upon specific evidence on which to secure his conviction by charging he had threatened to destroy the physical building called the Temple. What he had done was to say enough to prove to them he foresaw the time

[3] *The Parson's Handbook,* p. 11.

in the new age ahead when there would be no need of the Temple system.

It is possible therefore that by his actions and words at the cleansing of the Temple, Jesus meant to imply that the system of sacrifices, with its necessary purchase of victims for offerings, the noise and turmoil incident thereto, the slaughtering itself with its nonaesthetic sights, sounds, and odors, and the use of the many vessels in the entire proceedings, was a hindrance, a grave hindrance to the genuine worship of God. His use of the expression "all nations" may also have special significance. The sacrificial system actually acted as a barrier to the universal religion dreamed of by the later prophets, because it was so alien to the religious concepts of many peoples. It appears therefore that Jesus may have intended to say the system was an obstacle in the way of realizing a universal religion.

Additional important evidence that Jesus contemplated the disappearance of the old system of sacrifices is found in his statement at the Last Supper, "This cup is the new covenant in my blood, even that which is poured out for you" (Luke 22:20; cf. Matt. 26:28 and Mark 14:24). This implies that his own death would establish a "new" type of covenant, spoken of by Jeremiah (31:31), to take the place of the old covenant, in which his sacrifice for sin would make unnecessary the Temple sacrifices. Additional support for this point of view is found in the parables of the new patch and of the new wine spoken by Jesus: "No man seweth a piece of undressed cloth on an old garment: else that which should fill it up taketh from it, the new from the old, and a worse rent is made. And no man putteth new wine into old wine-skins; else the wine will burst the skins, and the wine perisheth, and the skins: but they put new wine into fresh wine-skins." (Mark 2:21-22.) By these parables Jesus meant to say it would be necessary to create new forms in which to express the new gospel he was preaching. One of the new forms to be needed was a new type of worship. It was not necessary for Jesus to attack the old system as such because he expected it soon to be unnecessary because of his own sacrifice, and to die in the free atmosphere of spiritual worship soon to be established. His own gospel when embodied in another system would make the old system obsolete.

Ritual. In connection with the Temple sacrifices things were done according to a definite procedure which was carefully prescribed and followed in the same manner each time. This action in connection with the worship is sometimes variously referred to as ceremonial and ritual. Unless the action was carried out in precisely the manner prescribed, it supposedly lost its value or failed to achieve its purposes. For instance, in the case of the burnt offering the animals had to be male and without blemish. The ritual consisted of the action of the priest and the action of the worshiper, both of which were prescribed in detail. The instructions concerned items such as the manner of laying hands on the victim; the place where the slaughter took place; how the carcass should be flayed and cut up, and the several parts cleaned; how the priest should sprinkle the blood upon the altar, dispose of the pieces upon the wood on the altar, or dispose of unsuitable parts; and how to burn the offering. They also provided for differences between private offerings and group worship, between daily offerings and offerings on the Sabbath and on other holy days and seasons; and the rules differed in some respects according to whether the offering was in the form of animals, vegetables, drink, or incense, and according to whether the purpose was the expiation of sin, the purification from physical uncleanness, or the consecration of persons and things. Similar instructions, worked out to the minutest detail, governed the sin offering, the guilt offering, the peace offering, the meal offering, and so on.

The question I wish to try to answer here is whether there is anything in the gospel records to indicate what Jesus thought about these rituals in connection with worship. Actually there is little in the record that deals specifically with such matters. Presumably if the sacrificial system was to be superseded by another system, the rituals connected with it would also be discarded. The very fact that Jesus so bitterly opposed the scribal and rabbinical systems and apparently criticized the Temple system so mildly may be explained by the fact that he was more interested in the synagogue than in the Temple. The synagogue was more nearly like what he had in mind for his future church, and he expected it, when modified, to become an instrument in the hands of Providence for creating a higher form of worship. But he expected the Temple system as a whole to disappear. With much justification it can be said that opposition to repeating the same prayers over and over in the synagogue and opposition to repeating the same ceremonies over and over in the Temple are in the same category: if Jesus opposed the one, we may properly conclude that on the same principle he would oppose the other. However, there is practically nothing in the records that precisely reveals his mind on these matters.

The question raised about ceremonial washings comes nearer to revealing his mind than any other single incident. The scribes and Pharisees asked him specifically why his disciples did not observe the traditions concerning the ceremonial washing of hands, cups, pots, and so on, before eating (Mark 7:3 ff.). That question manifestly grew out of the fact, well known to his contemporaries, that Jesus and his disciples were indifferent to these matters. In answer to their question he replied, "There is nothing from without the man, that going into him can defile him; but the things which proceed out of the man are those that defile the man" (7:15). That constituted an open rejection of the priestly system of ceremonial holiness. The priests interpreted it as an attack upon that system. In reporting the words of Jesus upon this occasion Mark added, "This he said, making all meats clean" (7:19), which shows that his followers, at least, interpreted his words to mean the rejection of ceremonial holiness. After stating that what proceeds out of the man, not what goes into him, defiles, Jesus added, "For from within, out of the heart of men, evil thoughts proceed, fornications, thefts, murders, adulteries, covetings, wickednesses, deceit, lasciviousness, an evil eye, railing, pride, foolishness: all these evil things proceed from within, and defile the man." Here again he enunciated the prophetic teaching of the inwardness of religion and laid down the principle that ritual ordinances cannot affect the inner man, where the real issues of life are determined. That was a revolutionary word. Taken along with all else Jesus said and did, it spelled the doom of the system of ceremonial purification and in principle the doom of the Temple ceremonials.

To complete the picture, it should be added that the Temple ceremonials did not play a major role in the religious life of the Jews in the days of Jesus. By that time the synagogue had become the most important religious institution in their lives. The synagogue worship was relatively free from ceremonials as such, although the service of worship in it was carried on in an orderly fashion even as to such details as the posture in prayer and standing while the scriptures were read. One of the providential preparations for the emergence of the Christian movement and its acceptance by large numbers of Jews throughout the Roman Empire was the manner in which the Temple had lost

51

its significance in their lives and had been replaced by the synagogue. The Temple and Jerusalem were symbols of the hopes and dreams and most of all of the unity of the Jews, but the ceremonials as such played a minor role in the popular religion of the day. This may explain in part why Jesus said so little about them.

B. INSTITUTION OF BAPTISM AND THE LORD'S SUPPER

It is often asserted that Jesus instituted both baptism and the Lord's Supper to be used in Christian worship to take the place of the Temple ceremonials and to supplement the somewhat barren worship of the synagogue. Let us see to what extent that assertion can be made with certainty on the basis of the information available in the four Gospels.

Baptism. The gospel records leave us with many unanswered questions about baptism. Christian baptism was preceded by the ceremonial washings required by the Mosaic law, by proselyte baptism, and by the baptism of John. But what connection there was, if any, between the pre-Christian forms of baptism and Christian baptism cannot be ascertained from the four Gospels. The baptism of John was administered to Jews in preparation for the coming of the messianic kingdom. It was taught in those days that if all the people of Israel repented for one day, the Messiah would come. John's baptism was called the "baptism of repentance unto remission of sins" (Mark 1:4). It would seem therefore to have been a symbol of purification, and if it was not the actual initiation into the new Israel, it was an act of rededication to prepare the way for that community. Jesus submitted to John's baptism supposedly in order to identify himself with the hopes and aspirations of the people that were associated with the ministry of John.

The Gospel of John states that though Jesus did not baptize, his disciples did (John 4:2). No other details are given that throw light upon the precise nature of that baptism or that indicate Jesus' attitude toward it. From the time of his own baptism until his death Jesus did not mention water baptism. Matthew's account of the final words of Jesus after his resurrection is the only one that says he commanded his followers to baptize (cf. Matt. 28:19 with Luke 24:45 ff.; John 20:19-29; Acts 1:6 ff.). Although some question the textual validity of this verse, I myself do not feel that this is justified. Even so, it is not possible solely on the basis of that one statement to determine precisely what part water baptism played in the thinking of Jesus. It does seem clear, however, that baptism took place out in the open and was not a rite performed in connection with public worship.

In the Gospels are found a number of passages concerning the baptism of the Holy Spirit. The Holy Spirit descended upon Jesus at his baptism. John stated that he himself baptized in water but that Jesus would baptize in the Holy Spirit (cf. Matt. 3:11; Mark 1:8; Luke 3:16; John 1:33-34). The accounts of the final words of Jesus to his disciples in Luke, John, and Acts all contain reference to the coming of the Holy Spirit. It has even been argued with some force that Christ's reference to baptism in Matt. 28:19 was not to water baptism but to the baptism of the Holy Spirit. Be that as it may, the Gospels do impress us with the fact that the baptism of the Spirit was of some importance to Jesus. What Jesus said in his teaching about inner attitudes, changing the quality of the hearts of men, the need of inner cleansing and the new birth—all of which are familiar ideas in prophetic religion—is intimately associated with the same idea of the coming of the Spirit.

The Lord's Supper.[4] Before undertaking to discover what Christ meant by his statements at the Supper, we need to identify the meal as to type. The studies of New Testament scholars upon this subject necessitate a somewhat radical revision of the traditional conception of its nature and give a possible clue to its proper understanding.

To begin with, the Synoptic Gospels and John's Gospel seem to contradict each other as to whether Jesus himself ate the Passover (cf. Mark 14:12 and John 18:28). Mark says Jesus and his disciples ate the Passover together, but John says that after the supper had ended and Jesus was on trial in the *Praetorium*, his followers did not go in "that they might not be defiled, but might eat the passover." This means that the Passover had not yet been observed. Thus John indicates that the Passover was held twenty-four hours after the Last Supper which he had been describing since chapter 13. If the supper was the Passover, as the Synoptic Gospels indicate, a number of facts in the record are difficult to reconcile with Jewish laws and customs. The Passover celebration began at sundown on one day and ended with sundown on the next. If the supper was the Passover, it was in process during the trial and execution of Jesus. Yet the Jewish law strictly forbade a trial of a criminal during the Passover celebration. One of

[4] Scriptural references: Matt. 26:26 ff.; Mark 14:22 ff.; Luke 22:17 ff.; and I Cor. 11:23 ff.

the disciples of Jesus had a sword at the time he was arrested (Matt. 26:51), yet Jewish law forbade the possession of weapons at such a holy season. Again, Joseph bought a linen cloth in which to wrap the body of Jesus for burial, yet the stores or bazaars were expected to be closed during this observance. Still again, it was a custom for the Roman ruler, in order to please the Jews, annually to release a prisoner in the morning that he might eat the Passover the evening of the same day. But Pilate released Barabbas many hours after the Passover feast began.

Furthermore there are certain details about the Last Supper which point to its being of a different nature from the Passover. The Passover was strictly a family festival; the Last Supper was eaten by a group of male friends. At the Passover the paschal lamb and bitter herbs were eaten; neither of these was mentioned in the description of the Last Supper. Unleavened bread was invariably used in the Passover, but the New Testament narratives state that ordinary bread was used at the Supper. Several cups were usually passed at the Passover, but only one at the Supper (Luke speaks of two cups). At the Passover meal each person present used his own cup, whereas at the Supper one cup was partaken by all. The passage of scripture concerning the exodus from Egypt, invariably used at the Passover, was missing from the Supper. The Passover meal followed the blessing of the cup and bread, but at the Supper the meal preceded the blessing of the cup and bread.

For these reasons the scholars, generally speaking, now believe that John was right when he said the Supper was held some twenty-four hours before the actual Passover. This theory resolves most of the problems listed above, which are involved in considering it the Passover. In recent decades the scholars have discovered that there was a meal known as the "kiddush" which fits into the picture admirably. The best treatment of this whole problem is found in W. O. E. Oesterley, *The Jewish Background of the Christian Liturgy*, pages 155-93. He says it was customary for people of like interests to organize "chaburoth" (singular *chaburah*, from *chabar* meaning "friend"), or societies of friends. These were for both social and religious purposes. They met together in private homes, originally on Friday afternoons before the beginning of the Sabbath at sundown. Their meetings consisted of a meal, somewhat similar in procedure to an ordinary Jewish meal, but more formal in nature, presided over by the "president." The meal was accompanied by religious discussion. At the table thanks were given, and a benediction was said over the cup of wine before it was passed for what was called the "sanctification of the day."

These meals to begin with had no connection with either the Temple or the synagogue worship, but later were associated with the synagogue. By a process it is not necessary to describe here, the meal became known as the "kiddush," closely related to the earlier "Kedushshah," or "sanctification of the Sabbath." So the "meal" and the "sanctification ceremony," held weekly and continued until the Sabbath began at sundown, prepared for and actually ushered in the Sabbath. In time a similar meal was held in connection with other important festivals and for the same general purposes. In time also each important festival had its own special "kiddush." Incidentally a "kiddush" meal was usually partaken of exclusively by male friends. In his detailed study Oesterley shows that the many problems in the gospel records may best be explained if the Supper is regarded as a "Passover kiddush," not as the Passover celebration itself. His study of the references to the Supper in the early Christian documents of the postapostolic age also substantiates this conclusion.[5] W. D. Maxwell says, "It is almost certain that our Lord and his disciples were accustomed to partake of this meal of fellowship on the eve of every sabbath and festival; the Last Supper, therefore, was the last of these meals shared together." [6] With this statement nearly all New Testament scholars now agree.[7]

We may safely conclude then that the Last Supper was held the evening before the Passover and was a preparation for the same. Since it was the pre-Passover meal and therefore closely associated with it and a traditional preparation for it, it is easy to understand how it might have been called the Passover in the narratives. The Jewish reader, being quite familiar with the practice, would clearly understand what was meant. The reader is encouraged to re-examine the Gospels and see for himself how easily this interpretation fits the accounts there given. If this interpretation is correct, there seems to be some significance to the fact

[5] *The Jewish Background of the Christian Liturgy*, pp. 155-93.

[6] *An Outline of Christian Worship*, p. 5. Used by permission of Oxford University Press, London.

[7] Cf. Gregory Dix, *The Shape of the Liturgy*, pp. 49 ff., where another detailed study of the "Chaburah" may be found; and E. S. Freeman, *The Lord's Supper in Protestantism*, pp. 8 ff. For a defense of the traditional view that the Supper was the Passover, cf. A. Edersheim, *The Temple: Its Ministry and Services as They Were at the Time of Jesus Christ*, Appendix, pp. 389 ff.

that Jesus did not take for his purposes the Passover, which was connected closely with the priestly system, but the "kiddush," which had no official connection with that system and which may have developed as an adjunct to it, or to fill the purpose not provided for in that system. This is one more bit of evidence, added to other evidence already given, to show that Jesus identified himself with the prophetic, not with the priestly, tradition.

Now the question arises as to precisely what Jesus meant by what he said and did upon this occasion. There are disagreements, often of a violent nature, over the answers to that question. Disagreements at this point usually account for disagreements over what type of worship is most in conformity with Christ's gospel. This subject will of necessity come up for consideration again. Just now we want to do one thing only, namely, search in the records for evidence that throws light upon what Jesus himself was thinking about it.

It seems certain that Jesus intended the Supper to be repeated in his memory. If it was the last "kiddush," as described above, then primarily its repetition was intended to be a fellowship meal. It is possible Jesus associated this meal with the idea of a kingdom banquet, which he mentioned a number of times (for example Luke 22:29 ff.). If so, he may have meant to say that he was the host and the disciples the guests at a fellowship meal which was symbolic of the future fellowship he and his followers were to have together in the building of his kingdom. Whenever they met together in the future to re-enact this meal, it was to remind them of his continuing spiritual presence.

Considerable discussion has taken place over the years among the exegetes concerning the precise meaning of the expression "This do in remembrance of me," used by Jesus at the Supper (Luke 22:19; I Cor. 11:24-25). It is maintained that the Greek word translated "do" when used in classical Greek meant to "offer" or to "sacrifice." The Greek word translated "in remembrance" (anamnesis) likewise is said to have meant "for the recalling of" in the sense of presenting a "memorial" or "sacrifice" before God. Those who thus translate the words in the New Testament insist that from the beginning they carried a sacrificial meaning, so that each time the meal is repeated, it is to be thought of as a "representing" before God of the original sacrifice of Christ. I am convinced, after exploring the pertinent linguistic facts, that G. G. Findlay is correct when he says that despite the use of the words in classical Greek and in the Septuagint translation of the Old Testament to connote sacrifice, their sacrificial sense in the New Testament "is without lexical warrant." [8] I am also convinced that Jesus did not intend the meal to be thought of in any sense as a re-enactment of his own sacrifice.

There can be no doubt, however, that he meant the bread and wine in all future Suppers to remind his disciples of his vicarious sacrifice. He said, "This cup is the new covenant in my blood, even that which is poured out for you" (Luke 22:20). This implies that his death would inaugurate a new type of covenant to supersede the old covenant heading up in the Temple sacrifices. Repetition of the meal then was to be a commemoration of his sacrifice and a reminder that it instituted a new covenant.

At the time was he associating his coming death primarily with the priestly sacrifices or with the prophetic idea of the Suffering Servant? Was he at the moment thinking of himself as a priest or as a prophet? There are no other facts in the Gospels to indicate that he thought of himself as a priest at any time. All his actions and words hitherto pointed definitely to the fact that he considered himself sent of God to fulfill the prophetic concept of the Messiah who would come as the Suffering Servant of God. He undoubtedly realized that in so doing he would also fulfill the true meaning and purpose of the Temple sacrifices and make them unnecessary. But there is no evidence to show that at any other time he thought of himself as a priest or as performing priestly functions. So it can be said with a measure of confidence that Jesus was not acting in a priestly capacity at the meal, nor dealing with symbolic actions which, when repeated in his memory, would require an officiating priest after the pattern of the Old Testament priesthood. John Wick Bowman rightly says therefore that as Jesus presided at the table, it was not as a priest but as the "Incarnate Word itself," as the "final and greatest of the prophets." [9]

Nothing else was said or done at the time that throws further light upon Christ's intentions. He offered no instructions as to when and where, or in what setting, or by what procedures the Supper was supposed to be observed. He gave no hint as to how often it should be held or under whose direction. It was a private meal with his most intimate

---

[8] See his commentary on I Corinthians in *The Expositor's Greek Testament*, ed. W. R. Nicoll, II, 880.

[9] *Op. cit.*, p. 135.

disciples. There were no intimations at the time that it was to become an act of public worship.

However, it is taught in one form or another by most Protestant bodies that Jesus instituted the Supper to be observed in his church to the end of the world. When this general position is further elaborated, it is usually said it was both his intention and his injunction that it be used as a liturgical rite in all future Christian worship with precisely the same procedures he himself used. It is still further explained that this means the two elements of bread and wine are to be handled, blessed, offered, and eaten by the use of the same words and the same series of actions in the same sequence as Jesus himself used them. The proper observance of the meal under the direction of the properly authorized individual is by most Protestant communions defined as a sacrament and regarded as one of the essential marks of a true Christian church.

Decided differences of opinion are held by various scholars and Christian groups concerning whether in the sense described above the Supper can be regarded as "dominical," that is, as having been established by the Lord. As already shown, it is not possible on the basis of the evidence found in the Gospels to be sure what were Christ's exact intentions. When the Supper is regarded as a dominical sacrament in some such terms as those above, that position must be regarded as the interpretation of the Christian Church as it looks back upon Christ's words and actions in the light of subsequent developments. Some would say the church was led to this interpretation by the Holy Spirit through the unfolding experiences of the developing Christian fellowship. They would insist that Jesus did not intend to set up a purely spiritual worship in which no use whatever was to be made of material or sensible forms, but that knowing the needs of human beings living in material bodies in a material universe, he deliberately set up for his followers a worship rite that appeals to the senses of hearing, touch, sight, and taste.

Others would say that this interpretation is difficult to accept if the Supper is considered in the framework of Christ's entire ministry. In the light of his chastisements of the scribes and Pharisees for their semi-worship of the Law, of his references to liturgical prayers as "vain repetitions," of all he said about spiritual worship, and of his attitudes toward ceremonies in general, it is doubtful whether he was instituting a liturgical rite to be meticulously observed by his followers in all regular worship services to the end of time. To have established such a binding liturgical

58

rite would have been incongruous with the whole tenor and purpose of his ministry. That would have placed his rite in the same category with the other barriers to genuine worship which he so severely condemned. These matters will be taken up in detail again at several places in succeeding chapters. Attention is called to them here because this is the point where divergent opinions about Christian worship originate.

C. Summary and Conclusion

The most impressive and most important aspect of the record of Jesus' ministry is the manner in which he sets forth consistently and continuously the principles of the prophetic faith. On their basis he judges everything in the religion of his day. At every point, whatever the subject under discussion, those principles emerge. The effect of their constant emergence becomes cumulative, so that by the time the records have been examined as a whole, those principles are literally etched upon the reader's mind. It can hardly be doubted that a similar etching took place upon the minds of his hearers. The nature of Christian worship cannot be understood nor its form determined except on the basis of those basic principles.

It cannot be said that Jesus approved of either the synagogue worship or the Temple worship of his day. But it can be said with some justification that his prophetic gospel points to a type of worship more like that of the synagogue than that of the Temple. The relatively simple, personal, informal, didactic, spontaneous, prayer worship of the synagogue has more in common with his gospel than does the sacrificial and ritualistic worship of the Temple. Christ's apparent eagerness to reform the synagogue and by comparison his relative indifference to the Temple may be an index into his thinking about worship. He was expecting his followers to use the synagogue practices as a foundation upon which to create a worship more consistent with the gospel he set forth, while he was expecting the Temple practices to disappear.

The problem of determining precisely the form Christian worship should take resolves itself into a question of what kind of worship the Christian gospel requires for its expression, what elements of worship best befit the nature of the gospel. Christ left no blueprint of what the worship should become. His chief concern was to write his gospel indelibly upon the hearts of his disciples. Once that was done, he entrusted to the new Christian community the responsibility of shaping that wor-

59

ship to fit their needs and to keep the gospel alive. To have laid down rules to guide them would have been a betrayal of the fundamental principles of that worship. We turn now to discover what the early Christians did with the responsibility laid upon them. The fate of Christianity is inextricably bound up with the nature of its cultus. Was Christianity to fulfill Christ's own hopes and purposes, or was it, like other lesser prophetic reformations that preceded his, to fail because of the lack of a cultus suitable to its nature? We turn eagerly to the New Testament to begin our search for the answer to that question.

3

New Testament Background: The Church

IT has become customary to say that New Testament worship was a combination, a merging of three types: worship in the Temple, worship in the synagogue, and a semiprivate worship in homes and other places where Christians met as a distinctive group. Let us see to what extent the facts justify this statement.

A. TEMPLE WORSHIP

It is stated in the Gospel of Luke that after the ascension of Jesus his followers returned to Jerusalem "and were continually in the temple, blessing God" (24:53). In the book of Acts we read that after the experience on the day of Pentecost "day by day, continuing stedfastly with one accord in the temple, and breaking bread at home, they took their food with gladness and singleness of heart, praising God, and having favor with all the people" (Acts 2:46-47). Shortly thereafter it is said again, "Every day, in the temple and at home, they ceased not to teach and to preach Jesus as the Christ" (Acts 5:42; cf. v. 21). Peter and John "were going up into the temple at the hour of prayer" (Acts 3:1) when they were accosted by the lame man. The teaching referred to undoubtedly took place in the outer court or on the porch of the Temple and had nothing to do with worship, unless, as some scholars believe, there was a synagogue in the Temple itself, in which case the teaching could have taken place at the point in the synagogue service where the members of the congregation were permitted to participate.

The prayers offered in the Temple were undoubtedly private prayers, of the sort referred to by Jesus in the parable of the Pharisee and the publican. There is not sufficient evidence to determine whether these private prayers were offered by individuals while the daily sacrifices were being performed by the priests or whether they were entirely apart from the sacrificial system. In Acts 21 it is reported that Paul joined several others in a ceremony of purification which ended in a sacrificial offering (cf. Acts 21:26). Aside from this there is no reference in the New Testament concerning any other Christians offering sacrifices upon any occasion, daily or on the weekly Sabbath or during the annual feasts. But the records are quite clear that the New Testament Church quickly abandoned the entire priestly system. Evidence for this may be submitted under three headings.

Discarding of Temple Sacrifices. For centuries God had been slowly preparing the minds of his people for the discontinuance of the sacrificial system. Although it had been revealed by God in their religious childhood, was hallowed by antiquity, had satisfied many of their deepest needs, and had provided them with dramatic and visible means of approaching God, its hold on the people had been weakening generation by generation. The factors contributing to this process were: (1) the prophetic teaching that sacrifice was in itself of no value unless accompanied by sincerity of heart and evidence of genuine repentance; (2) the destruction of Jerusalem and the Temple, leaving the people for many decades without the opportunity for sacrifices; (3) the development of a type of prayer worship in the synagogue which met their needs without the necessity of sacrifices; (4) the conception of God and of his requirements of man set forth by the prophets, which had its counterpart in the teaching of the Stoics and the Platonic school, which raised the question whether animal sacrifices were acceptable to him; and (5) the manner in which the public slaughter of animals offended the aesthetic nature and refined feelings of both Jews and Gentiles and raised a question as to its appropriateness in worship. Thus by the time of Christ a number of advanced religious conceptions, emerging from their maturing religious development, were combining to make the sacrificial system unnecessary. Christianity concluded the process by completely discarding the system in the name of a higher, nobler, and more efficacious sacrifice in the death of Christ.

Paul had very little to say about animal sacrifices. He was brought up in the synagogue school, and his interests were primarily with the legalistic system of the scribes and the rabbinical system of conduct. But he uses the expression "new covenant" twice, once in connection with his description of the Last Supper where he says Christ called the cup the "new covenant in my blood" (I Cor. 11:25) and once when he described himself and others as "ministers of a new covenant" (II Cor. 3:6). And in his epistles he sets forth in detail a theory of the atonement in which the death of Jesus is regarded as a vicarious sacrifice in behalf of sinful men which broke the power of sin and created at least potentially a new humanity. Thus we may say that Paul's position is as follows: Christ's sacrifice accomplished in a more satisfactory manner and a more enduring form than the old sacrificial system the reconciliation of man with God and the expiation of sin. We are not concerned with Paul's theory of the atonement as such but only with the fact that his theory definitely makes unnecessary the priestly sacrificial system. For the details concerning his theory the reader is referred to his epistles, especially I Corinthians and Romans.

The author of the Epistle to the Hebrews discusses at length the Old Testament sacrifices, shows wherein they were ineffectual, and states that they were typical only of the real sacrifice which was offered in the death of Christ, and that therefore they were transitory in nature. He also deals at length with the nature of Christ's sacrifice, showing that it is superior to the animal sacrifices because it is a spiritual instead of a material offering, because Christ offered a "stainless soul and a perfected obedience," rather than mere blood, and because as the great High Priest he offered himself once and for all, thus fulfilling the intentions of all other sacrifices and making the repetition of his own sacrifice unnecessary. Again, it is no part of my purpose to go into the details of his argument, but only to show he taught that Christ's sacrifice fulfilled and therefore abrogated the Temple sacrifices. For the author's theory of atonement the reader is referred to the Epistle to the Hebrews, especially chapters 7–9. Although the emphasis in the writings of John is on the incarnation instead of the atonement of Jesus, there are many references in these writings to the sacrificial death of Christ. Jesus is called the "Lamb of God, that taketh away the sin of the world!" (John 1:29). Twice he is spoken of as the "propitiation for our sins" (I John 2:2; 4:10). Thus John sets forth a doctrine of the death of Christ that parallels that of Paul and of the writer of Hebrews.

There are a number of references showing that the New Testament writers conceived of other types of sacrifice which were more acceptable to God than animal sacrifices. Paul uses the expression "living sacrifice" (Rom. 12:1) and explains that he means using the body as an instrument of Christian service. Peter speaks of Christians as a "holy priesthood" who "offer up spiritual sacrifices, acceptable to God through Jesus Christ" (I Pet. 2:5). In Hebrews reference is made to prayer through Christ as the offering up of a "sacrifice of praise to God continually, that is, the fruit of lips which make confession to his name," and of good deeds as "sacrifices" with which God is well pleased (Heb. 13:15, 16). Paul refers to the offerings of money sent him by the Philippians through the hand of Epaphroditus as "an odor of a sweet smell, a sacrifice acceptable, well-pleasing to God" (Phil. 4:18). He also speaks of his service to the Philippians as offering (literally "pouring out as a drink-offering") himself upon the "sacrifice and service of your faith" (Phil. 2:17). He says Christians are privileged to "fill up . . . that which is lacking of the afflictions of Christ" (Col. 1:24), that they could experience the "fellowship of his sufferings" (Phil. 3:10), and that they could here "suffer with him," and later be "glorified with him" (Rom. 8:17). All these references emphasize the fact that God desires and accepts the services and the sufferings of his children as a "spiritual" or "living" sacrifice of a higher quality than the animal sacrifices. Throughout the New Testament the writers uniformly agree that Christ abolished the old sacrificial system.

Discarding of Priestly System of Ceremonial Laws. This was done in due time, but not without considerable struggle. Jesus' followers were familiar with all that Jesus himself had said to make these laws unnecessary. But apparently they had not faced this question squarely until the response of the Gentiles to their preaching made it necessary. At the outset, and for several decades in succession, Christianity was regarded as a sect of Judaism, not as its rival. The Christian movement at first was simply an effort to convince their fellow Jews that the events that had transpired and were continuing to transpire were the fulfillment of their ancient prophetic scriptures. This was the burden of their early preaching, as the sermons reported in the book of Acts clearly indicate. After opposition from their kinsmen increased and they found themselves not only unwelcome in the synagogues but excluded therefrom, and after their movement began to spread among the Gentiles, they found it imperative to define their attitude specifically toward these and other Jewish customs. A conference of the leaders was held at Jerusalem to determine whether Gentiles would be required to follow Jewish ceremonial laws (cf. Acts 15).

Peter, fresh from his dramatic experience with Cornelius and his household at Caesarea, pleaded that they not "put a yoke upon the neck of the disciples which neither our fathers nor we were able to bear" (vs. 10). Paul reported how Gentiles under his ministry were accepting Christianity and bringing forth its fruits in their lives. After due discussion it was agreed to "lay upon [the Gentiles] no greater burden than these necessary things: that ye abstain from things sacrificed to idols, and from blood, and from things strangled, and from fornication" (vss. 28-29). But this did not settle the controversy, as is evidenced by Paul's Epistle to the Galatians. Paul there reveals that both Barnabas and Peter changed their minds somewhat and to please the Jews, reverted to some of their old customs. He also shows that a group of Jewish Christians, known as "Judaisers," had gone among the churches of Galatia, which were composed mostly of Gentiles and were the results of Paul's first missionary labors, and insisted with some results that it was necessary for them to abide by the Jewish laws in order to be full-fledged Christians. In his letter Paul takes the position that not only are Gentiles exempted from such laws but Jewish Christians also.

He asked his readers why they turned "back again to the weak and beggarly rudiments, whereunto ye desire to be in bondage over again? Ye observe days, and months, and seasons, and years. I am afraid of you, lest by any means I have bestowed labor upon you in vain." (4:9-11.) He appeals to them fervently: "For freedom did Christ set us free: stand fast therefore, and be not entangled again in a yoke of bondage. . . . For in Christ Jesus neither circumcision availeth anything, nor uncircumcision; but faith working through love . . . [and] a new creature" (5:1, 6; 6:15). Although twice it is stated Paul desired to be at Jerusalem for the feast of the Pentecost (Acts 20:16 and I Cor. 16:8), and although, as noted above, he joined several others in a ceremony of purification ending in a sacrificial offering (Acts 21:26), he felt no obligation in regard to these matters. Furthermore he laid no such obligation upon the early Christians. On the contrary he said to the Colossians, "Let no man therefore judge you in meat, or in drink, or in respect of a feast day or a new moon or a sabbath day: which are a shadow of the things to come; but the body is Christ's (Col 2:16). It can therefore be stated quite emphatically that the New Testament Church discarded the priestly system both of sacrifices and of ceremonials.

Discarding of Temple Priesthood. As indicated previously, the author of Hebrews argued that priests were no longer needed. Peter carried this idea still further by saying that all Christians are "an elect race, a royal priesthood, a holy nation, a people for God's own possession" (I Pet. 2:9). This idea recurs regularly throughout the book of Revelation (cf. 1:6; 5:10; 20:6). This is the basis of the doctrine of the universal priesthood of believers which teaches that, because of the mediatorial work of Christ, every Christian is privileged to approach God directly without intermediaries, and that each for himself can offer his own "spiritual" sacrifices to God. Nowhere in the New Testament is there any indication of a special order of priests or of any sacerdotal functions for such an order to perform. And as we shall see later, there is no suggestion that a priest was required for the administration of either baptism or the Lord's Supper, or that Jesus specified for the administration of either a set liturgical form, or that any specified person was put in charge of worship, or that he is essential to make that worship valid and effective. In the light of these facts there is no justification for the statement of Percy Dearmer, "The careful directions as to ornaments and vestments in the Pentateuch are familiar to every student; and there is no hint that the principle of such worship was dropped under the New Covenant." [1] If Christians discarded the whole priestly system, including the priests, it is hardly reasonable to suppose they would retain priestly vestments and ornaments: there was nobody to wear them.

In the light of the facts just given it is not fair to say, as one writer has said:

The way of worship within the Temple made a rich contribution to the way of worship within the Primitive Church. . . . The New Israel developed and moulded its worship after the pattern of the traditional worship. Especially marked was the contribution of fundamental thoughts and conceptions derived from the Temple cultus. The new way of worship was also to have its Lamb and its Altar, and many of the accompanying elements. Consequently, we find . . . the New Testament . . . replete with references to sacrifices, incense, blood, passion, atonement, high priests, bread, wine, white robes, seven lamps, golden bowls, and thrones. Though the Christians discontinued both the forms and the art of Temple worship, because in Christ the Temple

---

[1] *Op. cit.*, p. 11.

cultus found its fulfillment, they nevertheless continued to think and worship in the same general realm of ideas.[2]

This is misleading and is likely to confuse the casual reader. There is a vast difference between making use of some of the terminology of the old worship to explain the new and molding the new worship "after the pattern" of the old. The New Testament is indeed "replete with references" to terms used in the Temple worship, but with the express purpose of using those terms to explain that Christian worship is a nobler and higher type of worship.

The book of Hebrews says, for example, "We have an altar" (13:10). This is the only place in the New Testament where the word "altar" is used in connection with the church on earth. The entire setting of the verse—the book of Hebrews as a whole and the immediate context in which it is used—excludes any possibility of its referring to the use of an altar in a place of worship, or to any action comparable to the actual eating of food after the parallels of the Old Testament. That can be ascertained by reading the verse immediately preceding, which speaks of "grace" instead of "meats" (9), and verses 15 and 16, which speak of the sacrifice of "praise" and of doing good and of communicating (which means sharing with others). Clearly the writer is using figures of speech. To make them refer to a real altar with an actual sacrifice is to make him in this place contradict the main thesis of his whole book, namely, that Christ's sacrifice fulfilled and made unnecessary all other sacrifices. Like the other New Testament writers mentioned a few pages back, he is making use of the advanced notion of *spiritual sacrifices*. Such sacrifices are of a different order from material sacrifices. They are not in any sense offered on an altar. When used in the New Testament, the old Temple terms are figures of speech that signify something sharply to be distinguished from what those same terms refer to in the old cultus. If taken literally in their Old Testament sense, they do violence to the nature of Christian worship.

B. SYNAGOGUE WORSHIP

It is generally agreed that the Temple worship had little influence on either Christ or his early followers. But it is often asserted that Christians formed their own worship by taking over bodily the general order of

[2] S. F. Brenner, *The Way of Worship*, pp. 4-5. Copyright 1944 by The Macmillan Co. and used by their permission.

worship in the synagogue and adding to it the ritual of the Lord's Supper. Let us see how much justification there is for this position. Actually there is no mention in the New Testament of Christians in Palestine attending the synagogue. Some scholars explain this by saying that the followers of Christ in Palestine apparently ceased attending the synagogue after Christ himself was expelled from that body. But during his missionary journeys over the rest of the Roman world Paul and his companions consistently sought out synagogues and attended their services regularly.

Whether there was much actual sympathy between Christians and the service of the synagogue is a debatable question. Christians went there to convince their fellow Jews that Jesus was the Messiah and that Christianity was the fulfillment of the purposes of the law and the prophets. The opportunity to present these claims was given supposedly at that place in the service when the members of the congregation were permitted to participate in the discussion, or when they were themselves asked to read and interpret the scriptures. This procedure created grave antagonisms, resulting in uproars, stonings, beatings, imprisonments, and for some, actual death. Christians were charged with "having turned the world upside down" (Acts 17:6), with teaching people to "forsake Moses" and telling them not to walk after the "customs" of the Jews. Remember: these charges created uproars *in the* synagogue. Are we to conclude that among the "customs" Christians were trying to change none was associated with the worship in the synagogue? Jesus specifically indicated his dislike of liturgical prayers in the synagogue. That dislike was most certainly reflected in his followers.

Certainly the opposition of Jesus to the legalistic system of the scribes and Pharisees was reflected in his followers. The New Testament Church in time discarded this system entirely, as is evidenced by Paul's letters to the Galatians and Romans. Paul said in Galatians, "Christ redeemed us from the curse of the law, having become a curse for us" (3:13); and again, "The law is become our tutor to bring us unto Christ, that we might be justified by faith. But now that faith is come, we are no longer under a tutor." (3:24-25.) His most elaborate treatment of the subject, however, is found in his letter to the Romans. Here he tells of his own fruitless effort to find peace by strict obedience to the Law (ch. 7) and argues at length that we are justified by faith not by the works of the law (ch. 3), insists that Christians are not under law but under grace, that when the love of God is shed abroad in their hearts by the Holy Spirit (5:5), they will be obedient from their hearts (6:17) and spontaneously and from inner compulsion produce righteousness. Hence Christ "is the end of the law unto righteousness to every one that believeth" (10:4). Henceforth Christians need no external laws to compel them to be righteous but will voluntarily produce righteousness because they are constrained by the love and the grace of Christ to do so (chs. 6; 8; 13).

It is therefore an oversimplification of the problem of New Testament worship to state that the Christian Church took over bodily the form and order of worship to which they were accustomed in the synagogue. This will appear even more clearly as we proceed to examine the new worship developed specifically by the Christians for their own fellowship. They did some of the same things that were done in synagogue worship; for example, they prayed, they read the scriptures and expounded the same, and they had singing and almsgiving. But what they did with these same elements made the difference—and it was a tremendous difference—between the old worship and the new.

C. Christian Worship

It is evident from the records that Christians began quite early to gather together for worship as a fellowship. This began informally and at first was not intended to start a rival worship to the traditional types among their own kinsmen. After opposition increased and persecutions began; they were forced to organize churches and to develop worship services suitable for their own group. Just when the process of detachment from the Jewish institutions was completed is not clear. It probably began in a modest way at the outset, but by the time the New Testament documents were written, the process of creating a distinctly Christian order of worship appears to have been well along toward completion.

When the small band of Christians returned to Jerusalem after the ascension of Jesus, they met in the "upper chamber" of a private house and "continued stedfastly in prayer" (Acts 1:13, 14). After the experiences on the day of Pentecost "they continued stedfastly in the apostles' teaching and fellowship, in the breaking of bread and the prayers" (Acts 2:42). This was elaborated upon a few verses farther on, "And day by day, continuing stedfastly with one accord in the temple, and breaking bread at home, they took their food with gladness and singleness of

69

heart, praising God, and having favor with all the people" (2:46-47). These references imply a daily meeting in a private home in which they studied together, prayed, engaged in "breaking bread" and partaking of food. "Breaking bread" is supposed to refer to the "agape" or "love feast" which may have been the primitive form of the observance of the Lord's Supper. "Partaking of food" refers to an ordinary meal. When Peter was released from prison, "he came to the house of Mary the mother of John whose surname was Mark; where many were gathered together and were praying" (Acts 12:12). In his letters Paul refers a number of times to the "church" in somebody's "house" (cf. Rom. 16:5; I Cor. 16:19; Col. 4:15; Philem. 2). Only once in the New Testament is the expression "the house of God" used (I Tim. 3:15). A weekly meeting upon the "first day of the week" is mentioned several times as taking place both in Palestine and elsewhere (cf. John 20:19, 26; Acts 20:7; I Cor. 16:2). There is no mention in the New Testament of any yearly meetings or festivals.

There is no reference in the New Testament to indicate that anyone in particular was the appointed leader of worship. Paul's description of public worship in the fourteenth chapter of I Corinthians shows that any person present was privileged to offer prayer or otherwise participate (vs. 26). References are found to different church officers teaching, or exercising discipline, or carrying administrative responsibilities; but the records are completely silent concerning what officers, if any, led in public worship. If the statement in Acts 20:11 that when Paul "had broken the bread, and eaten, and had talked with them a long while, even till break of day," and then departed, refers to the observance of the Lord's Supper, this is the only place in the whole New Testament which indicates any particular individual presided at this observance. All other references to the "breaking of bread" simply state that it occurred, without saying how it proceeded or under whose leadership.

Likewise the records are silent as to any order for public worship, except that Paul states how Jesus himself conducted the Last Supper (I Cor. 11). The only instructions that may be compared remotely to rubrics are found in the principles laid down by Paul: "Let all things be done unto edifying"; "God is not a God of confusion, but of peace"; "Let all things be done decently and in order"; and the suggestion of mutual deference (I Cor. 14:26, 33, 40, and 30). Nor is there anything in the New Testament that tells us at what time of the day they were accustomed to meet for worship. Such are the general facts concerning early Christian worship. Let us now examine the records to find out what, if anything, is said specifically about the several elements of their worship.

Reading of the Scriptures. There is no specific mention of this in connection with Christian worship. But the frequent use of scripture in the sermons of the leaders, such as that of Peter on the day of Pentecost (Acts 3), that of Stephen just before his stoning (Acts 7), and that of Peter before the household of Cornelius (Acts 11), the many allusions to the Old Testament scriptures in the records of Paul's ministry and in his letters, and the statements such as the "word of the Lord was spread abroad throughout all the region" (Acts 13:49) and the people of Thessalonica "received the word with all readiness of mind, examining the scriptures daily, whether these things were so" (Acts 17:11), would seem to indicate that the reading as well as teaching and preaching of the scriptures was a regular procedure when they met together. It is said they "continued stedfastly in the apostles' teaching" (Acts 2:42), which may refer to what the apostles said about the ancient scriptures as well as about the teaching of Christ and the facts of his life. Paul requested that his epistles be read in the churches (Col. 4:16 and I Thess. 5:27). Of course only the Old Testament would be regarded as scripture, but "readings" undoubtedly took place.

Singing. In his letter to the Ephesians, Paul exhorts, "Speaking one to another in psalms and hymns and spiritual songs, singing and making melody with your heart to the Lord" (5:19). At the moment Paul is not referring to worship but to Christians addressing or conversing with one another in praise rather than in the profligate talk which characterized drunken heathens. It is not possible to make any precise or hard and fast distinctions between the meanings of the three types of music referred to. Hence it is not wise to imply too much from their use. "Psalms" may refer to the Old Testament psalms, such as were used in the synagogue worship. But more likely the word refers to the Christian psalms, similar to the psalms of Israel, which the worshipers were moved by the Holy Spirit to utter as their contribution to public worship and referred to by Paul in I Cor. 14:26. "Hymns" likely means songs of praise to Christ or to God contributed in the same manner. Both then would be "spiritual songs," or songs inspired by the Holy Spirit. It is possible that "singing" is to be distinguished from "making melody with your heart to the Lord," the former being the outward expression of praise, the latter the unexpressed praise or inward worship of the heart. Although it may mean simply singing with all your hearts, as indeed it is usually translated. The point is that the terms refer to the *spontaneous* singing which characterized the early Christians.

Paul used similar words in Colossians: "In all wisdom teaching and admonishing one another with psalms and hymns and spiritual songs, singing with grace in your hearts unto God" (3:16). The connection here is somewhat different from that in Ephesians. Caution should be exercised again not to make precise distinctions between the words. The idea is that the word of God is to dwell in them so richly that it will find spontaneous expression in religious songs, and that these should be used as the means of religious instruction and admonition. The last idea is important for spiritual worship. Music should have proper content and purpose and not be mere music. This Paul says in another way in I Corinthians: "I will sing with the spirit, and I will sing with the understanding also" (14:15). Singing in spiritual worship should have a didactic purpose.

Offerings. To the Corinthians, Paul wrote, "Now concerning the collection for the saints, as I gave order to the churches of Galatia, so also do ye. Upon the first day of the week let each one of you lay by him in store, as he may prosper, that no collections be made when I come." (I Cor. 16:1-2.) Since their earliest gatherings for worship were held upon the "first day of the week," called the "Lord's Day" because it was on this day that Christ's resurrection occurred, it is supposed Paul here refers to the custom of taking an offering in connection with these weekly services. He further elaborates upon giving in II Cor. 8–9, where he says, "As ye abound in everything, in faith, and utterance, and knowledge, and in all earnestness, and in your love to us, see that ye abound in this grace also" (8:7). In this same setting he utters his well-known words, "Let each man do according as he hath purposed in his heart: not grudgingly, or of necessity: for God loveth a cheerful giver" (9:7). Again this seems to refer to giving in connection with public worship. The collection he referred to in I Cor. 16 was to be used to relieve the poor Christians at Jerusalem. This was mentioned again in Rom. 15:26. And the practice of "giving" as a grace is mentioned apparently again in I Tim. 6:18. It should be noted that Christian giving is not the same as paying a tax or a tithe according to the provisions of a law, but is to be spontaneous, personal, individual, voluntary, and from a willing heart.

The People's Amen. In the chapter where he deals with a number of matters pertaining to public worship, Paul speaks of one person saying the "Amen" when another has "given thanks" (I Cor. 14:16). This is usually regarded as a specific reference to the ancient practice of the people participating in worship by using "Amen." Amen of course is a way of giving approval to something the leader or speaker has said, and it means literally "let it be so."

Confession of Faith. Paul says to Timothy, "Fight the good fight of the faith, lay hold on the life eternal, whereunto thou wast called, and didst confess the good confession in the sight of many witnesses" (I Tim. 6:12). He uses the expression "confession unto the gospel of Christ" in II Cor. 9:13. We find references to the "confession" of Christians several times in the epistle to the Hebrews (for example, 4:14; 10:23). At this early date this hardly meant that in their services of worship they were accustomed to recite together a well-articulated creed. But it does seem to mean that when they were received into the church, it was customary for them to make some sort of public statement of their faith. It is believed this statement of faith was offered in connection with baptism.

The Kiss of Peace. The expression "Salute one another with a holy kiss" is found a number of times in the letters of Paul (cf. Rom. 16:16; I Cor. 16:20; I Thess. 5:26). Peter changes the expression slightly to "Salute one another with a kiss of love" (I Pet. 5:14). It is believed this practice of exchanging kisses between the same sex, never with the opposite sex, was commonly a part of their public worship, either at the beginning or at the conclusion of the service, somewhat after the manner of our modern handshaking.

Prayers. The earliest reference to the prayers of the Christians as a group is found in the first chapter of Acts, already cited in other connections, where it is recorded they met in the "upper chamber," similar to the one where the Last Supper was held, where "all with one accord continued stedfastly in prayer." After the report of the stirring events of Pentecost it is stated, "They continued stedfastly in the apostles' teaching and fellowship, in the breaking of bread and the prayers" (Acts 2:42). A few verses beyond that we read, "And day by day, continuing stedfastly with one accord in the temple, and breaking bread at home, they took their food with gladness and singleness of heart, praising God, and having favor with all the people" (46-47). The "prayers" may refer to the

73

prayers they offered in the Temple. In his Gospel, Luke reports that after the ascension of Jesus his disciples returned to Jerusalem, where they "were continually in the temple, blessing God" (24:53). Peter and John were accosted by the lame man when they were going to the Temple at the hour of prayer (Acts 3:1-2). Or the "prayers" may refer to those the early Christians participated in when they attended services in the synagogue.

But the general concensus of opinion is that the expression refers to the prayers offered in their worship together as Christians. These could have been a mere repetition of the liturgical prayers held in connection with Jewish worship. But more likely they were prayers of their own for their immediate purposes and as an expression of their common needs. These may have been of the several kinds spoken of by Paul to Timothy: "I exhort, therefore, first of all, that supplications, prayers, intercessions, thanksgivings, be made for all men; for the kings and all that are in high place" (I Tim. 2:1). The word "thanksgiving" in the original is "eucharist" and is used frequently in the epistles of Paul (for example, II Cor. 4:15; 9:11; Eph. 5:4; Phil. 4:6; Col. 2:7; 4:2; I Tim. 4:3, 4). Twice the word is used in the plural, in I Tim. 2:1 and II Cor. 9:12. This may justify us in supposing that giving thanks had a special place in the service.

This gains some support from what Paul said in I Cor. 14:16, where in distinguishing between the intelligible and unintelligible expressions in worship, he says, in effect: If you bless with the spirit only and not with the understanding, how shall an unlearned man be able to say the "Amen" at the conclusion of your "giving thanks," seeing he cannot know what you are saying? This was manifestly not liturgical prayer taken from Jewish worship, but a form of free, spontaneous prayer. We may therefore quite legitimately suppose that the Christians *adapted* some of their traditional prayers for use in Christian worship, or that they *developed* prayers of their own better fitted to express the worship of those who had come to believe in the Christian revelation. We must believe that some of them were free, spontaneous prayers. Some of them might conceivably have been common prayers, handed down orally and participated in by the entire congregation. But the quality that made them Christian was that they were spoken "with the spirit," that they were genuine, sincere, spontaneous, prompted by the spirit, and not vain repetitions of the sort condemned by the Master.

74

Preaching. What is sometimes labeled the "instructional" or "didactic" part of public worship seems to have been carried on by several types of leaders in the New Testament church: preachers, teachers, prophets, and exhorters. Those scattered as a result of persecution went about "preaching the word" (Acts 8:4) or "preaching good tidings concerning the kingdom of God and the name of Jesus Christ" (Acts 8:12). Some of this preaching, like that of Jesus during his earthly ministry and of Peter on the day of Pentecost, was out in the open places or in the open court of the Temple, apart from any worship service. Some of it was in connection with the services in the synagogue. But some of it was in the distinctly Christian services established when they either were driven from or dissociated themselves from the synagogue worship. Barnabas and Paul, along with others, preached the "word of the Lord" at Antioch (Acts 15:35). Paul preached a lengthy sermon, as well as made extended remarks at the "breaking of bread" reported in Acts 20:7-11. Teachers and teaching are spoken of in the records numerous times (for example, Acts 15:35; Rom. 12:7-8; I Cor. 12:28; Eph. 4:11).

But prophets also did a great deal of speaking at public meetings. They are named among the New Testament leaders in nearly every list (cf. I Cor. 12:28 and Eph. 4:11), and prophesying occurs in the list of the religious expressions. There is an occasional reference to a prophet predicting the future. For example, Agabus is represented as foretelling a famine (Acts 11:27-28) and also predicting the imprisonment of Paul (Acts 21:10-11). One statement about itinerant prophets (Acts 11:27) may indicate that there were in those days groups of wandering prophets who after the fashion of the Old Testament prophets engaged in "ecstatic" prophesying. It is known that such groups did go about somewhat later, expecting to be hospitably entertained, being given precedence over local officials in the conduct of public worship, and making themselves, in time, a veritable nuisance. It is believed they rather quickly disappeared, although sporadic attempts were made in later history to revive them.

But prophesying seemed to be a form, and an important form, of apostolic preaching. Judas and Silas were called prophets of whom it was said they "exhorted the brethren with many words, and confirmed (meaning 'gave encouragement or comfort to') them" (Acts 15:32). Some of the converts began immediately to prophesy (Acts 19:6).

75

Philip the evangelist had four daughters who prophesied (Acts 21:9). Both men and women prophesied in connection with public worship, according to I Cor. 11:5, although in I Cor. 14:34 Paul lays down the rule that women should keep silent in the churches. Paul held prophesying in high esteem. He said, "Despise not prophesyings" (I Thess. 5:20). He urged his readers to "desire" the gift of prophesying "earnestly." Commending the prophet he said, "He that prophesieth speaketh unto men edification, and exhortation, and consolation," and, "He that prophesieth edifieth the church" (cf. I Cor. 14:3-4). Commenting on the effects of this ministry, he said an unbeliever who attends church is likely to feel reproved and judged by prophesying, "the secrets of his heart" may be made manifest, and he may "fall down on his face and worship God" (I Cor. 14:25). Evidently this was a form of fervent and effective evangelistic preaching. Preaching occupied such a prominent place in the New Testament Church that it can be said with assurance that their worship would not have been complete without it.

Contributions by Individual Worshipers. While dealing with the worship practices, Paul says, "When ye come together, each one hath a psalm, hath a teaching, hath a revelation, hath a tongue, hath an interpretation" (I Cor. 14:26). Other contributions by members of the congregation were hymns and songs, prophesying and exhorting. The number of these contributions became so numerous and those contributions were made with such eagerness, and responded to by others so vigorously, that it led to confusion and disorder and caused Paul to try to put restrictions upon the practice (cf. I Cor. 14). But the practice is another evidence of the spontaneous nature of New Testament worship. We must distinguish the principle itself from its abuse.

Speaking in Tongues. This was still another type of spontaneous contribution on the part of the worshipers and is put by itself because of the prominent place it occupied in the early Church. It was not the same thing as the speaking in foreign languages which took place on the day of Pentecost, but was an outburst of words which had no meaning either to the speaker or to the hearers. It was one form of hysterical frenzy, or of emotional ecstasy, which has appeared among many widely separated peoples over the ages, accompanied many of the revivals in the history of the Christian Church and is still practiced by

76

some modern sects. It was regarded by the New Testament Church as a divine gift (charisma) which resulted when some believers received the Holy Spirit. Paul admitted he was susceptible to it (I Cor. 14:18), but at the same time recognized it had little value and endeavored to curb it. The fourteenth chapter of I Corinthians, already referred to many times, was devoted to this purpose.

He urged the worshipers to remember that an outsider coming into the church where it was going on would probably consider the worshipers "crazy" (vs. 23). He reminded them it was not helpful to utter a lot of gibberish, meaningless alike to the utterer and to the listener, and exhorted them to cultivate those gifts, such as prophesying, that were really edifying to the Church. He said:

"If I pray in a tongue, my spirit prayeth, but my understanding is unfruitful. What is it then? I will pray with the spirit, and I will pray with the understanding also: I will sing with the spirit, and I will sing with the understanding also. . . . I had rather speak five words with my understanding, that I might instruct others also, than ten thousand words in a tongue." (vss. 14-15, 19.)

In connection with these strictures he laid down the principles, already referred to, which are still valid for the conduct of public worship: "Let all things be done unto edifying. . . . God is not a God of confusion, but of peace. . . . Let all things be done decently and in order" (vss. 26, 33, 40). The Christian Church seems to have accepted Paul's judgment of the practice. At any rate it gradually died out in the early Church, although, as stated above, it has broken out at fairly regular intervals ever since, especially during periods of revival or among groups that are revivalistic in nature.

It has led to other types of excesses such as jerking, dancing, rolling on the ground, swooning, and self-mutilation. It is to be regarded as excessive, uninhibited emotionalism which has little value except as a form of release to those who practice it. This Paul recognized when he said, "He that speaketh in a tongue edifieth himself" (vs. 4). It is always calculated to bring religion into disrepute in the eyes of thoughtful people. But we must be careful always to distinguish between this and properly controlled emotions in worship. It is open to question whether worship can be fully Christian in the New Testament sense of that term unless it calls the emotions into play.

Baptism. There is no detailed description of baptism in the New Testament. It was merely stated that it took place, presumably because the Christians believed it to be sanctioned and authorized by Jesus. But no effort was made to explain the practice further. It was administered at various times and places: by the roadside, in the house, out in the open places (cf. Acts 2:41; 8:36 ff.; 16:29-34). The trinitarian formula of Matt. 28:19 is not found elsewhere and there is no uniformity in the formula used (cf. Acts 2:38; 8:16, 10:38; 19:5; Rom. 6:3; Gal. 3:27). The statements that believers were baptized "into Christ Jesus" (Rom. 6:3) and "into Christ" (Gal. 3:27) seem to mean baptism was regarded as an ingrafting into the Church, the body of Christ. It was often but not always associated with the coming of the Holy Spirit (cf. Acts 2; 8:14-17, 36 ff.; 9:7-18; 10:44 ff.; 16:14-15, 29-34; 19:1-7). But the two are mentioned together so consistently it would seem to mean that water baptism became Christian baptism when the Holy Spirit came into the heart. If so, then the water baptism symbolized the more significant experience of the baptism of the Spirit and the new life that resulted therefrom. But there is no certain instance of it having been administered in connection with public worship, although it was administered following repentance and in connection with the public confession of faith in Christ.

The record is silent about a number of other things. It does not say that any sacerdotal significance was attached to the act, that it conferred grace, that it was a means to salvation, that its efficacy depended upon being administered by divinely appointed officials or upon the precise use of a particular formula repeated in exactly the specified form, or that it was utilized as a worship rite. It does seem clear, however, that it was part of the ceremony of induction into the Christian fellowship, that it was a symbol of repentance, of purification or cleansing, of acceptance of Christ and of newness of life in him. It was a badge, so to speak, that identified a person henceforth as belonging to the Christian brotherhood. And since the Church was regarded as the body of Christ, it symbolized entrance into the communal or corporate life of Christ himself. It was not called a sacrament, but the significant spiritual experiences associated with it prepared the way for it to be so regarded later.

The Breaking of Bread. This expression, first used in Acts 2:42, is somewhat indefinite. It may have meant the same as "eating bread"

(Mark 3:20) or "taking food" (Acts 9:19). Note, for example, it is said that when on board the battered ship, Paul took the bread and "gave thanks to God in the presence of all; and he brake it, and began to eat" (Acts 27:35-36). This was a customary Jewish practice in connection with all meals. But it is generally believed that it refers to what later was called the "agape" (translated "love feast") by Jude (vs. 12), apparently referred to again by Peter (II Pet. 2:13), and described at length by Paul as part of public worship (I Cor. 11). To begin with, this feast appears to have been held in the homes of Christians (Acts 2:46). They may have started it solely as a communal meal after the fashion of such meals among both Jews and Gentiles, to give expression to their sense of brotherhood and for the purpose of having needed fellowship with those of like minds and interests. Apparently it took place on the first day of the week (cf. Acts 20:7). Each family brought its own food (I Cor. 11:21). The food was shared by all in the same manner as it is in modern "potluck" or "favorite-dish" meals.

The longest description of the feast is that found in I Cor. 11, where it is definitely indicated as taking place in connection with their coming together "in the church" (vs. 18). In this chapter Paul connects it with the observance of the Lord's Supper. In fact, it may have been the earliest form of that observance. By this time it had developed into a form of public scandal. The worshipers apparently gathered together in small groups to eat food with their own friends, probably their rich friends, leaving the poorer people to look with envy and to go hungry. Some ate and drank to such excess that it was impossible for them to worship properly, especially when it came to partaking of the Communion proper. The agape spread rather widely and rapidly in all parts of the Church. Somewhere near the end of the second century, or by the time of Tertullian and Clement of Alexandria, it was detached from the observance of the Lord's Supper. But there is no evidence in the records that the two were separated in New Testament times.

In time it was discontinued entirely, partly because of its own abuses, partly because of the impracticability of large numbers of people coming together for this type of meal, and partly because it was opposed by some of the secular authorities. It was finally forbidden in the Western Church by the Council of Carthage in A.D. 397. The wisdom of attempting to use this type of meal in connection with formal worship is questionable, as the early Christians learned by bitter experience. But the

79

social values of such a gathering, especially for small groups, are obvious. John Wesley undertook with a measure of success to revive it as an institution. In a purely social form it is used by numerous modern churches with various age groups quite successfully. It should be noted that this is one more evidence of the dynamic, spontaneous expression of the deep spiritual fellowship of the early Church.

The Lord's Supper. As stated above, the agape and the Lord's Supper originally were held together. Paul deals with both together in I Cor. 11, as though the agape preceded the Supper, which may have been the usual procedure at the time. The Supper came in due time to be called the "Eucharist," meaning "thanksgiving"; but nowhere in the New Testament is the word "eucharist" used to indicate the Supper as such separate from the general prayers of thanksgiving. Once the expression the "Table of the Lord" is used (I Cor. 10:21), and once it is called the "Lord's Supper" (I Cor. 11:20). But aside from the term "breaking of bread" to cover both the agape and the Supper, the usual name for it is *koinonia* (Communion), meaning "fellowship" (cf. Acts 2:42). Paul called the church the "Body of Christ" and spoke of the breaking of bread as the "communion of the body of Christ" (cf. I Cor. 10:16). The individual's entrance into this church, the fellowship of believers, was symbolized by baptism. His continuing participation in that fellowship was symbolized by his observance of the communal meal. Since they believed that Christ himself was a member of that corporate group, the Supper was a vivid reminder of his continuing presence with them.

At this stage in their Christian development they were prepared to understand more fully what Christ meant when he said, "This cup is the new covenant in my blood: this do, as often as ye drink it, in remembrance of me" (I Cor. 11:25). As shown in the previous chapter, there is no lexical justification for taking the expression "this do . . . in remembrance of me" as a sacrifice to God. This seems even clearer in the light of the explanatory statement added by Paul, "As often as ye eat this bread, and drink the cup, ye proclaim the Lord's death till he come" (I Cor. 11:26). The word translated "proclaim" means "publish" or "preach." The action of the Supper was a form of testimony or preaching about the death of Christ. By its observance the meaning of that death was vividly remembered and dramatically proclaimed to all who were present. We may also quite properly suppose that as the worshipers ate the elements, they appropriated for themselves by faith the benefits of Christ's death and were spiritually nourished by his presence.

The use of the term "high priest" as applied to Christ by the author of the book of Hebrews is sometimes cited as evidence that the Lord's Supper was interpreted by New Testament Christians as a sacrifice. That author says Christ, our great high priest, offered himself on the cross for our sins and entered into heaven, the eternal holy of holies, where, having made the final and perfect sacrifice of himself, he stands before God ever to make intercession for us (cf. Heb. 4:14 ff.; 6:20; 7:25; 8:1 ff.; 9:24-26). This is said to mean that each time the Supper is observed on earth, it represents Christ's eternal act as the heavenly high priest perpetually presenting his accomplished sacrifice at the altar before the throne of God. These words are not to be taken literally but figuratively. In fact the writer is explaining how Christ fulfills and therefore makes unnecessary the Old Testament priesthood, altar, and sacrifices. Christ was not a priest in the literal sense. The cross was not a literal altar, and his death was not a literal sacrifice. Heaven neither contains nor needs a temple, a priesthood, or an altar. But if these priestly terms are taken as figurative language to express the reality of which the Old Testament system was a mere shadow (and this is what the writer himself was doing), they aid in grasping a concept that is almost too difficult for human minds. If taken literally, they not only take us back to where the imperfect priestly system left off but make mechanical what is a mystical, dynamic experience that taxes the ability of articulate speech to formulate.

There is something profoundly true in the thought of Christ's sacrifice as perpetual or eternal. The New Testament many times speaks of the love of God in Christ as existing from the foundation of the world (cf. John 17:24; Eph. 1:4; Heb. 9:26; I Pet. 1:20; Rev. 13:8). Christ revealed the eternal love of God. So long as the world is not redeemed, so long must men be reminded that God eternally *is* what Christ *was*, that he carries a perpetual cross on his heart, that he always has suffered and always shall suffer until his children are redeemed. But there is something intolerable in the thought that Christ stands like a high priest offering himself before God eternally to remind God of his suffering for sinful men. It is men, not God, who need reminding. *Christ is God!* Through the Supper the Christians reminded themselves and others that God forever suffers as Christ once suffered for man's redemption. This is one more illustration of how misleading it is to say the use of the terminology of the priestly sacrifices by New Testament writers to explain the sacrifice of Christ proves that they were perpetuating something comparable to that Old Testament system.

It may be said of the Supper, as it was of baptism, that the record is silent about many things. It does not say that the Supper was supposed to be observed at any particular time or place, that only properly appointed officials were authorized to conduct it, that it was thought of as a sacerdotal procedure, that the elements were consecrated for holy purposes or that when eaten they conveyed grace, or that it was regarded essentially as a ceremonial indispensable to Christian worship. There is, in fact, no clear indication that it was always a part of their regular worship, although some so interpret the statement, "Upon the first day of the week, when we were gathered together to break bread, Paul discoursed with them" (Acts 20:7). Although Paul does not say his description of its institution was an outline of the procedure in its observance, in all probability the observance followed some such pattern. And undoubtedly that outline became a fixed liturgical form within a relatively few decades. It was not called a sacrament, but the vital benefits associated with it laid the groundwork for it to be defined as such in the later theology of the Church.

D. Conclusion

We do not know and have no way of discovering whether the early Christians used all the above thirteen items in every service. We do not know in what sequence they placed the items in whatever order of service they arranged. We do not know precisely how they observed the agape and the Lord's Supper in the breaking of bread, or whether this was a part of every service of worship. But if these items were formed into a liturgy in the order listed above, the resulting service of worship would be of considerable length and would contain a variety of separate elements. So we conclude that the New Testament worship is not to be thought of as in any sense barren though, relatively speaking, it was somewhat simple.

Writers upon the subject of Christian worship have fallen into the habit of separating the elements of New Testament worship into two groups.

First, those elements which resulted from what they call the fusion, or union, of the worship of the synagogue and the experience of the Upper Room are placed in one group. These are usually listed as the reading and expounding of the scriptures, including preaching; the fixed prayers; the singings; and the formal observance of the Lord's Supper. These are set to one side, variously labeled the "stable," "permanent," "enduring," or "staple" elements of worship, and called the "norm" for Christian worship.

Second, all other elements, such as the unrestricted contributions of individual worshipers, the agape, speaking with tongues, and other spontaneous features of New Testament worship, are laid on the other side and variously labeled the "unstable," "ephemeral," "evanescent," "transitory," or "impermanent" elements of Christian worship. One writer goes so far as to say all the impermanent elements were associated with what he terms a "prayer-meeting" type of free worship described by Paul in the fourteenth chapter of I Corinthians, and all the more dignified and orderly procedures of the Lord's Supper and of the synagogue were associated with another type of worship which was not mentioned in the New Testament documents because it was taken for granted, presented no problems to be dealt with, and was universally accepted. This stable type is what survived and has been the standard for Christian worship ever since.[3]

This division is an arbitrary arrangement, an oversimplification of the problem, and a misreading of the New Testament documents. It is not clear where the dignified type of worship was supposed to have taken place. Some Christians continued to worship in the Jewish synagogues on the Jewish Sabbath until well through the New Testament period, while at the same time they worshiped with their own group on Sunday. If the type of worship not mentioned in the records is supposed to have taken place in the synagogues themselves, it can be asserted with considerable confidence that the evidence makes this an extreme improbability, if not an actual impossibility. This would mean that early Christian influence was strong enough to bring Christian elements into the synagogue worship. The violent arguments, riots, and persecutions which resulted from the testimony of Christians in the synagogues certainly make it all but impossible to believe that Christians succeeded in modifying the worship procedures of this institution. Presumably this

[3] See S. A. Devan, *Ascent to Zion*, pp. 47-48.

unmentioned type is supposed to have been engaged in by Christians at meetings where the spontaneous elements, including the agape, were omitted and where only the orderly, dignified worship took place. There is not a shred of evidence in the New Testament for the existence of such meetings.

All the evidence, and to this the New Testament scholars agree with practical unanimity, points to the fact that the agape and the Lord's Supper were never separated in New Testament times and that the type of service called the "breaking of bread," which was accompanied by excesses such as speaking in tongues and the vigorous spontaneous participation of individual worshipers, is the only type of general worship engaged in by the Christians as a group. Furthermore it is by no means certain that the synagogue worship was quite as free from "informal" elements as this theory supposes. The scholars agree that though many of its procedures by the time of Jesus were relatively fixed, it was nevertheless a democratic, lay-participation, relatively free type of worship. The worship was not under the leadership of any single person, and first and last there was considerable opportunity afforded for individual worshipers to make a personal contribution, especially when opportunity came to ask questions of the speaker and to pass judgment upon what he said. It was at this place in the service apparently that the "uproars" reported in the New Testament took place in the synagogues. If we are permitted to use the argument from silence, a precarious procedure, and start our imaginations to operating a bit, we can picture a synagogue worship that was both undignified and disorderly.

Be that as it may, the spontaneous elements of the New Testament worship cannot be disposed of quite as easily as is done by this theory. In fact, those who hold to the theory do not deny the force and vitality of the Christian movement and even concede that such "spirit-filled" movements have a function to perform in religion. But they insist that such "ebullience" cannot last long and that given time the great masses of mankind always turn away from the prophet and his "free" worship to the more stable, fixed, and traditional worship of the priests. There is much to be said for this position, as will be said again later. This constitutes one of the problems of worship for spiritual religion. But to say that this return to a priestly type of worship is inevitable, due to the necessities of human nature, is to deny the possibility of God accomplishing his purposes to create a new type of humanity in Christ.

84

And if we set aside the spontaneous, exuberant features of Christianity as being transitory, we do violence to the whole prophetic revelation and the purpose of God as it is progressively unfolded in the Bible and which came to its climax in Christ.

It is a superficial treatment of New Testament worship to separate it into two types of worship procedure, one formal and the other informal. Every element of Christian worship was affected by the impact of the Holy Spirit upon the Christians. The enthusiasm, the spontaneous outburst of spiritual power, put new vitality into their singing, their prayers, their giving, their preaching, their testimony, and all their relations with one another. The Lord's Supper as observed in the New Testament Church cannot be appraised properly apart from this enthusiasm, nor can New Testament baptism. Granted that the pattern of the synagogue worship was followed in general outline, Christian worship was something else. It was not synagogue worship to which was added another formal feature called the Lord's Supper; it contained a new ingredient of a different quality and force. For want of a better term let us call this new ingredient "spontaneity." It was this that put "life" into New Testament worship, that made it dynamic, enthusiastic, intimate, heartfelt, and that distinguished it from other types of worship.

Admittedly this worship was surcharged with emotion. Such intense emotion could not, and should not, remain long at white heat. Human nature is not psychologically constructed to stand such emotion continuously for great lengths of time. But to say that the vitality of movements such as New Testament Christianity is expected to "cool off" and to ebb away, and deliberately to plan a worship service that helps that process along by squeezing all spontaneity from it, is to block the redemptive effort of God and to defer its success. There is no way to redeem man without affecting his emotions. A man does not believe anything until he feels it. Everything creative in human life has to be charged with emotion to succeed. Worship is not complete until the worshiper's emotions are moved. We can speak of modern worship as being like New Testament worship in type only if its several elements—music, prayers, sermons, and so on—contain this quality of spontaneity. If worship is to be made fully Christian, fully alive, in the New Testament sense, it must provide an open channel for the incoming of the Holy Spirit, "who works when and where and how he pleases."

By way of summary New Testament worship may be characterized as (1) spontaneous, or free, worship in contrast to fixed worship; (2) prayer worship in contrast to sacrifice worship; (3) lay-led and lay-participation worship in contrast to priestly, or sacerdotal, worship; (4) preaching worship in contrast to ritualistic, or ceremonial, worship; (5) spiritual, heartfelt, or inner worship in contrast to outward, or formal, worship; (6) simple and direct worship in contrast to complex and "mysterious" worship.

4

Ancient and Medieval Background

THIS period will be considered in two parts: (A) Brief history of worship and (B) Specific phases of worship practices.

A. BRIEF HISTORY OF WORSHIP IN THIS PERIOD

Developments in the First Two Centuries. Oesterley says that following the New Testament times there was a period of fifty years "at the very least during which we are in almost complete darkness as to the details of the worship of the early Christian communities, as far as our knowledge from Christian sources is concerned." [1] The main—and practically the only—sources of importance up to the third century (ca. A.D. 200) are five, as follows:

The first letter of Clement of Rome to the Corinthians (ca. A.D. 96). At the close of Clement's letter, which is in the nature of an exhortation, not a document dealing with worship, is a prayer in which many phrases occur that are similar to those found later in the liturgies of the fourth century. It is a noble utterance, dignified and solemn, but is not a fixed liturgical prayer; nor is there any indication that it was the so-called "Great Prayer," or prayer of consecration later used in the celebration of the Lord's Supper, as is often asserted. He used the expression, "Holy, Holy, Holy, Lord of Hosts, every creature is full of Thy glory," which is quite similar to the wording of the *Sanctus* and may have been its early form. He also referred to the "offering" or "oblation" which later became a technical expression for the offering

---

[1] *Op. cit.*, p. 100.

87

of the elements of the Lord's Supper, but which in earlier times referred to the offerings taken for the poor.

The letter of Pliny the Younger, Roman governor of Bithynia in Asia Minor, to his Emperor Trajan (ca. A.D. 112). This letter embodies the result of his judicial investigations in Bithynia. He was not a Christian but an outside observer reporting on the general practices of the Christians. Hence he might not be expected to understand thoroughly what he was observing. He mentions two services. He says the Christians assembled at sunrise on an appointed day, presumably Sunday, though this is not specified; that they sang a song to Christ as God responsively, or antiphonally, and then made a vow by an oath not to do any evil work, nor to commit theft, robbery, and adultery, nor to break their word, nor to sacrifice property entrusted to them. Then he says that afterward, but does not specify when (possibly at the evening hour), they assembled again to eat "ordinary and innocent" food. There is nothing to indicate, as is often stated, that the first worship was the observance of the Lord's Supper. All one can legitimately conclude from these facts is that it was a simple worship service. The brief description of the second service does suggest it was the agape. All scholars agree that the agape and the Lord's Supper were not separated at this early date, so it is presumed this evening service was the same as the New Testament service of the "breaking of bread."

The teaching of the twelve apostles, usually called the *Didache* (dated roughly ca. A.D. 130). This work, supposedly of Jewish-Christian origin, consists of sixteen chapters dealing with religious instruction, directions for the celebration of baptism and the Lord's Supper with the agape, directions on discipline and the offices of various leaders, and an exhortation on watchfulness. The section dealing with worship is interesting for a number of reasons. It indicates that the agape and the Lord's Supper were still held jointly, states Christians met for this service "every Lord's Day," mentions Wednesday and Friday as fast days, gives a few brief prayers of thanksgiving and states that following those prayers the "prophets" were permitted "to give thanks as they wish." Some prayers then were still "free" prayers, and there is no suggestion of the organized prayer of consecration which assumed such liturgical importance later.

The "Apology" of Justin Martyr to the Emperor Antoninus Pius (ca. A.D. 140). This document contains still more details. At the close of his *Apology*, Justin describes public worship. He gives a full account

88

of baptism after which he gives the following description of the celebration of the Lord's Supper:

After the prayers we greet one another with the brotherly kiss. Then bread and a cup with water and wine are handed to the president of the brethren. He receives them, and offers praise, glory, and thanks to the Father of all, through the name of the Son and the Holy Spirit, for these his gifts. When he has ended the prayers and thanksgiving, the whole congregation responds: "Amen." For "Amen" in the Hebrew tongue means: "Be it so." Upon this the deacons, as we call them, give to each of those present some of the blessed bread, and of the wine mingled with water, and carry it to the absent in their dwellings. This food is called with us the *eucharist*, of which none can partake, but the believing and baptized, who live according to the commands of Christ. For we use these not as common bread and common drink; but like as Jesus Christ our Redeemer was made flesh through the word of God, and took upon him flesh and blood for our redemption; so we are taught, that the nourishment blessed by the word of prayer, by which our flesh and blood are nourished by transformation, is the flesh and blood of the incarnate Jesus.[2]

He also describes a regular Sunday service as follows:

On Sunday a meeting of all, who live in the cities and villages, is held, and a section from the Memoirs of the Apostles and the writings of the Prophets is read, as long as the time permits. When the reader has finished, the president, in a discourse, gives an exhortation to the imitation of these noble things. After this we all rise in common prayer. At the close of the prayer, as we have before described, bread and wine with water are brought. The president offers prayer and thanks for them, according to the power given him, and the congregation responds the Amen. Then the consecrated elements are distributed to each one, and partaken, and are carried by the deacons to the houses of the absent. The wealthy and the willing then give contributions according to their free will, and this collection is deposited with the president, who therewith supplies orphans and widows, poor and needy, prisoners and strangers, and takes care of all who are in want. We assemble in common on Sunday, because this is the first day, on which God created the world and the light, and because Jesus Christ our Saviour on the same day rose from the dead and appeared to his disciples.[3]

It appears the repetition of the details concerning the Supper means he is describing two different uses of the same, one after a baptism and

[2] Philip Schaff, *History of the Christian Church*, II, 235-36.
[3] *Ibid.*, pp. 223-24.

one in connection with the regular worship service. Notice should be given to his statement that none "can partake" of the Eucharist except the believers. This may hark back to Paul's warnings in I Corinthians[4] and may have been a purely voluntary restraint on the part of each worshiper. It is not stated that the unbelievers were excluded from the room or that the service was divided into two separate parts. In fact, a rather simple order of service is indicated, one in which the reading of the scriptures, preaching, prayer, and the Lord's Supper were joined together in one continuous service. Some of the prayers of the president were "according to the power given him," meaning "free" prayer; and the people offered "common" prayer, implying either a litany or a prepared or memorized prayer. Tertullian (ca. A.D. 240) mentions the same parts of worship and in addition refers to "vigil," a midnight service on Saturday (and possibly lasting the rest of the night) in preparation for Communion the next morning.

The Apostolic Tradition, often called the "Egyptian Church Order," compiled by Hippolytus of Rome supposedly sometime after A.D. 200. There are considerable differences of opinion about its date and its importance. It is not now, as formerly by some, regarded as representative of the Roman liturgical usage in the third century, but as the "work of an individual who deviated from the traditional form." Its chief interest is the prayer of consecration, the text of which is given in fullness. Yet it is not a fixed prayer, or as Hippolytus puts it, "It is not necessary for him [the president] to recite the same words, but, according to his own ability, so each one is to give thanks." [5]

This then is the total picture until shortly after the end of the second century, so far as the actual facts are concerned. To play square with those facts, it must be asserted that the information is entirely too fragmentary to use as the basis on which to reconstruct a complete liturgy for the period. Yet it has become customary for modern writers to set forth for this period a fairly complete order of worship consisting of two distinct parts, labeled respectively the "Liturgy of the Word" and the "Liturgy of the Upper Room." The casual reader is likely to suppose that such an order has come to light in some of the

---

[4] I Cor. 10:21—"Ye cannot drink the cup of the Lord, and the cup of demons: ye cannot partake of the table of the Lord, and of the table of demons." I Cor. 11:27—"Whosoever shall eat the bread or drink the cup of the Lord in an unworthy manner, shall be guilty of the body and the blood of the Lord."

[5] Maxwell, op. cit., pp. 21-23.

ancient documents. But such is not the case. What happens is this: In the documents of later centuries sufficient evidence is found on which to reconstruct a liturgy which may be fairly clearly divided into two distinct parts. With that scheme in hand as the pattern or key, and utilizing only the fragmentary evidence available, and by exercising a moderate amount of imagination, one can reconstruct the worship of all previous periods into a similar scheme. This process is carried on back even to the New Testament itself.[6] What one does when proceeding thus is to read into the earlier documents not what is justified by the facts but what one hopes to find to support a preconceived theory.

As we shall see in the next section of this study, which follows immediately, Christian worship in the third and fourth centuries can quite naturally be organized under the two categories indicated above. But the available evidence does not justify such an arrangement for the worship of the first two centuries. Gregory Dix, whose work *The Shape of the Liturgy* is probably the most extensive piece of research yet made into the documentary evidence, says that the two parts, which he calls the "Synaxis" (meaning "meeting") and the "Eucharist," were separable and that either could be, and frequently was, held without the other as late as the fourth century. But, he says, that "from the fourth century onwards the two were gradually fused, until they came everywhere to be considered inseparable parts of a single rite" (pp. 36-37, 439).

The point to be emphasized is that at this early date the liturgy was undoubtedly quite simple. Even those who have undertaken to reconstruct the liturgy on the assumption that it was divided into separate parts come out with a very simple outline.[7] The conclusions that can be properly drawn from the scant data are that the order of worship was still relatively brief; some prayers were still free; the agape and the Supper were still observed jointly; the service was continuous, not divided into parts, but a slow development was going on in the direction of an expanded liturgy; and a general outline was in process of becoming traditional.

[6] For an ingenious effort to prove that the book of Revelation exhibits a liturgy which is basically the same as that of later periods, the reader is referred to "A Note on the Liturgy of the Apocalypse," by Allen Cabaniss, in *Interpretation*, Jan. 1953, pp. 78 ff. The author's interpretation of the Apocalypse is to be questioned seriously. It shows to what lengths imagination can go when once released to read back into history what one wishes to find.

[7] For two such undertakings see Dix, *op. cit.*, p. 434; and Devan, *op. cit.*, pp. 56-58.

Developments in the Third and Fourth Centuries. The period of "secret" worship. Sometime after the days of Justin, but just when it is not possible to say with any assurance, a radical step was taken with reference to the practice referred to by Justin of none but believers partaking of the Communion. When the time came for the Communion, all but believers were actually sent from the room. The earliest reference to this strict separation is made by Tertullian, who died about A.D. 240. Tertullian attacked the practice of allowing baptized and unbaptized both to attend the same prayers, and demanded that believers should occupy separate places in public worship from the catechumens (those being prepared for church membership) and the heathen. The separation may have been hastened by Tertullian's influence. At any rate it did take place sometime after the middle of the third century. The first part of the service, consisting of scripture reading, preaching, singing, and prayers, was attended by everybody, baptized and unbaptized alike. The second part, consisting of the observance of the Lord's Supper, was attended by the baptized only.

Before the Supper began, all unbelievers and catechumens were summoned to the door by the announcement of the deacon, "Let none of the catechumens, let none of the hearers, let none of the unbelievers, let none of the heterodox, stay here," and were by him conducted from the room. After which the doors were either closed or carefully guarded. The first part of the service came to be called in the Western Church the "mass of the catechumens," the second part the "mass of the faithful." In the Eastern Church the usual designations were the "proanaphora" and the "anaphora," from the Greek word meaning to carry or to lead to a higher place. The word "mass" (Latin missa) occurs first in Augustine and in the records of the Council of Carthage about A.D. 398. Some believe it is derived from the formula by which the non-baptized were dismissed or is the equivalent of missio or dismissio. Augustine directed, "Take notice, after the sermon the dismissal (missa) of the catechumens takes place; the faithful will remain." The popular theory is that it is derived from the phrase "Ite, missa est," which comes at the close of the "Mass of the faithful." Afterward the word was used to designate exclusively the Communion service.

This practice of dismissing all but the actual believers has since 1679 been called the "Secret Discipline." A number of explanations have been offered for this secrecy. Some think the practice was adopted from the Greek and Roman mystery religions. These religions were secret cults. Initiates were pledged not to divulge anything about the esoteric ritual. Others believe it was the result merely of the growing sacerdotal and hierarchical spirit of the Church. Still others attribute it to the actual necessity of guarding the Christian teachings and practices against profanation in a heathen world. Perhaps all these explanations have some truth in them. But the most plausible explanation is that during the period from about A.D. 250-350 Christians were not only under suspicion but actually persecuted at times. It was to their advantage, even for their actual safety, to keep the intimate parts of their beliefs secret except to all who could understand them and enter into them sympathetically.

The secrecy was observed for at least a hundred years, possibly even longer. It appears in the liturgies of the fourth century but disappeared from the Western Church in the sixth century. The Eastern Church, however, retained the practice; and until this day her liturgies contain the ancient form for the dismissal of catechumens together with the special prayers for them. As we shall see later, she also still calls the sacraments "mysteries" and celebrates the mass in part behind the veil. Thus it is correct to say that sometime after the middle of the third century in both the Eastern and Western sections of the Church the worship was divided into two distinct parts. After this time we may appropriately label the two parts the "Liturgy of the Word," because it dealt primarily with the use of the scriptures; and the "Liturgy of the Upper Room," because it dealt exclusively with the Lord's Supper.

The expansion of the liturgy. So long as actual secrecy prevailed, the Christian writers said little about their liturgy. This partly explains why it is not possible to determine the approximate dates when certain practices were initiated. But by the time the secrecy was no longer necessary for security reasons, opposition to Christianity had ended, and it had become the official religion of the empire, the liturgy could once more be brought out in the open. When that occurred, it became evident that the liturgy had been considerably elaborated during the period of secrecy. The process of elaboration was accelerated in the next few decades by the sense of release. It is not possible to determine how much of the expansion occurred during the years of "captivity" and how much immediately followed. It is known only that by the end of the fourth century and the early part of the fifth century Christian worship had changed. Instead of a semiprivate worship it was now a fully public worship which had taken on more and more of the characteristics of a spectacle. Church buildings had become more numerous and more expensive. Furnishings and appointments had become more lavish and more ostentatious. Such things as lights, incense, jeweled altars, and golden chalices were being increasingly utilized; and rituals were becoming longer and more complicated.

It is believed this process of elaboration had been going on since subapostolic days. This is attributed chiefly to two influences. The first of these influences was Judaism. As we have already seen, that influence was a cause of controversy in the New Testament Church. The controversy came to a head in the Council at Jerusalem (Acts 15), where a compromise was effected. It broke out again in the churches established by Paul (for example, in Galatia). He had constantly to combat the Judaisers who attempted to attach the Jewish ceremonials to the new Christian movement. Paul opposed this effort on the ground that it was a reversion to a primitive religion which he classified with the rudimentary practices of pagans. But that by no means resolved the conflict.

C. Anderson Scott[8] has made a careful comparison of the *Epistle of Clement to the Corinthians* with the *Gospel* of *John* (the two being practically contemporary), the letters of Ignatius with the letters of Paul, and the work of the Apologists with the Synoptic Gospels. He finds that the Church of the subapostolic period "had taken over from Judaism principles which were in contradition to the teaching of Jesus" (p. 13). The preference of the leaders of that period for Jewish ideas caused Ignatius to say, "It is monstrous to talk of Christianity and practice Judaism." *The Epistle of Barnabas* was written specifically to warn Christians against adopting Jewish ideas and practices. Clement said that the practices of the day in a manner constituted the restoration in the Christian Church of the Temple worship of ancient Judaism. The increasing emphasis on ceremonials, the increasing employment of the idea of objective sacrifice and of the term "priest" and other Temple terminology, and the beginning of distinctions between clergy and laity and between different orders of ministers (found in the writings of Clement) all may be attributed in part to the influence of Judaism.

The second and perhaps the more important influence in the elaboration of the liturgy in the subapostolic period was the mystery religions

[8] *Romanism and the Gospel*, pp. 9-40.

then prevalent throughout the Roman world. These religions flourished for at least a thousand years, beginning about 700 B.C. Although they were more or less in decline when Christianity arose, there can be no doubt that for the first few centuries Christians carried on their activities in an environment in which these mystery cults were active and influential. There were many of these cults of varying degrees of strength and importance. The ones most often listed are the mysteries of Eleusis, Cybele, Dionysus, Isis and Osiris, Orpheus, Mithra, and the Great Mother.

All of them were based on myths and had their hero gods to whom were attributed many miraculous happenings and powers. They had solemn and impressive symbolic and sacramental rites, rituals and ceremonies. All these were secret, and initiates were pledged not to divulge anything they had observed or experienced behind closed doors. Many of their worship practices were impure, licentious, even orgiastic; but some were of a high moral and spiritual nature. Their appeal was due in part to the atmosphere of mystery and secrecy and to their dazzling and spectacular rites, and in part to their promise of salvation and immortality and to the new hope they engendered in disillusioned souls. They contained many ideas congenial to the Christian faith and are believed to have prepared the way to some degree for Christianity's favorable reception in the Roman world. They contained a number of striking—by some regarded as even deadly—parallels to Christian beliefs and practices. Among these the following may be mentioned: a dying and reviving god, a baptism of purification and regeneration, a ritual portrayal of death and resurrection into immortality, communion with the god by drinking water or wine and eating bread or some other kind of food, a returning god, bodily resurrection of the dead, a last judgment and a final rejuvenation of the world. When Christianity first appeared, it must have seemed to many pagans to be another mystery religion.

But it is easy to be misled by these superficial resemblances. There were many striking resemblances between these religions and Christianity. They had many things in common. Both made a similar appeal to some of the basic human needs and instincts. But it has by no means been proved that Christianity borrowed from the mysteries. For example, it has been conclusively shown that many of Paul's terms and concepts that are similar to those of the mysteries may more easily be traced to a Jewish origin. Furthermore there are some amazing differences between the two religions, and these are crucial. Whatever the resemblances that first appeared, it was later discovered by both pagans and Christians that there were irreconcilable differences. Christianity refused to come to terms with these religions. This refusal provoked persecutions of Christianity by part of the pagan world. On the other hand, the very recognition of fundamental differences impressed and appealed to another part of that world. In the long run the superior worth and power of Christianity enabled it to survive while the mystery religions disappeared. The victory of Christianity is usually attributed to the facts that Jesus was a historical person, not a mythical character; that the spiritual nature of the Christian sacraments was maintained in the face of the gross materialistic nature of the mysteries; and that the Christian sacraments were founded on faith alone, not on the magic operation of the ritual.[9]

While all these things are true, it must also be said that Christian worship was somewhat changed in the process. Few are willing to state categorically that pagan practices were taken over bodily by Christians. But it seems almost certain that Christians added colorful ceremonies, emphasized the "mystery" of the Supper and guarded it carefully from all but the faithful, and utilized sacramental terminology in their worship practices for the express purpose of competing with the fascinating rites and rituals of the mystery religions. Students generally would admit the influence to a greater or less degree, but would not agree as to whether that influence was desirable or undesirable. Some would say the worship of the Christian Church was somewhat paganized in the process. Others would say Christians made a necessary adjustment to the spiritual temper of the age, that they wisely accommodated themselves to the needs of the people of the Greco-Roman world whom they sought to win, and that this was a natural step in the development of their liturgy. Whatever the judgment as to the value of the influences, the net result was the same. The mystery religions helped to mold early Christian worship into medieval worship.

Scott's study referred to above shows conclusively that the process of "progressive departure" from the evangelical faith and free worship of the New Testament had already started in the second century and

[9] A brief but thorough treatment of the mystery religions may be found in Freeman, *op. cit.*, pp. 31-43; James S. Stewart, *A Man in Christ*, pp. 64-80; and H. A. A. Kennedy, "Mysteries (Christian)," in the *Encyclopaedia of Religion and Ethics*, IX, 72 ff.

was beginning even then to change the character of New Testament Christianity: its doctrines, its organization and administration, and its worship. On the one hand the church had adopted from Judaism certain pre-Christian principles, and on the other had taken over from the mysteries certain contemporary pagan principles that were alien to original Christianity. By the time the Christian Church emerged from its one hundred years of secret worship, many of the foundation stones upon which the medieval church was erected had already been well laid. The process of transforming New Testament Christianity to the apostate Christianity of medievalism had already been well begun.

This period is of crucial importance for the history of Protestant worship, for, as we shall see later, it is the period to which the leaders of the modern liturgical movement go to find the patterns for current worship practices. Some of these leaders assume that the liturgies which appeared at this time represented, certainly in general outline, the accepted worship procedures of the early Church, almost, if not altogether, from New Testament times. This assumption is based upon the additional assumption that the Christian leaders of the second, third, and fourth centuries were true successors of the apostolic leaders and that they preserved the New Testament traditions in their purity. As has been shown, neither of those assumptions can be sustained by the facts. Other leaders admit that the liturgy was more elaborate than the New Testament worship but either fail or refuse to recognize the alien nature of the added practices. Rather they insist that the elaboration was a perfectly natural development toward a mature liturgy. They believe that the guidance of the Holy Spirit may be discerned in the formation of the norm for Christian worship in the same way it can be in the formation of the New Testament canon. The Christian Church found out by experience that worship has to be adapted to the desire in human nature for ritual and color and action. They had at hand the two institutions of baptism and the Lord's Supper, authorized by their founder, which they developed into Christian sacraments and offered to the pagans and to the Jews as a substitute for the rites of their own religions. This ability to adjust to the practicalities of realistic situations is a fundamental principle of Christianity and demonstrates it to be a growing, living religion.

It must be admitted that there is considerable truth in this position.

97

But it fails to recognize the degree to which some of the new ideas and practices were alien to the gospel of Jesus and to the nature of New Testament Christianity. It also minimizes the fact that these very accretions to Christianity had prepared the way for the imminent transformation of the Lord's Supper into the Roman Mass and the abuses that followed. The question arises then whether Protestants can properly or wisely go back to the third or fourth centuries rather than to the New Testament itself for their worship principles and standards.

The Development of Various Rites from the Fifth Century Onward. The scholars have made a detailed, even meticulous, study of the liturgies that developed following the period of secrecy. It has become a highly specialized, technical, and skilled procedure, similar in many respects to that of the textual criticism of the Bible. The "rites" are divided into families, their courses traced, their differences noted, the reasons for these differences assigned, the probable dates set when and the places where local variations occurred, and how various practices began to settle down into uniformity or became traditional and led to fixed liturgies here and there. No good purpose for this study can be served by going over this ground in detail. Readers interested in so doing will find that Dix, *The Shape of the Liturgy*, offers the most complete analysis of the rites and that Maxwell, *An Outline of Christian Worship*, contains an excellent introduction to the subject.

For the sake of convenience Maxwell groups the rites under the names of the three great patriarchates, Antioch (Syria), Alexandria, and Rome. He cautions, however, that this does not mean the rites originated in these centers, but only that "the rites of one class belong to one family with so many characteristics as to suggest a common origin." His list is as follows:

I. ANTIOCH
1. The *Apostolic Constitutions*, Books II and VIII
2. The Byzantine rite (Constantinople)
   (a) Liturgy of St. Basil
   (b) Liturgy of St. Chrysostom
3. The Jerusalem rite
   (a) Liturgy of St. James
   (b) All other Syrian rites
   (c) The Persian rites (Nestorian)

II. ALEXANDRIA
   1. Sarapion
   2. The Liturgy of St. Mark
   3. All other Egyptian and Ethiopic rites

· · · · · · · · · · · · · · ·

III. ROME
   1. The early Roman rite
   2. The Gallican rites (All the non-Roman Western rites)
   3. The Lutheran Reformed and Anglican rites[10]

The rites under II. do not especially concern us since for the most part they are derived from one or more of the rites listed under I., and therefore contribute very few features that are distinctive. The liturgies under I. are those of the Eastern Church. Among these the most important is the first one on the list, the so-called Clementine Liturgy. It is important primarily because it is the earliest complete liturgy preserved to modern times. It is also important because it is the parent of all other Eastern liturgies and because between the time it appeared in the fourth century (ca. A.D. 380) and the eighth century, when the Eastern liturgy became fixed, no changes of any importance were made in the Eastern liturgy. From that time to the present it has remained practically the same.

This liturgy is contained in Books II and VIII of the *Apostolic Constitutions*, which is dated about A.D. 380. The *Apostolic Constitutions* professed to be a "bequest" from all the apostles "to all who among the nations have believed in the Lord Jesus Christ," handed down through the Roman bishop Clement. It is actually a collection or compilation of "moral exhortations, church laws and usages, and liturgical formularies, which had gradually arisen in the various churches from the close of the first century, the time of the Roman Clement, downward, particularly in Jerusalem, Antioch, Alexandria, and Rome, partly on the authority of apostolic practice." [11] These were supposed to have been transmitted orally at first, then committed to writing, and finally put in this form by some unknown writer or writers. It was not accepted by the whole Church at the time as authoritative, nor for that matter is it so accepted

[10] *Ibid.*, pp. 34-36. Used by permission of Oxford University Press, London.
[11] Schaff, *op. cit.*, II, 185.

at the present. But the Eastern Church took it as the rule in matters of discipline as it took the scriptures to be the rule in matters of doctrine. This accounts for the great influence it had on the Eastern liturgy. There has been considerable difference of opinion about whether the liturgy was ever a "living" liturgy. But the scholars seem now to be generally agreed that on the whole it represents the liturgy actually used in the city of Antioch and perhaps in the whole Syrian Church, about A.D. 350-80.

There are two summaries or descriptions of liturgies in the document, one in Book II and the other in Book VIII, which Maxwell [12] has put together and arranged into a general scheme, which, though it must be considered an arrangement of the observer, at least indicates what additions had been made to the liturgy by this time. The only addition of any consequence to the first part of the service was the increase in the number of scripture readings. The other additions had to do with the observance of the Supper and consisted of an increase in the number and kinds of prayers, of the use of vestments, of ceremonial and symbolic action, and of the elaborated structure of the eucharistic prayer. By this time therefore the Lord's Supper was beginning to overshadow in importance the other elements of worship.

The Western rites showed a corresponding growth. As we have already seen, there is little information about these rites for the first four centuries. After that time a number of Latin rites appeared here and there, the two most important of which are known as the "Roman," because it was apparently first used only in the city of Rome; and the "Gallican," which was used in the rest of the West outside Rome. For the next four or five hundred years the two rites influenced each other. But by the ninth century, because the Roman See had become so influential, the Gallican rites were suppressed under Pepin and Charlemagne, after which time they dropped out of use. Maxwell says that since the Gallican rite developed among "barbaric" people outside Rome, it is "more colourful, elaborate, and flamboyant" than the Roman rite, and that "as a whole [it] was more sensuous, symbolical, and dramatic than the Roman rite of the same period, and much lengthier." [13] Because of the comparative lack of texts it is not possible to be sure of all the details, but Maxwell has set forth a scheme which he believes approxi-

[12] Op. cit., pp. 27-28.
[13] Ibid., pp. 46, 48.

mates the rite as it was celebrated in France in the seventh century.[14] It contains some thirty or more single items. Both parts of the service had been lengthened, but as in the case of the Clementine Liturgy, the lengthening took place mostly in connection with the observance of the Supper.

After about A.D. 900 and continuing until the Reformation the Roman rite was in the ascendancy in the West. During this time the rite was "not absolutely fixed, but varied considerably in different dioceses and provinces, while minor changes were continually taking place. . . . But the rite as a whole did not assume its present fixed form until 1570." [15] As in the case of the Gallican rite there is considerable uncertainty about the details of the Roman rite because of the lack of documentary evidence. But Maxwell has given a brief outline of what appears to have been the liturgy of the fifth or sixth century, showing it to be the "simplest of all rites, terse, austere, rigid in its economy of words, structure, and ceremonies." [16] He also gives the scheme of High Mass as it was observed toward the end of the medieval period.[17] The liturgy of the sixth century contained some thirty separate items, that of High Mass almost one hundred. In the case of all the Western rites the expansion of the liturgies was due to the addition of responses and versicles, both spoken and sung; numerous collects, bidding prayers, and litanies inserted here and there; ceremonials; symbolic actions; censing, and so on, which will be described in some detail in the section that immediately follows. But the reader may be interested to learn that the following items were counted in the scheme of the High Mass mentioned above: The Lord's Prayer, two bidding prayers, fifteen other prayers, sixteen versicles (including all the well-known ones such as the *Gloria, Sursum corda,* the *Kyries*) eight psalms sung or spoken, two graduals, eight scripture selections spoken or sung, nine collects spoken of separately and four other groups of collects, and twenty-five responses of one kind or another.

B. Specific Phases of Worship Practices of This Period

Places of Public Worship. For the first two centuries Christians worshiped in private homes, or in secluded outdoor places such as quarries

[14] *Ibid.,* pp. 49-50.
[15] *Ibid.,* pp. 45-46.
[16] *Ibid.,* pp. 56-57.
[17] *Ibid.,* pp. 69-71.

Lincoln Bible Institute

101

and sandpits, or in the crypts of the catacombs. This was due partly to their inability to finance the building of suitable places of worship because of their poverty and smallness of number, partly to the fact that they were oppressed and their religion was classified as "unpermitted," and partly to choice. For one thing, they had an aversion to heathen art. Their leaders boasted that they did not have temples and altars like the heathen. For another thing, they were proud to be the possessors of a spiritual religion which was independent of place and required neither buildings nor rituals. "Heathens, like Celsus, cast this up to them as a reproach; but Origen admirably replied: The humanity of Christ is the highest temple and the most beautiful image of God, and true Christians are living statues of the Holy Spirit, with which no Jupiter of Phidias can compare." [18] Justin Martyr was asked by the Roman prefect, "Where do you assemble?" He replied, "Where each one chooses, because the God of the Christians is not circumscribed by place, but being invisible fills heaven and earth and everywhere is worshipped and glorified by the faithful." [19]

The catacombs, first excavated as burial places for Christians, served as places where they could retreat in times of persecution and conduct their worship unmolested. They were not suited for this purpose because the rooms could accommodate no more than twenty or thirty people each. Hence they must have served primarily for the gathering of small groups. After they were no longer used as cemeteries, they became the object of interest because they contained the tombs of the martyrs and saints. Here began what has been called the "devotional use of the catacombs," pilgrimages to the graves and services held and chapels erected in memory of the dead. Jerome relates how as a mere boy (ca. 350) on Sundays he used to accompany groups of Christians who visited the graves in the crypts at Rome. Pope Damascus (366-84) even erected staircases and repaired and decorated the catacombs for the use of pilgrims.

The private houses in those days had oblong dining rooms. Some of them even had semicircular niches similar in shape to the apse of later church buildings. An elevated seat for the leaders and a table for the Communion were easily provided. Hence homes of Christians, especially the larger homes, were adaptable for the worship of small groups. Dix[20]

[18] Schaff, op. cit., p. 199.
[19] Hastings, Dictionary of the Bible, IV, 941.
[20] Op. cit., pp. 21 ff.

believes these homes furnished the general pattern for the later church buildings. He emphasizes the significance of private homes and not pagan temples or even the Jewish synagogue furnishing the model for Christian churches. He also cites a document, dated about A.D. 303, which lists in the court the various articles used in worship in private homes. The list indicates a variety and a large number of expensive chalices, bowls, lamps, tunics, veils, slippers, and so on, used, showing how complicated the worship had become by that time.

As the need for larger buildings arose, the Christians are believed to have rented public buildings such as mortuary chapels and rooms of the guilds or fraternities common in those times. These usually were equipped with a seat and a reading desk for the presiding officer. The Communion table was usually placed in the center of the room, or "in the midst," around which they gathered for their symbolic meal. In the catacombs they used sarcophagi with flat stone tops for Communion tables, which may explain the cubicle tomb-shaped tables in some of our modern churches. Later they rented Roman basilicas, or court and merchandising halls, which were rectangular in shape with a semicircular extension at the end, which later provided one model for the apse of their churches. The first houses of worship built especially for Christian worship were modeled after these basilicas, or after the arrangement in private homes where worship was held. The first mention of such buildings is found in the writings of Tertullian and Clement of Alexandria. Hence it is believed they began to build their own houses of worship sometime in the latter part of the second century. After the middle of the third century, when the persecution and restraints of Christians ceased for a while, the building of churches expanded rapidly. The era of church buildings began in earnest with Constantine the Great (fourth century), who built magnificent church structures in Jerusalem, Bethlehem, and Constantinople. The style of these buildings was basilican.

In the places of worship, whether homes or basilicas, or churches modeled after them, the presiding officer was on the platform (bema), where there were seats and a reader's stand (ambo, or pulpit). Sometimes the Communion table was placed on a low platform in the body of the building up a step or two from the floor level, which is usually attributed to the Jewish influence. The clergy and the elders sat round the apse back of the table. Sometimes the table was placed in the center of the main platform, and the officiating ministers and elders sat behind

103

it with extra seats around and on the sides, the people coming forward to the table to be served. Sometimes the entire service, including the sermon, was conducted from behind the table. Later this became known as the "basilican" position or posture, as distinguished from the "eastward" position in which the celebrant stood in front of the altar or table, facing east, with his back to the people.

One of the best established facts about the whole history of worship is that the early Christian ministers sat behind the table, and that the table was unmistakably a table, not an altar and not treated as such. It is believed that this position was adopted to carry out the symbolism of the church's fellowship together around the table—the officiating minister, the elders, and the people all sitting as equals around the Lord's table. So well authenticated is the ancient historicity of this practice that the pope is in this position when conducting the Mass at St. Peter's in Rome, and in recent years as a result of the revival of interest in liturgics in Roman Catholic circles, many of those churches are pulling their altars away from the wall and the officiating priests are conducting Mass in the same position as the pope. According to Dix every pope for the first thousand years celebrated Mass "facing the people across the altar," and the altar had on it no candle, no cross, no vases of flowers, no bookstand.[21]

Dix also has a most interesting explanation of how the "eastward" position originated. He thinks it had no ecclesiastical meaning whatever to begin with but rather began almost accidentally in Gaul and the Rhineland during the eighth and ninth centuries. For some centuries it was customary to place the bodies and relics of the martyrs under the altar. Later the relics were placed on the altar, and still later they were taken off the altar and placed on pedestals behind it. This "blocked" the access of the person celebrating the Communion to his usual position behind the altar. Whereupon the bishop's seat was placed on the side between the altar and the people, so that he could go to the front of the altar to perform his duties in connection with the Communion.[22] Whatever the origin of this practice, it has long been considered a priestly act, one in which the minister turns his back upon the people and goes to an altar as their intermediary to do for them what they are not privileged to do for themselves.

[21] Ibid., p. 421.
[22] Ibid., p. 591.

The Greek word for chair is "throne." The clergymen sat in "thrones" behind the table. In time these chairs were made larger in size than ordinary chairs. When distinctions between laymen and clergy became more pronounced, something of the royal dignity associated with kings' thrones became associated with these chairs, the bishop being privileged to occupy the largest of the thrones because of his exalted position. In time the platform became the sanctuary proper for the celebration of the holy mysteries; the table became an altar; the choir (chorus), that part of the chancel reserved for the clergy; and the nave, that part to be used by the laity. Probably as early as the fourth century an actual barrier was set up, and laity were forbidden to enter the enclosure of the altar, and a screen or veil was used to hide the altar from the view of the people. The latter practice seems to have grown out of a superstitious fear of the sacrament and the mysterious miracle there taking place. In the East it became a conviction that the people ought not to see what was taking place at the table, and in the West that the people ought to see it simply because it was so wonderful and awe-inspiring.

The Liturgies. Basically they had the same general outline. One of the most significant facts about the liturgies is that there was a surprising unanimity as to general outline in all of them. All of them provided for scripture readings, prayers, singing, sermon, confession of faith (in time), almsgiving, congregational participation (in all the early centuries), and the observance of the Communion. Some believe this was the general outline almost from the New Testament times. The observance of the Communion also followed the same general pattern: bringing in the elements, thanksgiving, recital of the institution, general prayer of consecration, fraction, and actual Communion (called "delivery"), so that the basic structure was common to all. I shall refer to the significance of this again later.

The lengthening and expansion of the liturgies. As already indicated, an expansion of the liturgies apparently began quite early. At first it proceeded slowly. At times, notably in the first few decades after the hundred years of "secrecy," it proceeded rapidly. So rapid was it at that time, in fact, that it is the source of some astonishment that changes could take place so rapidly in a day when the means of intercommunication between the several parts of the Church were so few and so slow. This rapid spread of practices in ancient times and by ancient means should remind us that it does not take centuries, but only decades, for new customs to sweep over the whole of the Church. It should occasion no surprise therefore if we discover that liturgies changed from the simple to the complex within a matter of a comparatively few years. It should be emphasized that most of the differences between the liturgies can be attributed to the handling and interpretation of the expansions, not to any disagreements as to what basic elements should be included in the liturgies. The expansion resulted from the following:

The elaboration of the regular, or stated, features, such as the readings from the scriptures and the prayers. At first the readings were from the New Testament and from the Old Testament. The number and length of these selections (lections) increased rapidly, being chosen from each section of the Bible in this order: the law, historical books, Job and the wisdom literature, the prophets, Acts, the Epistles, and the Gospels. The prayers too increased in number and length and became more elaborate in structure. As has been mentioned several times, informal or free prayers continued through all the early centuries. Rather quickly prayers of several types—of thanksgiving, of adoration, of petition, of confession, and of intercession—were used, as well as litanies. The consecration prayer in connection with the Communion became fixed as to form and consisted of the thanksgiving and adoration, the memorial of the passion (anamnesis), the oblation or offering, the prayer for the descent of the Holy Spirit (epiclesis), and intercessions for the people and for the Church. Some of the texts of this prayer are available and reveal its great length and careful structure. The extended participation of the people also added length to the service. This participation had been a regular feature from the beginning, but was multiplied into a variety of symbolic and dramatic actions, some of which will be described shortly.

The inclusion of new features. The expansion resulted also from the inclusion of new features. It is customary to speak of some of these additions as liturgical "fragments" or "variables." They were of many kinds and were inserted here and there in the order of service according to the desires or theory of the church in a particular area. The names of these variables are usually the first word or two in Latin. Among them may be mentioned the following:

Sanctus: Holy, holy, holy, Lord God Almighty,
        Heaven and earth are full of thy glory;
        Glory be to Thee, O Lord.

Sursum corda: Minister: Lift up your hearts.
People: We lift them up unto the Lord.
Minister: Let us give thanks unto the Lord.
People: It is meet and right so to do.
Salutation: (The usual greeting between Christians as they met)
Minister: The Lord be with you, or, Peace be with you, or, The grace of the Lord Jesus Christ, the love of God, and the communion of the Holy Ghost be with you all.
People: And with thy spirit.
Kyrie eleison ("Lord have mercy"), the Amens, the Lord's Prayer, the secrets (collects said at the end of the offertory), the Post-Communions (collects spoken just before the dismissal), and the ejaculation, "Thanks be to God."

Some of these are called "versicles," which are dialogues between leader and people usually in the language of scripture. Some were spoken or sung, often antiphonally. A principal one was:

Benedictus qui venit: Hosanna to the Son of David.
Blessed is He that cometh in the Name of the Lord.
God is the Lord, and hath appeared unto us.
Hosanna in the highest!

The gradual was a psalm sung on the step (gradus). Others that were sung were the Alleluia, the offertory psalm or anthem, the Communion psalm, the Magnificat of Mary, the Benedictus of Zacharias, the Gloria in Excelsis of the heavenly hosts, the Gloria Patri (traditionally sung after the Psalter to add the Trinitarian formula to the Old Testament readings), the Nunc Dimittis of Simeon, and a number of others which may be found in the liturgies of the several periods. In time almost every element and action in the worship came to be "framed" (preceded and followed) by a variable of one type or the other—with the result that practically every known variable was used in every service.

Still other additions consisted of the prothesis, or preparation of the clergy, which usually, but not always, took place in private and consisted of prayers said while the ministers vested or prepared the elements. While this was going on, the people were being censed to prepare them for worship. This censing took place also at several places in the service itself, notably before the elements were brought in. The custom of censing seems to have originated in the Old Testament idea of incense used as a sin offering. Undoubtedly also, as was the case in Old Testament times, it served a purely fumigatory purpose in a day when ventilation and sanitation were relatively unknown. It is believed by some to have been one method of giving peculiar honor to the bishop. The first use of censing is found in the fourth century. There were also added certain preparations for the reading of scriptures, consisting of various prayers and singings, including the deacon's litanies. Also added were biddings to prayer, the recital of the creed, and the diptychs, reading of lists of names of the living and the dead.

The ceremonials. These were the most time-consuming of all the additions. They soon grew into lengthy processions and became dramatic spectacles. They seem to have begun in a simple manner as signs of respect, such as, for example, standing when the Gospels were read. But afterward they became dramatic action. This action occurred principally at three places in the service: (1) when the ministers entered (in the West); (2) when the gospel book was carried from the table to the place where the lesson was read (in both East and West); and (3) when the elements were brought to the table (in the East). The action before Communion as developed in the East was the most elaborate of all. At first the sanctuary was divided from the nave by steps, then by a curtain that could be drawn as desired, then by a solid screen known as the iconostasis. This screen was decorated with raised pictures of Jesus, Mary, the apostles, and the saints, known as icons. Behind this screen was the altar or table, and here the clergy prepared the elements for the Communion and gathered for their ceremonies. In the screen they placed three doors, the center one immediately opposite the table being called the "Royal Door," across which could be drawn a veil when the door was open.

When the Gospel was about to be read, the deacon, bearing the Gospel Book, and accompanied by the celebrant and a procession of ministers and acolytes bearing crosses, lights, and incense, came through the north door of the iconostasis and passed down to the centre of the church, where amid censing and prayer the Book was ceremonially blessed and kissed. The procession then returned through the Royal Door to the Holy Table, and, the door still remaining open, the deacon read or sang the Gospel. The Gospel ended, the doors were closed.

This was known as the "Little Entrance." The ceremony connected with the bringing in of the bread and wine, known as the "Great Entrance," was even more imposing.

This time all the ministers took part, the acolytes bearing lights, the thurifers incense, and the other ministers carrying the instruments of the Passion, the cross, the spear, the scourge, and the thorns. As at the Little Entrance, the procession passed through the north door of the iconostasis, the celebrant bearing the Cup, and the deacon the paten upon his head. Both Cup and paten were veiled. When the procession returned from the church to the sanctuary amid clouds of incense, it entered the Royal Door, which was then shut and veiled, remaining so until the celebrant and his ministers had communicated. Then the doors were flung open as celebrant and deacon came through the Royal Door to give communion to the people.[23]

This ceremonial may be observed, substantially as in ancient times, in modern Orthodox churches. In the West, first in the Gallican rites and later in the Roman rites, the elevation of the Host was accompanied by bell ringings, censings, lights, and genuflections.

The Development of Symbolism. Everything used in the service and every bit of action in the service came to be invested with an air of mystery and were looked upon as sacred and holy. "Holy" was applied to the water, to the Communion itself, to the elements in the Communion, to the table, to the sanctuary, to the garments, to the Bible, and so on. Everything was regarded as having a figurative or symbolic meaning. W. H. Frere describes the symbolism in the Eastern liturgy as follows:

The entry of the Gospel, brought in with great procession and preceded by lights, shows the coming of the Saviour into the world; the Book is regarded as representing the presence of the incarnate Lord. The *Trisagion* of the congregation corresponds to the *Gloria in excelsis* of the angels; the *prokeimenon*, or respond, to the prophecies of the Old Testament; the Epistle to the apostolic witness. The *Alleluia* gives the attestation of David; and the reading of the Gospel is the climax of the first cycle. In the second, the Lord is symbolized by the gifts of bread and wine. The Holy Table is the sepulchre of Christ; the corporal is the linen cloth enwrapping his body. The veil of the paten is the kerchief round His head. The larger veil, or Aer, which covers both paten and chalice, is the stone with which St. Joseph closed His sepulchre. The Great Entrance is the Way of the Cross; the laying of the paten and chalice on the altar is the burial. The consecration corresponds to the Resurrection; and this symbolism is worked out fully through the Anaphora. In later days there was still further development of this symbolism.[24]

Yngve Brilioth gives the allegorical explanations of the various stages

[23] Maxwell, *op. cit.*, pp. 40-41. Used by permission of Oxford University Press, London.

[24] *The Principles of Religious Ceremonial*, p. 54. Used by permission of Morehouse-Gorham Co.

in the eucharistic rite as found in the exposition of Amalarius of Metz, the disciple of Alcuin:

The main idea was that the liturgy itself should be used so as to bring to remembrance the passion of Christ; the first part of the mass, however, deals with the history of Christ before his entry into Jerusalem. Some confusion of the order of events is inevitable. While the Introit symbolises generally the coming of Christ and his ministry, the *Gloria* shows the joy in heaven after his Resurrection; and when the Bishop sits down in his throne, there is symbolised the session of Christ at the Father's right hand. The Epistle, Gradual and Gospel, signify the proclaiming of the Old and the New Covenants, and Christ's own preaching. The salutation before the Offertory is the greeting of the crowd at the Triumphal Entry. When the priest offers the oblation, Amalarius sees the entry of Christ into the temple to offer himself to the Father. In the *Sanctus* he is greeted with the people's praise; the first part of the canon recalls the beginning of the Passion, and the disciples' flight. The remainder of the service symbolises the death of the Lord, the centurion's confession, the taking-down of the body, the burial, the resurrection, the appearance at Emmaus, and lastly the Ascension.[25]

The sign of the cross, which was used early, apparently as a part of the baptismal rite, came to be used on rising, bathing, going out, eating, and in other daily affairs; and the cross was used as decorations on tombs, ornaments, helmets, crowns, coins, scepters, seals, public buildings, and so on, as though its use had magical virtue, or was effective against demons, or worked as a charm in preventing injury or in insuring success. The crucifix, which cannot be traced further back than the middle of the sixth century, was similarly used. Other Christian symbols were the dove, the ship, the palm branch, the anchor, the lyre, the cock, the hart, the vine, and the branches. Then there came into use historical and allegorical pictures from mythology and the Bible, allegorical representations of Christ, pictures of the Virgin Mary, and so forth. After this it was but another step to the practical worship of these objects or to their use as fetishes. This became, in fact, a form of Christian idolatry. Much symbolism developed around the sacrament of baptism. Before baptism the candidate was required to take a solemn vow in which he renounced all evil and confessed faith in the triune God. Then his head was immersed three times in the water. His forehead and breast were signed with the cross to indicate he was a soldier of the Christ under

[25] *Eucharistic Faith and Practice*, p. 83. Used by permission of the author and the London Society for Promoting Christian Knowledge.

the banner of the cross. He was given milk and honey and salt in token of his sonship with God and citizenship in the heavenly Canaan, and given a lighted taper and a white robe. Then followed thanksgiving, benediction, and the brotherly kiss.

As one looks back upon all this, it appears almost as if nothing in worship could be done directly or quickly, but that everything had to be done in a dramatic, symbolical fashion, the form or the ceremony becoming the thing of central interest. In many instances the whole procedure was a form of magic, a superstition. If there was virtue in one prayer, there was still more virtue in many prayers. If the reading of the scriptures was a good thing, the reading of many scriptures was a much better thing. Thus item was piled upon item, action upon action, ceremony upon ceremony, until there was not time to do all that seemed to be needed to please God and secure his favor. So several things had to go on simultaneously. Many of the prayers were said during the singing of the deacon's litanies. It is disturbing, if not an actual shocking thing, for a Protestant who attends for the first time a present-day service in an Orthodox Church to discover that several things are going on at the same time. The people are buying and placing candles here and there, the attendant removing candles burned out and placing them in receptacles, the people coming and going, filling bottles with holy water (for example, on the day the baptism of Jesus is celebrated), while the reading and the prayers are going on. It has been estimated that the services of the third and fourth centuries probably lasted three hours. The more developed services of later centuries might easily have lasted longer if it had not been that the sermon and the instruction were shortened.

Changes in the Lord's Supper. Most radical of all the changes in worship resulted when the simple ceremony of the Lord's Supper of the early Church was transformed into the Roman Mass. Just how long the alteration was in process, it is not now possible to determine; but it certainly was a gradual change extending over several centuries. Slowly the Supper had been becoming the central and culminating act of the worship service. More and more of the other acts of worship were associated with the Supper and used to point to it. From the early days of the agape the people had brought the elements that were used in the Supper, each worshiper bringing a portion. In time these might have come to be thought of as "offerings." Almost from the start the praise and thanksgiving to God for his great love in Christ had been regarded as spiritual

111

sacrifices. The dedication or offering of themselves to God as living sacrifices had long been an important part of their Communion prayer. The collection for the poor, which became a traditional part of the observance, could easily have been considered an offering to God. More and more the table was taken away from the people. The area about it was being reserved for the exclusive use of the ordained minister and his helpers. Ere long he was functioning somewhat after the fashion of the ancient priest at the altar. Finally the theory of transubstantiation arose whereby the elements were supposed to be transformed into the actual blood and body of Christ and endued with magical powers. As a result of all these developments the Supper ceased to be thought of as a memorial meal and was conceived of as an objective sacrifice by the priest in behalf of the people.

There is no unanimity of opinion as to when this process of transforming the meaning of the Supper was completed. It was well on its way by the latter half of the third century, was nearing completion by the end of the fourth century or at the latest by the end of the fifth century, and thereafter was widely held until about the year 750 when it became definitely a part of the official doctrine of the Church. At that time John of Damascus refused to allow the "elements after consecration to be called types or symbols of the body and blood, since consecration effects a fundamental change in them." [26]

Modifications in basic conceptions of worship. The importance of this change-over in the understanding of the Supper, and consequently in the nature of worship, cannot be overemphasized. It was a watershed in the history of Christian worship, remaining until the present as the fundamental barrier to unity between Evangelical and Roman Christians. It is not possible to say to what extent the theology of the Supper had developed by this time. But even if hitherto it was conceived of as a sacrament, it was still only a spiritual thing. It was a meeting of spirit with Spirit. But now the experience was reduced to the level of the mere material. The elements became a physical offering to God endued with miraculous powers. The whole proceeding was transformed into magic. The ideas of the Supper as a symbol of the fellowship of believers with one another and with their living Lord, as a dramatic commemoration of his atoning sacrifice, and as a vivid reminder of his spiritual presence

---

[26] Quoted by E. S. Freeman, *The Lord's Supper in Protestantism*, p. 51.

gave way entirely to the idea of a priestly sacrifice. Once that idea was given full sway, the whole priestly system of medieval Christianity followed logically. And that marked the ultimate elimination of such characteristics of evangelical worship as spontaneity, evangelistic preaching of the gospel, committal of life to Christ under the influence of the Spirit, and congregational participation.

This change of conceptions constituted a right about-face of the Church in the whole matter of worship. From here on the culminating act of worship, almost its sole purpose, centered around the action of the priest in presenting the sacrifice and performing the miracle. Christ's presence became localized in the bread and wine rather than in the hearts of the believers. Attention was focused at the single spot where the priest was at his work. Many worshipers deliberately planned to arrive at the place in the service where the sacrifice occurred. They gave little heed to the other parts of the service because these were regarded as acts of officiants perparatory to the great moment.

The most important thing in worship was to see the miraculously transformed elements that were lifted high for this purpose. Worshipers ceased to be participants and became spectators. University students are said not to have taken time to communicate or even to attend Mass, but would call out to the priest, "Heave high, Sir, heave it high," so they could get a glimpse of the holy objects and thus perform their sacred duty for the day. The host (transubstantiated bread), regarded as the actual body of Christ, was transported through the streets, gazed upon with wonder, and treated with idolatrous and superstitious awe. It was sometimes carried away by the worshipers and used as a charm against demons. It was actually supposed to be efficacious as a physic or as a poultice.

Christian worship became something radically different from the worship of the New Testament Church. It was diverted into a different channel. Its purpose and direction were shifted, or reoriented. A whole set of alien ideas became associated with it. The very nature of Christianity itself was modified.

Changes in procedures of worship. When the underlying purpose of worship changed, procedures changed. The Liturgy of the Upper Room was expanded still further. The canon or rules of action increased and

113

became more involved. The table was pushed back against the east wall of the apse and became an altar before which the priest officiated. Churches were built primarily so that people could see, not so they could hear or take part. Sanctuaries became deeper and deeper, leaving the people farther and farther away from the altar. Rood screens were erected to shield the Holy Mystery. A railing barred all but the priests and servers from the chancel. Music became more elaborate and more complicated and was rendered by trained voices or merely intoned by the clergy. Three tones were specified for use by the celebrant in High Mass: the *vox sonora* to be used aloud in the plain-chant melodies, the *vox submissa* to be heard by those near but not loud enough to disturb the singing, and the *vox secreta* to be heard by the celebrant only.

The priest faced the altar and spoke inaudibly to the people. Latin was the language of the liturgy and was not understood by the people. Hence the whole service of worship, including the music, was in a foreign tongue. Preaching deteriorated and practically disappeared. Because the wine was not as easy to recover as the bread in case of an accident, the bread alone was given to the laity. This came to be known as "communion in one kind only." In time, though the people looked on at the weekly Mass, only the priest communed. He communed regularly in their behalf, but they were expected to commune only a few times, or even once, a year. It can be readily seen therefore how the whole concept of worship was modified. Worship was given a new focus. It was set into a different framework. It was carried on in surroundings and through actions that were reoriented to new purposes.

The number of observances was multiplied. Since each Mass supposedly provided sacerdotal merit, many Masses provided much more merit. Hence the number of Masses multiplied rapidly. More Masses required more priests and more places for Masses to be held.

So side chapels and chantries were formed, collegiate churches were founded for the purpose, and altars were placed in the bays of the naves of the cathedrals and abbey churches. . . . Masses were also said to achieve definite ends. As early as Hippolytus we hear of special masses for the dead, but in the Middle Ages these were increased out of all reckoning. As each mass was held to have value as an act of merit, it was now seriously computed how many were required to bring a soul through purgatory to paradise, and to what extent a mass could alleviate the pangs of a soul condemned to eternal punishment. There were masses for success in temporal affairs: for one going on a journey, for recovery from sickness, for the capture of thieves and the return of stolen goods, for rain or fair weather, for the release of captives; and here again the number required to achieve the object was solemnly determined. Masses were said even to bring about the death of persons; these were condemned and forbidden by the Synod of Toledo in 694. Private masses became, as Heiler says, a cancer feeding upon the soul of the Church.[27]

Worship Without Communion. The instincts or good judgment of some of the religious leaders, possibly under pressure from the people, remedied the situation to some slight extent by providing services of worship without the Lord's Supper and more in keeping with the spiritual and more personal worship of the early Christians.

The dry Mass. The Mass was observed in three forms: (1) The High Mass, which was the sung Mass, requiring the bishop and several other clergymen as well as a number of helpers and a highly trained choir. (2) The Low Mass, the Mass in an abridged form, without the choir, by one priest assisted by one or more servers, the celebrant speaking the parts, mostly inaudibly. By the time of the Reformation this had become the popular service because of its brevity and because it became the custom to give the people Communion only at this Mass. (3) The dry Mass, which was a low Mass said without either the consecration of the elements or the Communion, and therefore with those parts of the service connected with the Communion entirely omitted. This provided a service similar in general outline to the synagogue service and that of the early Christians. In the East a similar service was devised known as the Liturgy of the Presanctified, in which the elements were used; but they had previously been consecrated in another service.

The prone. The priests also provided a simple worship service known as prone, which became popular in both France and Germany. It did not appear in the text of the Mass, but was inserted after the reading of the Gospel and was spoken from the pulpit by the celebrant. Not the least important feature about it was that it was in the vernacular. It consisted of bidding prayers, the Epistle, the Gospel, the creed, the sermon, exhortations, and the Lord's Prayer. If one chose to enter the church for this part of the Mass only, as undoubtedly many people did, he would

[27] Maxwell, *op. cit.*, pp. 67-68. Used by permission of Oxford University Press, London.

be able to worship in somewhat the same manner as Christians did before the service became so elaborated.

The quire offices. This was still another type of simple worship which was developed by the monks, who left the world to enter monasteries where they gave their whole lives to nothing but worship. Quire offices, or hours of prayer, were arranged for stated periods during the twenty-four hours of each day. The first to appear was Vigils, from *vigilare*, meaning "to watch at night," mentioned by Tertullian. Six others were added later as follows: Nocturnes, at the cockcrow; Lauds, at daybreak; the three hours mentioned in Acts (cf. Acts 2:1, 15; 3:1; 10:9, 30); Terce, the third hour, Sext, the sixth hour, and None, the ninth hour; and Vespers, at sunset. These services usually consisted of hymns, scripture readings, and prayers. The multiplication of these services together with the fact that they were developed to such a high degree in the monasteries prevented their becoming as popular as they might otherwise have been. But at least they were a welcomed relief from the long, complicated, nonpersonal services of the Mass. Dix calls these services the "Puritan," or "private," or "purely personal" worship, as distinguished from the corporate worship of the Church.

There is some difference of opinion about which of these briefer services is the prototype of the Sunday morning services, with the Lord's Supper omitted, of the Reformed churches. The dry Mass is usually assigned the role, but in all probability the others also played their part at least to the extent of providing precedents.

Vestments. The term "vestments" technically means vestures worn by clergymen in the performance of strictly ministerial functions.[28] Christian ministers wore no vestments for the first four or five hundred years. This was due to a definite policy throughout the entire Church that ministers should conduct worship in the garments of everyday life. This was done to prevent distinctions between ministers and laymen, thus applying to their worship the Christian doctrine of the priesthood of all believers. It was also done to prevent the adoption of ceremonials similar to the worship apparatus of the pagan religions about them, thus applying their Christian convictions that worship should be simple and spiritual. Sometime during the sixth or seventh centuries the attire of

[28] For a detailed study of the history of vestments see (1) *Historic Dress of the Clergy*, by George S. Tyack, an older book (1897) but accurate; and, (2) Dix, *op. cit.*, pp. 398-410, a thorough and recent treatment of the subject.

clergymen became special liturgical vestments by the simple practice of conservatism on the part of the clergy. When laymen adopted the new styles of dress of the folk about them, the clergymen refused to do so on the ground that the dress was that of "worldly" and "barbarian" people. So they retained what they considered "civilized" attire. In time their dress became old-fashioned, even "archaic," and finally the distinctive garb of clergymen. Thus by the seventh or eighth centuries what were once ordinary street clothes had evolved into ecclesiastical vestments. Dix reminds those who would stress the necessity of clerical vestments to distinguish clergymen from other Christians that the older dress of clergymen was intended to do exactly the opposite.[29]

A number of articles of clothing worn by the clergymen were originally garments worn for purely utilitarian reasons. The headgear, for example, was originally a cap to keep the head warm while the minister was conducting a long service in an unheated building. However, according to Dix it has been proved that no liturgical headgear whatever was worn by clergymen at the liturgy anywhere before A.D. 1,000.[30] The stole originally was called *orarium*, something to wipe the face with, and was a primitive handkerchief. The wrapping around the neck called the amice originally was used to prevent the stole from getting soiled as it touched the skin. The maniple was designed to provide a handkerchief for the priest, who had no place to keep such an article in case he needed it. It was made so it could be slipped over the wrist to prevent it from falling off. As time passed, it became ornate and costly, was not suited for the purpose for which it was first made, and became a mere vestment.

The dress of other professions, such as academic dress, dress of monastic orders, dress required for all sorts of weather, also became mixed up with the development of clerical vestments. That is, they began as something else, were worn for one reason or another by clergymen, and then by a process of evolution were popularly regarded as clerical in nature. Once garments became mere clerical vestments, they became subject to mystical and metaphorical meanings which they were supposed to symbolize. Insignia have had the same general history. The church was slow adopting them also, and for the same reasons they were slow in adopting vestments and ceremonials that even to a slight degree paganized their simple, spiritual religion. Such practices as carrying the

[29] *Ibid.*, p. 410.
[30] *Ibid.*, p. 410.

cross in ceremonials, preceding the bishop with attendants bearing lighted torches and incense, the use of lights and torches at funerals, the use of candles on the altar, and the episcopal ring were taken over from the secular pagan society about the Church and in open imitation of that society. None of the practices just mentioned can be traced back further than the fifth century.

There were actually few vestments invented for clerical purposes. According to Dix the mitre, cope, gloves, and surplice were deliberate clerical inventions and were invented for the specific purpose of distinguishing clergymen from other Christians.[31] We are justified in saying that the Christian leaders of the Church of the first few centuries would regard this deliberate effort to make a distinction between clergy and laity as a betrayal of their fundamental doctrine of the priesthood of all believers.

The point to be emphasized is that there was no such thing, somewhere back in the dim and distant past, as a "historic dress" of the ministry which can be regarded as official or standard. The record is one of slow evolution in this matter. Efforts were made here and there by the public officials to force uniformity by legislation and the imposition of fines, but without any permanent success. There was no uniformity as to type, kind of materials, shape, number of garments, color, decorations, ornaments on the garments, and so on. Over the centuries there were continuous changes with the Church always tending to resist changes of styles, holding tenaciously to the ancient form merely because it was ancient, even though the reason for its adoption in the first place was a purely utilitarian one. So reasons offered for adopting a particular attire for ministers in our own day to be convincing must be reasons other than the fact that they are standard according to historical traditions.

C. Conclusion

Two things need to be said by way of summary and conclusion as we come to the end of this long period. First, worship practices were continuously in a state of fluidity. There was no "norm" for worship which the Christian Church everywhere adopted. The tendency in all the recent literature on the subject of worship is to take the position that standards for our modern worship practices may be sought and found in ancient practices. In many modern books on worship we meet with the quotation

[31] *Ibid.*, p. 410.

from Vincent of Lerins (A.D. 434), "Great heed must be taken to retain within the Catholic Church that which has been believed always and by all," which is quoted with approval and implies that what was everywhere practiced—"always and by all"—is our guide for modern worship procedures. But we have seen that with the exception of the Eastern liturgy the liturgy was never fixed anywhere.

Always worship procedures were undergoing changes. Experimentation with the liturgy by various sections of the Church was continually going on to adapt it to what they considered their own needs. Dix believes that borrowings from church to church began even in the first century. "And after that in every century every liturgy borrowed where it chose, without the intervention of 'authority' in the matter at all, till we come to the edicts of Byzantine emperors and Charlemagne." [32] These borrowings back and forth, changes here and there, continued almost up to the very threshold of the Reformation itself. We noted that if the liturgical variables and the elaborations that developed around the original elements are eliminated, there will always be found in all the rites an underlying common outline. If there is a pre-Reformation standard therefore, it must be sought in this structure common to all, not in the detailed practices.

Second, it must be said that dissatisfaction with worship was a major cause of the Reformation. The Reformation was a revolutionary movement of large proportions which, once it started, involved all the major interests of the people—economics, politics, learning, social arrangements, as well as religion. In his study of the Reformation George P. Fisher says that it was primarily an "event within the domain of religion." [33] Of the several aspects of religion under which the Reformation might be considered, worship is the most important because all other phases of religion, including theology and polity, are intimately bound up with worship. The low estate to which worship had fallen was the aspect of religion about which revolved many of the forces that provoked the movement.

As intermediaries between God and the worshipers the priests became powerful. They not only exercised authority ruthlessly and recklessly, but exploited it with utter disregard for the fundamental purposes for which worship exists. Starved spiritually and morally by their own system, they

[32] *Ibid.*, p. 587. Used by permission of A. & C. Black, Ltd.
[33] *The Reformation*, p. 8.

became venal and corrupt, used their authority to tyrannize the souls of men, to enrich the Church at the expense of the spiritual and material welfare of the people, and to control politics and economics for their own selfish ends. Before the Reformation therefore many groups of sincere Christians here and there were trying to disentangle themselves from the unchristian religion of their church and were making determined efforts to find ways of worshiping God for themselves and from their hearts, apart from the complicated sacramental worship of the sanctuary.

Hence among the special causes of the Reformation, Fisher gives an important place to the anti-sacerdotal sects, such as the Catharists of northern Italy and southern France (there known as Albigenses), the Waldensians in Italy, and the societies of praying women known as Beguines and of praying men known as Beghards in the Netherlands. These groups uniformly renounced the authority of the priesthood, but also strove to recover the simplicity of worship demanded by their own hearts. They were composed largely of common people, plain and un-learned, whose large number and persistence indicated a profound dis-satisfaction with religion as it was and a deep craving for a more simple and vital type of Christianity. The very rise of these sects was an omen of an approaching revolution. When it came, it affected the whole religious system of the medieval Church at the heart of which was their method of worship.

In his recent brief study of Protestantism, James Hastings Nichols gives an important place before the Reformation to what he calls the "Evangelical Undertow." [34] He mentions many of the sects already re-ferred to as well as the Lollards in England and the Hussites in Bohemia. All of these were movements in which laymen had a prominent part. He says there was a "rebellion against the vast secularization of the church," that it was a "great evangelical revival of the laity," that they tried in their worship to recover the "sense of the church as a religious fellowship rather than a mechanical dispensary of *mana*," and that in these sects a host of Christians before the Reformation found "communion with God more or less independently of the mechanical sacraments" and the "clerical closed shop union and its ceremonies."

Now let us turn to a study of the Reformation to discover what that movement undertook to do in regard to worship.

[34] *Primer for Protestants*, pp. 34 ff.

5

Reformation Background:
Sixteenth and Seventeenth Centuries

IN the conclusion of the last chapter we noted that worship was an important factor in the Reformation. When the adaptation of worship forms to the principles of the Reformation was undertaken, the results were varied. Without any intention of their own the reformers found themselves in the midst of a major revolution, the full significance of which no one in those days quite understood. They started out to reform abuses of the church to which they belonged and ere long found themselves all unwittingly undertaking the gigantic task of creating forms of worship adequate to express the new-found faith of a new organization. The old forms had more or less been woven into the very fabric of their souls. In spite of their desire to rectify errors and correct abuses they were held back by their traditions, training, and practice. The reformers did not intend to go as far as their successors did, nor as far as circumstances necessitated. In fact, they could not break as far away as some of those who came after them. As was to be expected, when the process of reconstruction began, there were all shades of opinions, violent differences of judgment, several degrees of enthusiasm involved. They were more agreed on what they wanted to do than on how to do it. The results, as is the case in all revolutions in human thought, were not altogether satisfactory as we look back, but probably all that could be expected under the conditions that prevailed. They approached their task with both courage and caution. Many essential things were accom-

121

plished, but the job was not completed. Many liturgical experiments were made with variable results.

A. LUTHER

In some ways Luther was the most reluctant of all the great reformers to make changes. And often after advocating the necessity of changes, he repudiated them either publicly when his followers undertook them, or in his own practice. Before he himself undertook to reform the liturgy, his followers did so. A number of German Masses appeared, most of them revised in accordance with Luther's own publicly expressed opinions. But he disagreed with many of the changes and insisted on going back to the customary ways. When he saw he could not stop the movement, he undertook to guide it by his own rite, *Formula missae*, which was published in 1523. It was supposed to create new forms for the new faith, but in actual fact was not a new creation at all, but a shortened version of the Roman Mass which retained many of the old features, including the Latin language. He made further changes in his second rite, *Deutsche Messe*, issued in 1526, which was intended to act as a check upon his followers who were eager for radical changes.

He gave a prominent place to the preaching and reading of the scriptures. He endeavored to recover the New Testament idea of fellowship in the Lord's Supper, insisted on the words of the institution being said audibly, openly declared himself in favor of a Mass in the vernacular, advocated that the Lord's Supper be celebrated daily throughout the Church, and repudiated the Roman Catholic doctrine of transubstantiation with its correlative teaching that the Mass was a repetition of the sacrifice of Christ. Most of all, he urged the need of new spiritual songs in the vernacular and was successful in stimulating the composition and the singing of hymns, which was one of the original contributions of the Reformation to worship. But generally speaking he was the most conservative of the reformers.

He advocated the Latin Mass for certain days and retained vestments, lights, altars, shrines and pictures, crucifixes, bells, and so on, unchanged. Though he consented to have the altar pulled away from the wall so that the celebrant could conduct the Supper in the basilican position, he himself continued to use the eastward position. Many other Lutheran liturgies appeared in the various cities and provinces of Germany which were different from those of Luther himself and which differed in details from one another. At no time was liturgical uniformity achieved in Germany. Both variety and freedom prevailed. This has been true of Lutheran worship ever since, both in Europe and in the United States. The outline of Luther's *Deutsche Messe* of 1526, as given by Maxwell, is as follows:

Liturgy of the Word
Introit or German hymn
Kyrie eleison
Salutation and collect
Epistle
German hymn
Gospel
Apostles' Creed (Elements prepared now)
Sermon or homily

Liturgy of the Upper Room
Paraphrase of Lord's Prayer
Exhortation
Recitation of Words of Institution, accompanied by
    Fraction and Delivery
Communion, hymns sung meanwhile
Post-communion collect
Aaronic Blessing.[1]

B. ZWINGLI

Simultaneous with the Reformation in Germany under Luther another reform movement was taking place in Zurich, Switzerland, under Zwingli. Zwingli arrived at his reformed principles, not out of a deep personal struggle as did Luther, but as a result of his humanistic studies. His education consisted of Greek and Latin classics and studies in humanism represented by Erasmus, with whom he had great sympathy. He approached his position more rationalistically. His teaching and preaching were more restrained and did not at once involve a severance from Rome. He proceeded cautiously, acted temperately, and had less violent clashes with the leaders of the Church. But once he arrived at his positions, he held to them tenaciously and followed them through to their conclusions more consistently than did Luther. He denounced the "Papacy and the mass, invocation of saints, justification by works, fasts, festivals, pilgrimages, monastic orders and the priesthood, auricular con-

[1] Maxwell, *op. cit.*, pp. 79-80. Used by permission of Oxford University Press, London.

fession, absolution, indulgences, penances, purgatory, and indeed all the characteristic peculiarities of the Roman Catholic creed and cultus." [2] He was influential in securing a decree of the Council in Zurich against the use of images and the sacrifice of the Mass.

His first revision of the Mass appeared in 1523 under the title *An Attack upon the Canon of the Mass*. He regarded the consecration prayer as inadequate because of its sacrificial ideas, its incoherence and contradictions; and proceeded to produce a more suitable substitute. It is regarded by some as too didactic and theological, but it was a thorough revision. Still later (1525) he published the first German rite to appear in Zurich under the title *The Action or Use of the Lord's Supper*. This became the pattern for all later Zwinglian worship. He did not believe the Lord's Supper was necessarily the norm for Christian worship and was therefore in favor of less frequent Communions. He originated the custom of "sitting communion," the people being served by the deacons while they remained in their pews. One of his most radical changes was to discontinue the use of the organ and abolish congregational singing for which he substituted the antiphonal recitation of the psalms and canticles.

The ordinary Sunday morning service of Zwingli consisted of scripture reading, prayer, and a sermon followed by a confession of sins. When Communion was held, the table was prepared following the sermon; and then the Communion service proceeded in the following manner:

(1) A prayer for grace to accomplish rightly the "praise and thanksgiving which thy only Son our Lord and Saviour Jesus Christ commanded us, the faithful, to make in memory of his death." (2) The reading by a minister of I Cor. xi. 20-29. (3) *Gloria in excelsis*, recited antiphonally by the celebrant and people—singing being altogether banned at Zürich. (4) The reading of John vi. 47-63. . . . (5) The Apostles' Creed, repeated antiphonally, by the men and women; and followed by (6) an exhortation by the deacon [followed by the Lord's Prayer]. . . . (7) Prayer by the deacon, for a worthy communion. . . . (8) Recital by the celebrant of the words of institution, followed by (9) the distribution. (10) Psalm 113 . . . recited antiphonally by the men and women. (11) The celebrant, "We thank thee, O Lord, for all thy gifts and thy goodness, who livest and reignest, God for ever and ever." "Amen." "Go in peace." [3]

[2] Fisher, op. cit., p. 141.

[3] Brilioth, op. cit., pp. 161-62. Used by permission of the author and the London Society for Promoting Christian Knowledge.

C. Strasbourg

Some of the most significant work pertaining to reformed worship took place at Strasbourg. Though Lutheran influence prevailed to begin with, the reformers there were quite independent. The first revision of the Mass there was made in 1524 by Diebold Schwarz. It was less radical than future rites but went further than did any of Luther's revisions. It retained a number of the familiar things such as vestments, genuflections, washing of the celebrant's hands, and most of the ceremonial. But it excluded everything indicating the Mass was a sacrifice, excluded invocations to the saints and to the Virgin Mary, directed that the Mass was to be said audibly, and made other changes. From 1524-25 nine or ten editions of the German Mass appeared at Strasbourg, each differing in some details from the others. Martin Bucer's influence, which had become manifest earlier, became pronounced when he was made the superintendent in 1530. He brought in the Zwinglian ideas, so that the later rites became a sort of middle way between Luther and Zwingli. Under Bucer's influence changes continued to be made for several years to come.[4]

Here new terms began to appear to take the place of the Roman terms: for example, instead of the word "Mass" they used the "Lord's Supper" or the "Holy Table," and instead of "priest" they used the word "minister." The worship was conducted in the basilican position from behind the table, which according to one observer did not differ in shape from ordinary altars. It was of course moved away from the wall to make room for the minister. Psalms and hymns were sung. Lections disappeared. The sermon was given a prominent place in worship. Saints' days were abolished. Eucharistic vestments were discontinued. The black gown or cassock, which had previously been used for outdoor wear and for preaching, was retained. The Eucharist was the norm for public worship, but it soon came to be celebrated monthly in the parish churches, though weekly Communion was still celebrated in the cathedral. The people formed a continuous line down the nave of the church and came forward to the table where they received the elements either kneeling or standing. When a service was held without the Communion, it consisted of

---

[4] The actual text of the Mass as celebrated at Strasbourg during this period, a detailed analysis of its various parts, a description of the action, critical comparisons with the Roman Mass it supplanted, and a general appraisal of its contents may be found in Maxwell, op. cit., pp. 91-111.

the Eucharistic service with those parts omitted which had to do directly with Communion. This shortened service is of importance because it was at least one of the possible patterns for the Sunday morning worship in many of the reformed churches.

D. CALVIN

The Strasbourg rite is also important because it had so much influence on both the Calvinian and the Scottish rites. When Calvin was banished from Geneva, he went to Strasbourg, where he taught theology and after 1538 ministered to a group of French exiles who had been driven out of France because of their reformed views. When the authorities finally permitted these exiles to celebrate the Lord's Supper monthly, it became necessary to have a service book in their own tongue. Since Calvin neither spoke nor read German, this book was provided by a friend who translated the Strasbourg rite in both Latin and French. This rite was quite satisfactory to Calvin, to begin with because it embodied many of his views concerning corporate worship as he believed it took place in the early Church. The first edition of the rite which appeared in 1540 he called *The Form of Prayers and Manner of Ministering the Sacraments According to the Use of the Ancient Church*. It went through at least three editions, the second in 1542, the third in 1545.

When Calvin was recalled to Geneva, he published in 1542 a modified form of the Strasbourg rite, which also went through several editions after 1547. This is known as the Geneva rite and is not to be confused with the 1542 edition of the Strasbourg rite. A number of changes were made in the liturgy to make it conform to Calvin's reformed faith, but for the most part they were slight alterations of sequence or position of the several items, or other slight variations from the Strasbourg rite. He added what Maxwell calls a "long and tiresome paraphrase of the Lord's Prayer." He introduced a metrical version of the Decalogue that disappeared after 1542. He omitted the *Kyrie eleison* and *Gloria in excelsis* after the psalm. He added the *Nunc Dimittis* after the Communion, reversing the order of the Strasbourg rites at this point. The most significant change was the omission of absolution and the substitution therefor of a prayer for pardon.

The outline of the 1542 edition according to Maxwell was as follows:

126

The Liturgy of the Word
Scripture Sentence: Psalm cxxiv. 8
Confession of sins
Prayer for pardon
Metrical Psalm
Collect for Illumination
Lection
Sermon

The Liturgy of the Upper Room
Collection of alms
Intercessions
Lord's Prayer in long paraphrase
Preparation of elements while
Apostles' Creed sung
Words of Institution
Exhortation
Consecration prayer
Fraction
Delivery
Communion, while psalm or Scriptures read
Post-communion collect
Aaronic Blessing.[5]

Perhaps this is the proper place to notice that the shortening and the simplifying of this and of the liturgies of the other reformers were achieved by the omission of the ceremonials, the reduction of the versicles and responses to one or two, the elimination of numerous responses by the choir, the reduction in the number and kinds of prayers, the simplification to some extent of the consecration prayer, and the reduction in the number of scripture lections, not to the elimination of any of the basic elements of the liturgy.

As will be seen in some detail later, Calvin's idea of the Lord's Supper was at variance with the ideas of Luther and Zwingli. In fact, these differences provoked a long controversy, known as the Eucharistic controversy, which divided the reformers, involved political leaders, and greatly retarded the progress of the Reformation. It was Calvin's desire to replace Mass not with a preaching service, as is often stated, but with a service composed of both the preaching of the Word and the Communion. It is claimed in fact that of all the reformers he was the one who

[5] *Ibid.*, pp. 114-15. Used by permission of Oxford University Press, London.

most earnestly opposed the division of worship into two parts. He believed the Communion should be held weekly. Although he was unable to have his way at this point because of the opposition of the magistrates of Geneva, he continued to hold to the idea that it should be a part of the weekly worship service. He circumvented the decrees of the magistrates that Communion should be celebrated quarterly by arranging the dates of Communion for each church in the city so that one wishing to observe it more frequently could do so by attending Communion at parishes other than his own. On the Sundays Communion was not held the service was really a Communion service without the parts belonging specifically to the consecration and the Communion itself; that is, it was an Ante-Communion service. As at Strasbourg, the people came forward to the table and received Communion standing or kneeling, receiving the bread from one minister and the cup from another. The order for receiving Communion was that which had been traditional, some think from the fourth century; namely, the minister received first, then the elders, then the people.

This rite of Calvin's became a pattern, generally speaking, for the worship of Calvinistic churches on the continent and later in the British Isles and in America. Many variations were made locally, but the general outline of the rite has remained substantially the same even into our own times. It is often stated that Calvin set the pattern of worship, though not always of doctrine, for Baptists, Congregationalists, Methodists, and Disciples, and of course Presbyterians, in the entire English-speaking world.

E. SCOTLAND

The history of the Reformed rites in Scotland is somewhat complicated and all intertwined with that of the English rites. A reform movement began in Scotland about the same time it began in England. Some were favorable toward the Continental reformers and some toward the English who had revolted against the pope. With the apparent approval of John Knox the *Book of Common Prayer*, the second book of Edward VI, was adopted by the "Lords of the Congregation," the nobles and barons of the reforming party, in 1552. Although Mary tried to suppress the book, it was used by a large number of Scottish churches.

In the meantime there was developing on the Continent another liturgy which was to have considerable influence in Scotland. The successor of

Calvin at Strasbourg was Valèrand Pullain, who later had to flee with his congregation, composed mostly of Belgian Walloons, to London. When the persecution of Protestants under Bloody Mary began, they fled again, this time to Frankfort-on-the-Main, where they were joined by a group of English refugees. A controversy arose between those who wished to use the English prayer book and those who wished to use the Calvinian rites. Meanwhile Knox, who also had to flee, arrived in Frankfort in 1554. He soon became the acknowledged head of the Calvinists in the controversy which could not be satisfactorily resolved. By 1555 the Anglican party got the upper hand and Knox was banished. He went to Geneva, then back to Scotland, and returned to Geneva in 1556, where he was made the minister of a group of English exiles, and later in the same year returned again to Scotland to begin his notable career.

During this so-called Genevan period of Knox's life a Calvinian form of service which had been previously drawn up at Frankfort was revised, much of the work, however, being done by one William Whittingham, a layman who later was ordained and became the Dean of Durham. This book was the first Reformed rite in English and was published under the title *The Forme of Prayers and Ministration of the Sacraments, etc., used in the Englishe congregation at Geneva; and approved by the famous and godly learned man, John Calvin.* Knox was somewhat enthusiastic about the type of worship at Geneva. Hence upon his return to Scotland he was responsible for introducing there the *Forme of Prayers,* commonly known as the *Book of Common Order,* sometime after 1560. This book came into general use in Scotland and superseded the second Book of Edward.

The influence of Calvin's liturgy and of the English *Book of Common Prayer* are both detected in this book by the scholars, but it is agreed that there is also evidence of independent thinking. The scheme of the liturgy is only slightly different from that of Calvin in Geneva. Ordinary bread and wine were used in the Lord's Supper. Communion was celebrated quarterly instead of monthly as in the English church at Geneva. The epiclesis was deleted from the consecration prayer. The people received sitting, except that the table was put in the nave, or between the two sections of the divided choir, and the people came forward in groups and sat around it. Worship services without the Lord's Supper were the same as the Communion service with those parts pertaining to the Communion proper being omitted. The Christian year was formally abandoned. The book was not a fixed and absolute formulary but left much to the discretion of the ministers. It was widely used for the next eighty years.

During those eighty years several efforts were made to revise it. In fact it went through three score or more editions in Scotland and some fifteen or more editions in English for the English Puritans abroad. It is not necessary for our present purposes to cite the history of this book. Rather let us move on to the more important book *The Directory of Public Worship*, which was produced by the Westminster Assembly about the middle of the next century, and which was the next liturgy of prime importance in Scotland. During those intervening years the Puritans in England had been pressing continuously for a revision of the prayer book. That revision finally came about with the active assistance of the Scottish leaders during the reign of Charles I.

In 1637 King Charles undertook to enforce the use of a newly completed *Book of Common Prayer* (a revision of some value regarded as the work of Archbishop Laud) upon the Scottish people without consulting the Scottish Church but solely upon the authority of the crown. This issued in a national revolt, the signing of the *Solemn League and Covenant*, the deposing of the bishops, the re-establishment of Presbyterianism, the return to the use of the *Book of Common Order*, and open warfare. Charles was soon faced by rebellion also in England and in the end was overthrown. In 1643 Parliament called the Westminster Assembly of divines to consult and recommend the form of government, a confession of faith, and the form of worship for the English Church.

The ordinance of Parliament calling the Assembly stated specifically the purpose was to bring the practices of the English Church "nearer agreement with the church of Scotland and other reformed churches abroad." At a crisis in the Assembly, Parliament made a bid for Scottish allegiance and dispatched commissioners to invite their assistance. They brought back with them a copy of the *Solemn League and Covenant*, which the English houses had to subscribe to before the Scottish commissioners would join the Assembly. That covenant was declared to be

For the defense and preservation of the Reformed religion in the church of Scotland . . . for the reformation of religion in the Kingdoms of England and Ireland, according to the word of God and practice of the best Reformed church; and for bringing the church of God in the three kingdoms to the

130

nearest conjunctions and uniformity in religion, Confession of Faith, Form of Church government, directories of worship and for catechising.

Much of this was the very language of the Puritans and was manifestly due to their growing influence in both Scotland and England.

The Assembly finally recommended a form of Presbyterian government and also produced a *Confession of Faith and Catechism* and a *Directory for the Public Worship of God in the Three Kingdoms.* These were accepted by the Scottish Assembly and by the English Parliament in 1645. It looked for a time as if a common Presbyterianism for England and Scotland would be effected. But the disturbed conditions under Cromwell and the restoration of the Stuarts followed, and except in a few sections of England the recommendations of the Westminster Assembly never became operative in England. But from this time until the last few decades of the nineteenth century the *Directory* was the standard for worship in Scotland. Those who have made a detailed analysis of the *Directory* find that it was influenced by Calvin's Genevan *Forme of Prayers,* by the English *Book of Common Prayer,* and by the positions of the Puritans who at the time were carrying on a persistent effort to secure the revision of the English prayer book. In fact it is often roughly described as a prayer book of the moderate Puritan party in England.[6]

The preface of the document pays a tribute to the *Book of Common Prayer* but asserts the time had come to take another step in the same direction that book had itself taken nearly a century before toward the advancement of the Reformation, and to "answer the gracious providence of God, which at this time calleth us for further reformation." The changes incorporated were largely those that had been demanded by the Puritans since the days of Elizabeth. The document discontinued liturgical vestments, all Saints' days, the sign of the cross, the marriage ring, private baptism, godparents, lections from the Apocrypha, and the administration of the Lord's Supper to the sick. A rubric designated that the table was to be "conveniently placed that the communicants may orderly sit around it or at it." The position while communicating was not prescribed, though kneeling seems to have been rejected and standing or sitting permitted. The Scottish custom was adopted of the minister communicating first and the rest of the communicants

[6] See Horton Davies, *The Worship of the English Puritans.*

distributing the elements from hand to hand. The double consecration of the bread and wine respectively, an Independent practice, was not permitted.

Although it was supposed to be a standard of worship only, it did give rather precise directions concerning both the order and the content of every service. The directions for the "performance" of the minister's whole duty specify that it must be done "painfully (carefully)," "plainly," "faithfully," "wisely," "gravely," "with loving affection," and "as taught of God." It explained that the directions concerning prayers were in order that the ministers might have help without becoming "slothful and negligent in stirring up the gifts of Christ in them" (meaning the gift of extempore prayer). It thus aimed to provide for both extempore and fixed prayers. The ordinary Sunday morning service structurally was quite similar to the pre-Communion service in the Calvinian rite, being slightly enlarged by the General Prayer and the Lord's Prayer and an additional lection. It outlined the order for the two sacraments, gave directions for the "Preaching of the Word," for the burial of the dead, and for keeping solemn fasts and for singing the psalms. It added an appendix "touching Days and Places for Public Worship," the church calendar being entirely abolished. The order for the Communion service was practically the same as the Calvinian rite, being lengthened slightly by an additional exhortation, by an additional metrical psalm, and by a more carefully constructed prayer (its parts were prayers of access, thanksgiving for creation and redemption, the Word and the sacraments, the anamnesis and the epiclesis). On the whole it was a *via media* between the free worship of the Puritans and the liturgical worship of the Anglicans, and was a serious effort to find an order of worship acceptable alike to Puritans, Presbyterians, and Independents.

The Scottish General Assembly accepted it with certain reservations. But even so, many changes, some of them extreme, followed its adoption by the churches. Some churches went so far as to discontinue the recital of the Lord's Prayer and the reading of scriptures in public worship. Extemporaneous prayers became the accepted practice. In time some of the Sunday morning services were reduced to the singing of a metrical psalm, a prayer, another psalm, the sermon followed by the long prayer, another psalm, and the benediction. Communion was observed infrequently, usually once each quarter in most of the churches.

It was the general guide for worship in Scotland until the revival of interest in worship began in the latter part of the nineteenth century.

F. ENGLAND

The English worship had a unique history, due to the fact that the English Reformation had a character all its own. But it was closely related to what was going on in Scotland and on the Continent. Henry VIII's break with the pope was primarily political, not religious or theological. He and Parliament were concerned with maintaining their freedom from the political power of the pope rather than with the great doctrines that engaged the attention of the Continental reformers. The Act of Supremacy passed by the English Parliament in 1534 simply cut the English Church off *en bloc* from the pope's authority and control. The English Church continued to conduct its services according to Roman principles and practices. Thus England could be called neither Protestant nor Roman Catholic. This may possibly account somewhat for the fact that many Anglicans ever since have regarded themselves as occupying a middle ground between Romanism and Protestantism and have therefore disliked being called Protestants.

Previous to the Reformation there was no absolute uniformity in worship throughout England, although it was Roman in character. There existed five service books, all in Latin: the *Breviary*, the *Missal*, the *Manual*, the *Pontifical*, and the *Primers*. At the time of the break with Rome these were "not all uniform, but varied according to different places and usages. . . . With such a number of books and with many different uses, with some of the clergy reformed and some intensely Romish, with the cup denied to the laity in some churches and tendered them in others, something had to be done—and the first and prime matter was of course in relation to the Mass." [7] A number of minor steps to relieve the situation were taken from 1536 to 1544. But the first major step was taken in 1548 when a commission headed by Thomas Cranmer, since 1533 the Archbishop of Canterbury, changed the Latin Mass into a Communion service in English. This was called the *Order for Communion*.

As soon as this first important document had been finished, the commission undertook to revise for use in English all the services of the Church. This task was completed, passed by both houses of Parliament

[7] Nolan B. Harmon, Jr., *The Rites and Ritual of Episcopal Methodism*, p. 21.

133

after debate and slight emendation, given royal assent, and printed. It appeared in 1549 and has become known as the *First Prayer Book of Edward VI*. It is believed to have been chiefly the work of Cranmer, although he was ably assisted by others. Their purpose, as expressed in the preface, was to purge out what they considered untrue and superstitious, to translate the services into the vernacular, to simplify the ritual, and to bring about uniformity of use. It was understood to be and was received at the time as a compromise between the new and the old.

It retained the term "Mass," the blessing of the ring in the marriage ceremony, provision for Masses for the dead, and other features not acceptable to the reformers. But it also made a number of other changes desired by them. It eliminated prayers for the mediation of the Virgin Mary and the saints and greatly reduced the number of saints' days. It provided for a service on Wednesdays and Fridays without Communion, provided there were no communicants. This consisted of that part of the Communion service preceding the Communion proper and became known as Ante-Communion. Although it provided for the celebration of the Communion at least every Sunday and Holy day, the people were required to commune as a minimum only once a year. It expressed the doctrine of sacrifice as a "sacrifice of praise and thanksgiving" and the offering of "ourselves, our souls and bodies, to be a reasonable, holy and lively sacrifice unto" God.

But this first book though popular was not uniformly used in the Church. Hence a revised edition known as the Second Book appeared in 1552. As the result of a combination of Puritan pressures from Continental reformers, from the foreigners (including Bucer) who were refugees in England, pressures that were strongly antipapal in general and more Zwinglian than Lutheran in the Communion rite, a number of changes were incorporated in the new book. The word "Communion" was substituted for "Mass." Eucharistic vestments were abolished. Prayers for the dead were not permitted. The epiclesis in the consecration prayer was deleted as were also a number of variables such as the *Agnus Dei, Benedictus qui venit, Christ our Paschal Lamb,* and *Peace.* The minimum number of Communions for the people was raised to three times a year. Altars were replaced by wooden Communion tables, which were to stand east and west or at right angles to the former position of the altars, the celebrant being directed to stand at the north side. Later when the tables were restored to the original position of the altar, the celebrant was directed to stand at the north end, which is the position still in use in Anglican churches.

A curious controversy arose over what became known as the "black rubric" in this second book. The rubric says the minister shall first receive the Communion in both kinds, then give to the other ministers and then deliver to the people in their hands "kneeling." Knox and others protested vigorously against kneeling because it indicated adoration of the elements. The rubric was left as written, but a lengthy statement, supposedly drafted by Knox, was inserted, declaring that the kneeling does not mean adoration of the elements or that Christ's real flesh and blood are in the elements and therefore to be adored, and that Christ's material body is in heaven and cannot be in more places than one at a time. This rubric was omitted from the 1559 version but reinserted in the 1662 revision.

The second book, though generally acceptable, did not come into wide use in England primarily because of the restoration of the Roman rite when Catholic Mary came to power shortly after its appearance. When Protestant Elizabeth in turn became the ruler, the second book was slightly revised and published in 1559. This new version came into common use. The principal changes at that time were the omission of the "black rubric" and the restoration of the privilege of using "Eucharistic vestments." The book of 1559 remained in use until 1662, at which time the final edition of the *Book of Common Prayer* was published.

The interval of approximately a hundred years between the appearances of the last two books has been called the period of "Puritan pressure" [8] because during those years it was the consistent policy of Puritans, both within and without the Church, to try to bring about additional changes in the prayer book so that English worship would conform more completely to that of the Apostolic Church. As a matter of fact the Puritan movement originated as a party opposed to the prayer book. The Puritans are sometimes divided into three groups: the moderate Puritans, who remained in England and tried to reform the established Church from within; the Separatists, who left the Anglican Church and established their own worship in secret conventicles; and the semi-Separatists, who went into exile voluntarily on the Continent and set up churches after their own ideal.[9] The moderate Puritans were greatly

[8] *Ibid.*, pp. 29 ff.
[9] See Davies, op. cit.

influenced by the other two groups, but made their fight in their own way while remaining in England. They had two main purposes: namely, to restore English worship to the purity, spirituality, and simplicity of the New Testament Church, and to rid that worship of its Roman characteristics, or "papal errors" as they were usually called.

As already indicated, their influence was felt in the revision of the prayer books in 1552 and 1559. This influence came partly through the Continental refugees who found an asylum in England under the protection of Cranmer. It also came partly through Knox and other Marian English exiles who had found a refuge in the low countries and in Switzerland, where they had been greatly influenced by the work of the Continental reformers. Although they failed in 1559 to bring about other reforms they sought, their efforts continued unabated.

A list of the major items in their list of needed reforms should be made before proceeding further. They were against the use of vestments by the ministers. They were opposed to the pronouncement of absolution by the minister, to auricular confession, and to bowing at the name of Jesus. They sought to abolish three ceremonies which were enforced by the *Book of Common Prayer*: kneeling for the reception of the elements in the Lord's Supper, the signing with the cross in baptism, and the use of the ring in marriage. They wanted to substitute sermons preached for homilies that were read and demanded at least one sermon each Lord's Day. They stood for radical revisions in the lections, especially the elimination of readings from the Apocrypha. They were opposed to the Lord's Prayer as a liturgical formula, which they believed Jesus did not intend it to be. They preferred long prayers to collects, disliked litanies, and wanted the prayer book to provide for extempore prayers as well as for fixed prayers. They took exception to private baptisms, to putting the questions to the child, and to the custom of godparents standing as sponsors in infant baptism.

They sought a number of changes in the observance of the Lord's Supper: changes in the words of delivery so as to eliminate all unscriptural phrases, eliminating kneeling in the reception of the elements, increasing the number of observances beyond three times a year, and preventing its observance by unworthy communicants and its being given to the sick. They believed that marriages and burials were civil not religious ceremonies and took exception particularly to the bridegroom's saying, "With my body I thee worship" and to the words in the commital service

136

"in the sure and certain hope of the resurrection to eternal life," which they considered presumptuous. They objected to confirmation as being in effect a third sacrament and to ordination because they believed Anglican orders clearly were not found in the New Testament. They desired to eradicate saints' days because they diminished the glory due to God and denied the sole mediatorship of Christ. For them there was only one festival of the Church in the new dispensation, and that was the Lord's Day which commemorated the resurrection of Christ. On that day they believed they rehearsed the whole drama of salvation from the creation of God to the resurrection of Christ. Hence they sought the discontinuance of all the other festivals of the church year. They demanded that the word "minister" be substituted for "priest" or "curate," and that the "Lord's Day" be used instead of Sunday."

In a number of ways they went beyond the Calvinistic reformers on the Continent. Calvin approved of a set form of prayers, of the festivals of the Christian year, of the pronouncement of absolution by the minister, of confirmation, of Communion to the sick, of auricular confession, of weekly Communion, of funerals and marriages as ecclesiastical activities, and of the use of vestments. He permitted the use of the signing of the cross in baptism, of the ring in marriage, and kneeling while receiving the elements, three ceremonies the Puritans opposed as superstitions. In many instances the Separatists such as the Barrowists, the Brownists, and the Anabaptists went even further than the moderate Puritans. They opposed all liturgical forms. The Anabaptists opposed infant baptism and stood only for believers' baptism and in their zeal to adhere strictly to New Testament practice made foot washing into an ordinance. Most of these groups went much further than the moderate Puritans in trying to attain to what is sometimes called the "pneumatic" or "charismatic" worship of the New Testament, terms used to denote the grace of God operating in the souls of the early Christians by the Holy Spirit.

The efforts of the Puritans to bring about changes continued through the last decades of the sixteenth century and until 1662 when the final revision of the Book of Common Prayer took place. They not only made lists of the changes they advocated but, what is more significant, actually produced a number of liturgies embodying those changes. In 1582 Thomas Cartwright tried unsuccessfully to get Parliament to approve a prayer book along the lines of the Genevan book. In 1585 the moderate

137

Puritans presented to Parliament a prayer book published by Walde-grave in London. It was entitled *A Book of the Form of Common Prayers Tendered to the Parliament* and was intended to persuade Parliament they were not opposed to the prayer book as such but only to its failure to provide also for extempore prayer. The Puritan Church in Middleburg, Holland, used a prayer book that permitted both ex-tempore and fixed prayers which went through several editions (1586, 1587, 1602). This too was proposed as the prayer book of the common-wealth but without success. As has already been shown, the *Directory* of the Westminster Assembly permitted the use of both kinds of prayer and otherwise gave specific and detailed directions concerning orders for services and for offices. All these liturgies were designed de-liberately to prove to the Anglicans that the Puritans believed in orderly worship.

The story of the *Directory for Worship* produced by the Westminster Assembly was told in some detail when the history of worship in Scot-land was studied. It was adopted as a substitute for the prayer book by Parliament in 1645 and continued in use, though by no means uni-versally, for some sixteen years. But the execution of Charles I, the establishment of the commonwealth and the protectorate under Crom-well, and the restoration of the Stuarts under Charles II in 1660 fol-lowed and made the change-over both short-lived and ineffectual. With the return of the Stuarts there was a demand made for the restoration of the prayer book. The Puritans attempted to prevent this and pro-posed still again that a modified book be produced. This like the other efforts was unsuccessful. Their influence was strong enough to force a conference for the revision of the book rather than a reprint of the book of 1559, but not strong enough to bring about the major reforms they sought.

In 1660 before returning to England, Charles I made a declaration intended to prepare the way for religious unity. This encouraged a group of Presbyterian ministers to believe he was favorable to their cause. So they drew up the "First Address and Proposals of the Min-isters," which they presented to him at Breda and in which they approved a liturgy in principle, but set forth briefly their well-known objections to the *Book of Common Prayer.* The Anglican bishops replied, some-what chiding the ministers for their proposals. This provoked a rebuttal from the ministers. The interest created by these documents provoked

Charles to call a conference of bishops and ministers at Savoy in 1661. At this conference the ministers presented their "Exceptions Against the Book of Common Prayer" in two parts: (1) general principles and (2) a detailed criticism. This has been described as probably the "most thorough examination of the Prayer Book ever undertaken." [10] It embodied everything in the book the Puritans wanted to see deleted or added or modified, down to the exact words and phrases. It dealt with prayers, lections, saints' days, feasts and festivals, procedures in connection with the Lord's Supper, ceremonies, and the use of psalms. The bishops were practically unmoved by these proposals. They made some seventeen concessions of a minor nature which did not satisfy the main demands of the ministers.

During these trying days Richard Baxter as a sort of last resort prepared the Reformation of the Liturgy, not as a substitute for the prayer book, but to provide alternatives to the forms in that book. It was said to have been prepared in fourteen days, but if so it was done with a rich background of both study and actual experience in the use of the liturgy he proposed. So it was by no means done hastily nor carelessly. It is regarded as a landmark in the history of Puritan worship because it shows that they believed in an orderly, dignified, even a semiliturgical worship, and also believed this kind of worship to be in harmony with the simple, spiritual, and pure worship of the New Testament, for which they stood. This effort, like the previous ones, was futile. The revised prayer book was published in 1662 without the main reforms so long sought by the Puritans. That edition of the book with minor changes has remained the official prayer book of the Anglican Church down to the present time. It reinserted the black rubric with some alteration in wording. A number of other rubrics were modified, the most important of which had to do with making the Ante-Communion the principal Sunday service henceforth in the parishes and reducing the actual celebrations of Communion to three or four times a year. Most of the changes left unmodified the general scheme of the Anglican worship.

This proved to be the last effort of any importance by the Puritans in England to revise the prayer book until another century had passed. It is interesting but unprofitable to speculate as to what course the history of worship might have taken in England if the proposals of the Puritan ministers had been accepted by the Anglican bishops. Most of

[10] Davies, op. cit., p. 148.

those proposals had already been incorporated in the groups later to be known as the "Free Churches," especially the Presbyterians and Independents (Congregationalists), and were to be incorporated in the worship of the Methodists, who will be considered in the next chapter. During the seventeenth, eighteenth and nineteenth centuries the worship in English nonconformist groups developed along the same general lines as that of the churches of Scotland and of the United States, where worship was until recent decades prevailingly nonliturgical.

Hence as far as the documents of the Anglican Church were concerned, the Protestant Reformation as it applied to worship ended in 1662. An attempt was made in 1927-28 to revise the *Book of Common Prayer*, but the proposed revision was rejected by Parliament. However, since then the revised *Order for Communion* proposed at the time has been used as an alternative to that of 1662 in some dioceses. Like all other bodies the Anglican Church has been divided into high church (liturgical) and low church (nonliturgical, more or less) groups. And the use of the prayer book has varied widely according to the prevailing custom in various parishes.

Let us now stop a moment to try, somewhat by way of summary, to see within broad limits what happened to worship in the Anglican Church as a result of the Reformation. When all the changes had been made, the English worship was left somewhere between the Reformed and the Roman worship, although it is to be remembered that attempts have been made to prove it is properly to be classified with the Reformed worship.[11] In many ways that Anglican position is a compromise and intentionally so. In general their worship practices resemble those of Lutheranism more than any other Protestant group, but their interpretation of the Lord's Supper is more like that of Zwingli. In the end they repudiated both transubstantiation and sacramentarianism (a term loosely used to describe Zwingli's doctrine). They refused to think of the Supper as an objective sacrifice, but retained the idea of it as a subjective sacrifice in the sense of a self-donation of the worshiper. They retained the epiclesis but changed the consecration prayer to make it conform somewhat to that used by the other reformers.

They exscinded many papal or medieval notions, such as prayers for the dead and to Mary and the saints. They eliminated introits and

[11] For example, see N. Dimock, *The History of the Book of Common Prayer.*

graduals and replaced them with hymns or psalms. They reduced the number, but did not entirely eliminate saints' days. They simplified the liturgy somewhat, turned altars into tables, provided for regular Sunday worship without Communion, and permitted Communion to be celebrated only a few times a year, discarded many ancient forms but retained many others, and retained a generous amount of medieval symbolism and ceremonials. Although they provided fixed prayers and other formularies, a considerable amount of freedom was allowed, or at least was exercised, in their use.

G. What the Reformers Accomplished

Let us now take a bird's-eye view of the first two centuries of the Reformation to discover what the reformers accomplished or tried to accomplish. It is not proper to speak of what the reformers "did" or "thought" as though they were uniformly of the same mind in all matters. It can only be said that some reformers took one position and others took another, that the early reformers accomplished this and the later reformers accomplished that. That is, we must distinguish between different reformers at different times and places and the Reformation as a whole. When viewed as a whole and at long range, the astonishing thing is that the leaders agreed at so many points and moved so consistently in the same general directions.

They abolished the priesthood. They substituted the word "minister" for the word "priest." All sacerdotal functions of the priest—confession, absolution, indulgences, penances, officiating at a sacrifice—were eliminated. Preaching was restored to a prominent place in the worship service. The services in the vernacular were restored. Congregational participation, especially in the form of hymn singing, was increased. Eucharistic vestments were generally, though not universally, discontinued. Saints' days were either reduced radically or abolished entirely. Prayers for saints were forbidden. The Christian year was abandoned, except that in some places the chief annual festivals were retained. Extemporaneous or free prayer was revived. Symbolism and practically all the ceremonials were abolished. The service as a whole was shortened radically by reducing the number of responses, versicles, and other variables as well as by reducing the number and types of prayers and the number of scripture lections.

141

Church buildings were modified. At the beginning of the Reformation, Protestants took over the Roman Catholic church buildings in their communities. For the most part these had long chancels with altars at the east end, with choir stalls on either side, and with high pulpits extending out into the nave from near one corner of the chancel. These buildings were simply improvised for their own worship. Many of these buildings, which were originally Roman Catholic but were later taken over by Protestants, are still in use in many parts of Europe. When Protestants began to construct buildings of their own, some used as a model those to which they had been accustomed; but many undertook to erect buildings which would be specifically suitable for worship in accordance with Protestant principles. This resulted in sanctuaries with a low platform, on which there was a central pulpit, back of which were the chairs for the officiating ministers, and behind these the choir and organ lofts, with the Communion table in front of the pulpit on the floor level of the people; or in sanctuaries with divided chancels that were shallow, with Communion tables away from the wall, and with seats behind them for the ministers and elders. These buildings were erected not merely so the people could see as in medieval times, but so they could hear and could participate in the intimate fellowship of worship.

Altars were turned into tables. It was unanimously agreed that an altar was out of place in a Protestant church. Hence altars were pulled away from the east wall, seats for the ministers were placed behind them, and regardless of their shape were treated as tables. This was done by all the reformers without any exception. The Lord's Supper, and often the entire service, was conducted from the Basilican position from behind the table. Since at first the tables were altars used as such, there was no difference in appearance between the old altars and the table. A young French student who worshiped with the Protestants in Strasbourg in 1525, describing the worship in a letter to his friend, the Bishop of Meaux, said, "The Table is set well forward, in a place in full view of the church, . . . in order that they may not be thought to be in any way like those who make a sacrifice out of Christ's Supper, but the Table does not differ in any way from ordinary altars." [12] At the time altars were frequently hugh cubical blocks of stone, shaped like tombs. When the time came to construct tables for their new houses of wor-

---

[12] Maxwell, *op. cit.*, p. 97. Used by permission of Oxford University Press, London.

ship, some of the reformers still made them in the shape of altars, although they were made of wood, while many others made them look like tables.

The interpretation of the Lord's Supper was changed. The main source of misunderstanding and division among the reformers was their differences in interpreting the Lord's Supper. Yet it is amazing how far their agreements went. It was unanimously agreed that Communion in both kinds should be restored to the people. It was likewise agreed that it must be observed around the table in such a manner as to carry out its original meaning as a fellowship. They repudiated the idea that the Supper was an "objective" sacrifice, that it was a repetition of the sacrifice of Christ, and also repudiated the accompanying doctrine of transubstantiation. But they could not agree on whether and how it was to be interpreted as a "subjective" sacrifice. Augustine is said to have stated to the newly confirmed communicants in his day, "There you are upon the table; there you are in the chalice." This idea that the bread and the wine were in some manner an "offering" or "oblation" of the individual worshiper had gained wide acceptance by the time of the Reformation. Both Luther and Calvin accepted this medieval view, but Zwingli eliminated it entirely from his liturgy of the Supper.

The reformers agreed that Christ was present in a real sense at the Communion but could not agree on any definition of "how" or "where" he was present. Luther and Calvin believed he was present in some unique manner in the bread and wine, and that in some mysterious way the elements do convey grace to the participant. Luther's doctrine, known as consubstantiation (the comingling of the two substances of the body and the blood of Christ and of the bread and wine), together with his doctrine of ubiquity, or the immanent presence of God everywhere in all created things, issued in the position that Christ's body and blood were *really*, not merely *spiritually*, present in the sacrament and that the benefits of these are received by the communicant when he takes the bread and wine, whether he is a believer or not. The latter idea is known as the *ex opere operato* doctrine of the schoolmen, which said the elements when consecrated operated automatically in conveying grace, whether the recipient was a believer or not. It is generally agreed that Luther's view differed little in a metaphysical sense from the medieval view.

Calvin, who tried to act as a mediator between Luther and Zwingli, believed that the reception of Christ is *spiritual*, but *real*, but to the

143

believer only. While he speaks of the elements being visible *signs*, or *symbols*, of spiritual realities, or *seals* guaranteeing the words of Christ, he also speaks of them as conveying what they signify. They really are means of grace. God uses them to feed the soul just as he uses fire to warm the body or the sun to give us light. So they become a "life-giving influence" by the secret workings of the Holy Spirit. There is a distinction between the interpretations of Calvin and Luther without too much difference. In the last analysis it takes a good deal of fine theological and semantic forensic to distinguish between their views and the doctrine of transubstantiation. The net result is the same in the end: the actual presence of Christ in the elements and their use as a vehicle of grace.

Zwingli took the position that Christ's presence in the sacrament is not physical but spiritual, that he is apprehended by faith in the heart of the believer, and that the apprehension has to do with mind and consciousness, not with material substance. He went to great length to explain what he meant by this so as not to be misunderstood. Yet he has often been both misunderstood and misrepresented. The most recent thorough study of Zwingli's doctrine of the Supper has been made by Cyril C. Richardson of Union Theological Seminary.[13] By numerous quotations from Zwingli's writings and a careful philosophical and theological appraisal of the same, Richardson shows that "great injustice is done Zwingli by the assertion that his view differed from the other notable reformers in a denial of the presence of Christ at the Supper" and by the charge that his position is purely mental or psychological or subjective. Zwingli's basic position was that the Holy Spirit cannot be "mediated" by sensible forms or by things. Things cannot be the "bearers or vehicles of spiritual power." "Faith is fed by spirit, not by flesh." It "has to do immediately with the spirit or consciousness." Christ's presence at the Supper is a "spiritual presence." He is there as divine Spirit. The believer "holds him in his soul like a treasure."

What part do the bread and wine play? "This is my body" means "This signifies my body." The bread and wine are symbols only and have no essential or organic relation to what they signify. The expressions "eat the flesh" and "drink [the] blood" of Christ (cf. John 6:53 ff.)

[13] *Zwingli and Cranmer on the Eucharist*, lectures published by Seabury-Western Theologcal Seminary, Evanston, Ill., 1949. I am greatly indebted to this pamphlet for much of the material used in my summary of Zwingli's position.

144

are figures of speech and are not to be taken in a literal sense. They do not bring Christ near, for he is always and everywhere present. The sight and eating of the bread and wine stimulate the believer to become aware of his presence. They remind him of the historic fact of Christ's death and of the grace there offered, but do not bring that grace. That grace is brought directly by the Spirit of God to the spirit of the believer. · The elements are not the physical channel of the grace but are instrumental in provoking the communicant to accept that grace by faith.

Trying to clarify his meaning, Zwingli once said, "You eat the body of Christ spiritually" (that is, by faith). And "by faith" means apprehending by mind or consciousness. This harks back to what Albertus Magnus, one of the the medieval scholars, said—that the substance of Christ's body passed into the "mind," not into the stomach or the digestion. In another place Zwingli said the believer eats the "body of Christ sacramentally," or "in the heart and spirit with the accompaniment of the sacrament." Zwingli would have protested vigorously against interpreting this as a *purely* "mental" or "psychological" or "subjective" experience. He would have insisted, as Richardson puts it, that faith "is not an emotional state created by ourselves, not an intellectual acceptance of the principles of truth." Faith is "being grasped by God through the action of the Holy Spirit." Faith is initiated not by man but by God. It takes place within the consciousness, but is not consciousness. Rather the consciousness is a "concomitant of faith."

It is a misrepresentation of Zwingli's point of view to say, as is often done, that his conception of the Supper is narrow, or that it is a "bare memorial," or that it lacks the experience of the "real presence," or that it is devoid of joy, thanksgiving, and mystery. He called the experience a "faith-mysticism" instead of a "substance-mysticism." It is true only to say that it is strictly a spiritual experience devoid of all semblances of materiality or substance. But Zwingli would insist that it is as real, as vital, as warm, as joyful, as the experience of the presence of Christ ever is or ever can be. In the last analysis therefore the presence of Christ is *real* to the three major theologians, but they differ in their terms used to explain how and where he is present.

The general structure of the consecration prayer was retained by the reformers, but on the whole they were careful to revise the wording so as to eliminate everything that could be construed as a physical miracle, although again Zwingli went further in that direction than either Luther

145

or Calvin. The wording was changed so as to imply not that the elements were being offered as a sacrifice to God but that the communicants were offering themselves as an expression of gratitude for what Christ had done. Also the prayer for the descent of the Holy Spirit, the epiclesis, was changed so that it would imply that God was sending the Spirit not upon the elements but upon the communicants. Thus the prayer was made to conform more nearly to that of the first few centuries, when, according to Oesterley, it was a prayer for the presence of God with the worshipers, not for the Spirit to come upon the elements themselves.[14]

Both Luther and Calvin wished to make the Lord's Supper an integral part of the regular weekly service. Zwingli believed it was possible to have a complete worship experience without the Communion and was therefore in favor of infrequent Communion. It is a mistake therefore to say, as is so commonly done, that the purpose of the reformers was to restore the Lord's Supper as the "norm" of public worship. It was the purpose of some, but not of all, reformers so to do. And in practice at least, if not in theory, Zwingli's views prevailed. In all the Protestant churches, including the Anglican, infrequent Communion became the common practice and has, generally speaking, continued to be until the present time. It can be said therefore that in spite of their differences the reformers did change the Supper to make it more nearly conform to the New Testament meaning.

Having considered the major changes the reformers made in the liturgy, let us attempt to understand what they were trying to do. It is well known that the expressed purpose of all the reformers, both the earliest and the latest, was to restore worship to its New Testament form. Undoubtedly to the extremists this meant to reproduce the exact actions and procedures of that worship. For example, many groups insisted the Lord's Supper must be observed in precisely the same manner and sequence of both words and actions as it was in the Apostolic Church. This same principle applied to the various elements included in worship. Only those and all those found in the early Christian worship were to be utilized. But it is doubtful whether this was the sole purpose of the great majority of the reformers, and for two reasons. First, they did not restore such New Testament practices as the agape and

[14] Op. cit., pp. 228-30.

speaking in tongues; and second, they continued to use the Eucharistic prayer, the Lord's Prayer, and some of the versicles and responses, such as the *Gloria* and the *Nunc Dimittis*, all of which were definitely older than the New Testament. Yet there was a striking similarity between the orders of worship of the reformers that finally emerged and the New Testament practices. This will be obvious if the reader will compare the list of New Testament worship practices found in Chapter 3, with the outline of the 1542 liturgy of Calvin found earlier in this chapter. Evidently they were trying to formulate a worship of the same general type as that used in the New Testament. It seems quite certain also that they were seeking an order of service far simpler and shorter than that of the fourth and fifth centuries, because they omitted so many of the lections, responses, versicles, prayers, and so on, which characterized that order.

In spite of the fact that Calvin himself desired a "stated form of prayers and of the administration of the sacraments," from which ministers "be not allowed to vary," it is a question whether a "fixed" liturgy was at any time the *chief* concern of the reformers. At any rate they did not agree on a fixed standard; all of them felt perfectly free to experiment with the liturgy and to make use of or to reject at will certain types of worship material and to vary worship procedures. As was the case in the period from New Testament times to the Reformation, the liturgy was continuously in process of change during the Reformation period. The most reasonable explanation of what they had in mind is this: they were striving to create for their age a worship based on the same general principles as that of the New Testament and by this step to put Christian worship back on the main track from which it had been switched during and after the fourth and fifth centuries. Whether we are justified in saying this was their deliberate purpose, we can certainly say that was what they succeeded in accomplishing. They put Christianity back in its original course. They reshaped Christian worship more nearly according to its original type.

6

Reformation Background:
Eighteenth Century to Present

THE Reformation in Christian worship was by no means completed when the last revision of the English prayer book was published in 1662. But since no changes of any great significance in worship practices occurred in England in the next two centuries that did not have their parallels in America, we now turn to the story of what took place here in the next 175 years.

A. Eighteenth and First Half of Nineteenth Centuries

Most of the Protestant groups in Europe were in process of being transplanted to America from the early decades of the seventeenth century. Throughout that century and until the crucial years of the formation of the Republic of the United States of America, these groups were slowly taking root in American soil. They carried certain principles of the Reformation more nearly to their logical conclusions than did the same groups in Europe. This is recognized by both secular and church historians. This was due to the perfectly natural progress of a momentous revolutionary movement, to the particular stimulus that came from the conditions of pioneers in a new land, and to the emergence of new forces in Western civilization.

The reformers did not and could not immediately see all the implications of what they had undertaken. They moved cautiously. They formulated their opinions tentatively, then revised them in the light of their open debates, their exchange of judgment, and their common expe-
148

riences. They were carrying on many experiments simultaneously under different political situations and were to a large extent limited by those situations. There was general agreement at some points but violent disagreement at others, so that adjustments and compromises had to be made. It was sometimes decades, at other times a century or two, before the reformers realized some of the implications of their positions. Moving away from Europe to this continent enabled them to think more clearly and to experiment with less restraint than did the earlier reformers—with the result that significant extensions of the Reformation took place in the United States.

An outstanding example of this is found in the length of time it took the various religious bodies in America to realize what their tenets logically led to in the matter of freedom of thought and of worship. After a number of experiments involving some social turmoil and injustice the churches in the United States devised the plan of complete separation of church and state that has very aptly been described as a "free church *and* a free state existing side by side and independently *in* a free nation." [1] Under this plan churches are supported not by taxation but by the voluntary gifts of their members, and the status of an individual in civil society is in no way dependent upon his connection with any religious group. Hence after several centuries of experience the Reformation produced in the United States a type and amount of religious liberty not hitherto known either in Great Britain or on the continent. It may be rightly claimed that in nearly every way the reformation in worship came nearer to its completion in the American churches than in Europe. In fact, many believe the Reformation moved out of its youth into its maturity in the United States. Here, unfettered by the heavy hand of the past, profiting by and building upon the costly experiments of others through more than two centuries, and stimulated by the challenging adventure of building a new type of society, Christians were able to give the principles of the Reformation their maximum chance to develop to their logical conclusions.

Previous to the revolt of the American colonies the various religious bodies were more or less closely related in an official way to the bodies in their mother-European countries. But when the colonies won their independence, those groups one at a time and in very quick succession began to organize themselves independently. Under the impulse of

[1] Winfred E. Garrison, *A Protestant Manifesto*, p. 198.

the spirit of democracy in the air they did not hesitate to do their own independent thinking. At the same time this was taking place, the whole Western world was being affected by the Wesleyan movement and the great evangelical revival that grew out of it. This movement gave a great impulse to freedom, to new spiritual life, and to new forms of practical Christian work. Its influence spread rapidly through the British Isles, to the continent of Europe, and to the American colonies. It led to the great revival which began in the United States about 1796, that continued unabated for more than a decade, and that did not spend itself fully until well toward the middle of the nineteenth century or even beyond.

The combined efforts of the French and American revolutions and of the evangelical revivals created a new factor and force in religion which carried the Reformation in worship further along toward a climax. That climax was reached about the middle of the nineteenth century. It resulted in what has come to be known as evangelical worship. This is not to say there was no worship in Europe previous to this that could rightly be given that label. Such worship did exist in certain groups in pre-Reformation times, some of them going well back toward New Testament times. It existed also in its more vibrant forms among the Separatist groups throughout the entire period of the Reformation. But it came to a climactic development or fulfillment in the United States, which justifies us in calling the worship of the churches of the whole nation outstandingly and distinctively evangelical. This worship has its roots in the work of the original reformers and still more in the work of the later Puritan reformers. But it is to be traced straight back to the charismatic aspects of New Testament worship. The worship of every religious body in the United States of whatever type became to a lesser or greater degree evangelical in nature.

Only a few denominations in this country adopted a fixed liturgy or a book of forms. One of these was the Methodist Episcopal Church, whose history constitutes a striking extension of the Reformation. Previous to the Revolutionary War the Methodist societies in America had been more or less under the care of the Episcopal establishment. Because of its natural associations with the Royalist cause the Episcopal Church in the colonies was practically destroyed when the British were defeated. This left the Methodists in a predicament. They began immediately to ask Wesley for men to minister to their needs. So in 1784

John Wesley and two other priests of the Church of England ordained two deacons, two elders, and two superintendents to care for the Methodists of North America. In that same year Wesley prepared a "liturgy" for their use as they traveled over America, advising that it be used and that the Lord's Supper be administered on every Lord's Day. The liturgy was entitled *The Sunday Service for the Methodists of North America, with Other Occasional Services.*

It contained an abridgment of the English *Book of Common Prayer,* twenty-four of the thirty-nine Articles of Religion and forms for ordination. When its text is carefully compared with the text of the English book, it is discovered to be literally an expurgated edition of that book. Although Wesley added and substituted a few words and phrases, for the most part he simply deleted what he considered objectionable. What is still more significant: When collated and studied in the light of the history of the English book, his deletions turn out to be largely the changes sought by the Puritans for the book of 1662 but refused by the revisers. So in a very important sense the *Sunday Service* of Wesley successfully completed the reformation in worship long sought by the moderate Puritans of England—a reformation that came to a halt in the Anglican Church more than a century before.

If the reader will check the list, given earlier, of changes the Puritans of the seventeenth century wanted made in the English prayer book, he will have a fairly complete list of the things Wesley discarded. A few changes should, however, be given special mention. He provided for extempore prayer, which was not permitted in the Anglican liturgy. He turned the pronouncement of absolution into a prayer for pardon, thus altering its sacerdotal nature, by changing from the third person to the first person and making it read, "O Almighty God, our heavenly Father, who of *thy* great mercy *hast* promised forgiveness of sins to all them that with hearty repentance and true faith turn to *thee; have mercy upon us;* pardon and deliver *us* from all *our* sins; confirm and strengthen *us* in all goodness; and bring *us* to everlasting life; through Jesus Christ our Lord. Amen." He adopted with some slight changes the prayer of consecration which in the English order is not so much a prayer of consecration of the elements as a recognition of Christ's sacrifice as "full, perfect and sufficient . . . for the sins of the whole world," and a prayer that those who by faith receive the elements "in remembrance" of that death "may be partakers of Christ's body and blood."

The book is as significant equally for the manner in which it was treated as for its actual contents. Within a comparatively few years the Methodists dropped the word "liturgy" from their ecclesiastical vocabulary, generally ceased to use the printed prayers and resorted to extempore prayer, and otherwise laid aside other parts of the order for Sunday service at their discretion. Considering the origin and the nature of Methodists, it was hardly to be expected that they would be bound by a fixed liturgy. Wesley's break with the Anglican Church in which he was an ordained minister was made in part to free himself from sacerdotal formalism. The Methodist movement from one angle may rightly be called a revolt against formalism. It was characterized by the spirit of democracy and freedom then prevailing. Methodism became a pioneering church in more than one way. It was thoroughly infused with evangelistic fervor and with new spiritual force. The spiritual life that characterized it was too vital to be confined within the limits of a fixed order of worship. Methodists were not at the time and never have been tied to the liturgy for their worship services. Article XXII of the church says, "Every particular church may ordain, change, or abolish rites and ceremonies, so that all things may be done to edification." Thus their service book has in practice been little more than a directory for worship.

But they did keep and continued to use the rituals for the other services, or "occasional services," as Wesley called them. The book became to all intents and purposes a book of discipline. But even the rituals for the other services were used freely. Ministers were never tied to them strictly. The sanctuaries of Methodist churches have consistently been pulpit-centered with the table on the floor level of the people. The people traditionally have communed kneeling at the rail, but the revised book of 1892 provided, "Let persons who have scruples concerning the receiving of the Sacrament of the Lord's Supper kneeling be permitted to receive it either standing or sitting." It should be observed in passing that Wesley's book was adopted by the Methodists in England also and there used in somewhat the same fashion as in the United States.

In 1789, about five years after the Methodist societies in the United States adopted Wesley's book, a general convention of the Protestant Episcopal Church adopted an American revised version of the English *Book of Common Prayer*. The basis of this book was the book of 1662,

152

but it was revised in the light of both the Irish and Scottish books and the "American opinions of the bishops and deputies composing the convention that adopted it." The first edition was not actually published until 1793. The principal alterations were those made to conform to the new political conditions. In 1892 another standard edition was published in which a wider choice of prayers and lections was provided. But despite the adoption of a service book the worship of the Episcopal Church for fifty years or more was in practice evangelical. One historian has described that church as being thoroughly "evangelical" in its nature until nearly the middle of the nineteenth century, and of having become concerned greatly about the ministry, the sacraments, and ritualism only when its evangelicism lost its power to resist the inroads of Catholicism by those we now call "Anglo-Catholics." [2]

The American Lutheran Church also had a fixed form. An effort was made from the very start to secure uniformity in the use of a liturgy. A printed liturgy was not available at the time but was current among the pastors in manuscript form. This liturgy has been traced back to the liturgy used by the Lutherans in parts of Germany and in Scandinavian countries. But actually there were wide variations in the liturgies used in the various churches, and at the outset individual congregations were permitted to decide for themselves what form of liturgy to use. In 1885 a *Church Book* was published for English-speaking Lutheran churches in the United States and was adopted for the express purpose of bringing usage into uniformity. But this was not mandatory and could be used in full or not according to the desires of any particular congregation.

While the Lutherans have been more or less liturgical, they have not escaped the influence of the free spirit of American churches in general. They cannot be said to be sacerdotal in their services. They have retained the altar but also the pulpit and have stressed the preaching of the word of God as strongly as any Protestant group and have preached it often with evangelical fervor. So far as the Lord's Supper is concerned, they rejected both transubstantiation and consubstantiation and have asserted their belief in the "sacramental presence of Christ." This presence is regarded as a mystery beyond their comprehension, and they have not tried to tie their people to any single formulation of this doctrine, but have left it to the consciences of the believers.

[2] See E. Clowes Chorley, *Men and Movements in the American Episcopal Church.*

They have, however, repudiated all magical or quasi-physical explanations of the virtue of the sacraments.

The only other groups in America of any size that have had an elaborate liturgy are the Dutch and German Reformed Churches.[3] Their liturgies go back to those of the sixteenth century and include forms for the Lord's Supper, for ordination, marriage, and so on, and provide printed prayers. But all forms except the sacramentive were optional as to use and soon fell into desuetude.

In 1788 the first general assembly of the Presbyterian Church in the United States was organized. At that time the *Directory for Worship* prepared by the Westminster Assembly was adopted with certain modifications to adapt it to the times. All Presbyterian bodies used that as a guide somewhat in the same manner as their Scottish forebears. Throughout the nineteenth century their worship, like that of the other bodies in this country, was informal, nonliturgical, and evangelical.

No other leading bodies had anything comparable to fixed formularies of worship. Congregationalists were uniformly Puritan in their worship practices. They opposed the sacerdotal idea of the ministry, used simple, nonliturgical, and even spontaneous orders of service, although every church was privileged to adopt the order of service most agreeable to its members. Extempore prayer was customary. They were greatly affected by the evangelical revival in all its aspects, admitting as members to their churches only regenerated persons and communicants to Communion only on the basis of a genuine Christian experience. The Evangelical churches, as could be expected from their very name, were strong for apostolic evangelism. They stressed spiritually awakened and quickened souls, repentance, sound conversion, regeneration, a radical change of heart, and the new birth. Their worship was simple and orderly, but free from all ironclad forms and all artificial aids or restraints. Baptists were among the most informal of all groups. With their roots going back through the Separatists of the Reformation period to the pre-Reformation sects like the Anabaptists, the Bohemian Brethren, and the Waldensians, they were consistently antisacerdotal, anticreedal, nonliturgical, and thoroughly evangelistic. They permitted only regenerated or converted members and stood for individual acceptance of Christ.

---

[3] One of the smallest Christian churches, the Moravian, not only has an extensive liturgy containing many ancient forms but is famous for its highly developed church music and noted for its missionary zeal.

They kept the Lord's Supper as a memorial feast after the manner, as they believed, of the New Testament practice. The Disciples of Christ, founded a few decades beyond the revolutionary days by Alexander Campbell, were likewise free and informal in their worship, nonsacerdotal in their ministry, and permeated with evangelistic fervor. The Lord's Supper was regarded by them as a memorial feast, but almost alone of all the early American churches they made the Supper a part of every weekly worship service.

It is now in order to make some generalizations about Christian worship in the United States. Speaking in general, and with the exception of two or three groups, that worship may accurately be called non-liturgical or Puritan or, better still, evangelical. When church buildings were erected, the sanctuaries with the central pulpit and the Communion table on the floor level of the congregation were customarily adopted, even in a large number of the Episcopal churches. The Lord's Supper has been observed by most of the denominations either monthly or quarterly, the main exception to this being the Disciples of Christ. The liturgy of the Lord's Supper has been simple but orderly with little attention to the structure of the Eucharistic prayer, with no semblance of sacerdotalism, and with the major emphasis on it as a fellowship. Until almost the end of the nineteenth century the prevailing sentiment in most denominations was against the use of art and symbols, candles, and the like except the symbol of the cross; and even the use of the cross was violently opposed in many sections of the country; and against ceremonial and dramatic action.

An outstanding characteristic of American churches in this period was the deliberate attempt to keep ministers and laymen on the same plane. In some denominations laymen were given a large place in the general handling of the affairs of the church. In many local churches laymen were permitted to assist ministers in the conduct of certain phases of public worship. As a matter of principle ministers dressed in the same manner as laymen to avoid giving the impression that they were of a different order. In only a few sections of the country was it customary for the minister to wear the black gown while conducting worship. The orders of service were simple, often informal, without the use of versicles and responses except the "Doxology" and the *Gloria*, with little use of prayers other than the invocation, the Lord's Prayer, the long pastoral prayer, and the benediction, and usually with a responsive

155

reading and one scripture lection. The central act of worship was the sermon. The worship service was distinctly a preaching service with emphasis upon evangelism. Most American denominations made little or no use of the Christian year. They paid no attention whatever to saints' days and had few annual festivals except Christmas and Easter, and even these were opposed by some denominations and given only slight attention by others. They had no books of common worship to guide their ministers and to be used as prayer books by the worshipers, and no fixed or standardized orders of service. In short, the worship of the overwhelming majority of Christian churches in the United States was of the Puritan, informal, spontaneous, spirit-filled, evangelistic type of worship of the New Testament. In short, it was evangelical worship.

B. Liturgical Revival Since Middle of Nineteenth Century

Since the latter part of the nineteenth century a revival of interest in worship has been going on throughout Christendom and has affected every church of whatever name or kind. The year 1855 is often given as the date at which the revival began in the United States. In that year Charles W. Baird published *Eutaxia or the Presbyterian Liturgies; Historical Sketches by a Minister of the Presbyterian Church*. In this book he cited the Calvinian liturgies used by Presbyterians in the early days of the Reformation and pleaded for their use in a restored liturgical worship. This awakened interest in the subject both in the United States and in the British Isles. He followed this in 1857 with a proposed book of worship entitled *A Book of Public Prayer, Compiled from the Authorized Formularies of Worship of the Presbyterian Church, as Prepared by the Reformers, Calvin, Knox, and Others*. About the same time a controversy arose in the German Reformed Church at Mercersburg, Pennsylvania, over the desirability of reviving a liturgical church service. This too resulted in 1858 in a proposed prayer book, *A Liturgy or Order of Christian Worship*.

From that time there was increasing discussion of the subject, and sporadic experiments in liturgical reformation were made in many churches of many denominations. In the Presbyterian Church this resulted in the *Book of Common Worship*, first published in 1905. This has gone through several editions since, the last one in 1946. Although this has been officially published, it has not been mandatory but leaves the ministers and congregations free as to form and order. A comparison of the several editions shows an increasing tendency to go back to ancient forms and an effort to standardize the order, especially for the Communion service, according to the practice of the early reformers. Similar books have been put out in Scotland, South Africa, Canada, and elsewhere among many Evangelical and Reformed churches. Within recent years a group of Congregational ministers put out for free churches a book of forms which will be referred to again shortly. The churches that have been the most informal and nonliturgical have also been affected, and their worship practices have been modified to some extent by the influence of the liturgical movement.

The significant phases of this revival may be summarized under the following headings.

The Arrangement of Sanctuaries. Numerous churches have set up divided chancels, with the Communion table placed at the center against the wall and with the pulpit and lectern pushed out into the nave on either side. Frequently the table is made in the form of an altar and treated as such. The table is now quite commonly spoken of in many church publications as an altar. The expression is frequently heard, "We Protestants also have an altar." When the table is against the wall, the Communion service is conducted by the minister from in front or at the north end of the altar. At certain places in the service the minister and people face the altar, even bow to it, and in some instances make the sign of the cross as they do so. In some churches the chancel proper is fenced off from the congregation with some sort of railing.

The Use of Arts and Symbols. Turning the table into an altar has resulted in the increased use of art and symbols. Altar guilds have been organized in some of the hitherto most Calvinistic churches, notably the Congregational-Christian Churches, and are being recommended by informal groups within other denominations. It is the avowed purpose of all such groups to bring the arts back into the Protestant churches. Pamphlets and booklets are printed containing photographs and other types of information concerning the use of textiles, glass, sculpture, flowers, music, painting, choral speech, poetry, and so on, in Protestant worship. Workshops and summer camps are held to create interest in bringing back into modern Protestantism the medieval idea of craft guilds. It is even asserted by one writer that our theological seminaries ought to be enlisted in this campaign. He says:

The seminary has so far failed to understand that the *minister's primary function is that of the artist and not the scholar* [italics mine]. What is needed at the seminary is a whole department of the religious arts. The best possible equipment must be given to this department. It will include a library of prints, films, slides and records; workshop rooms with paints and drawing boards; a chapel with all the appointments of worship; an organ, a piano and library of music; a little theatre with all the means of production; and of course, competent instructors to work with the students.[4]

A manual put out for altar guilds gives detailed instructions about the altar and the various ornaments that go with it, about liturgical colors, and about what guilds may do to perform most efficiently their duty of looking after the church's altar. An illustration of a vested altar is given, with twenty-two different items numbered and named as follows: cross, office lights, vases, communion lights, missal stand, mensa, fair linen, corporal, paten, pyx (or ciborium), cruet (or flagon), chalice, burse, frontlet, frontal, orphrey, fringe, dossal, dossal bar, retable, throne, and pall. The booklet gives minute details about all these articles and their proper use and care. Eleven pages are devoted solely to the instructions about the care of the several cloths used on the altar.[5]

An introductory chapter to *A Book of Worship for Free Churches*, published in 1948 by a group of Congregational ministers and referred to earlier, is perhaps the most elaborate treatment of "Symbolism in Worship" by the leaders of any American Protestant body. It explains in detail the altar and its various decorations; the use and meaning of of the several monograms placed upon crosses; bookmarks and other ornaments; the various symbols used in windows; carvings and stone work such as the hand, the dove, the tongue of fire, the triangle in its various forms, the crown, a fish, a vine, a door, a rock, a star, the sun, light, bread, a chalice, a cluster of wheat and grapes, the quatrefoil, the eagle, the rooster, the anchor, the ship, the olive branch, green sprigs of grass, and the palm. Attention is given to the symbolic meaning of numbers one to eight in their various uses, to the symbolic meaning of the various parts of the building—the narthex, the vestibule, the nave, the chancel, the center aisle, the baptismal font, the chancel with its three steps, its choir and sanctuary, and the twelve pillars. The symbolism of the traditional colors—white, red, violet or purple, black, and green—

---

[4] Clarence Seidenspinner, "Art and the Protestant Church," *Christendom*, Winter, 1946, pp. 36-44.

[5] See Carl F. Weidmann, *A Manual for Altar Guilds.*

is also described. All these symbols are commended to those who are willing to use them in their traditional meaning and manner and with proper restraint. What they mean by "proper restraint" is not explained.

Changes in the Lord's Supper. Almost without exception the leaders of the liturgical revival in all denominations advocate making the Lord's Supper the norm for the weekly worship service. All the other parts of the service, they maintain, are merely preparatory for and lead up to the observance of the Supper. A lengthened and fixed liturgy for this part of the service is suggested. Special emphasis is given to the structure of the Eucharistic prayer, including the oblation, the anamnesis, and the epiclesis. Some writers do not hesitate to insist that the Supper be thought of in terms of a sacrifice, both subjective and objective, and quite boldly declare this is justified by the New Testament use of the Jewish terms and concepts associated with the Temple sacrifice. Generous use is made of the traditional versicles, responses, and collects associated with the observance of the Supper. The number of private Communions for occasions such as deaths, weddings, and departures on long trips is increasing rapidly. So the liturgy of the Lord's Supper, the uses made of it, and the prevailing interpretations of it are becoming more and more like those of the early medieval Church.

Lengthened Liturgy. The order of service is enriched by the use of collects, bidding prayers, litanies, and other types of printed prayers; by the use of versicles and responses of all types; by an increase in the number of scripture lections; and by "framing" each part of the service with a bidding, a benediction, or an ascription. Dramatic or ceremonial action is advocated by many, as is also the intoning of prayers. Many musical introits, chants, responses, and other numbers by the choir are added, much of the music being difficult and medieval in nature. All sorts of Latin terms and expressions are reappearing in the printed order of worship. The ministers are encouraged to eliminate extemporaneous or free prayer and to make use of the fixed formularies of all kinds now being made available. In one book of worship the order for the regular morning service without Communion has some thirty separate items, the Communion service has twenty-four items preceding the Communion, while the Communion itself has six items preceding the consecration prayer, the seven parts of the prayer, the several actions of the actual Communion, interspersed with a prayer and benediction, the post

Communion prayer or prayers, a closing hymn, and the benediction—making a total of some forty separate items in one service.[6] The result is an elaborated order of service that is rapidly approaching in length and complexity the medieval mass. In fact, a Presbyterian minister recently openly advocated the development of a Protestant Mass and recommended that a converted Catholic priest be engaged to instruct Protestant ministers in how to conduct it properly.[7]

Changing Ministry. All this carries with it changes in the traditional conception of the functions and responsibilities of Protestant ministers. The use of a distinctive street attire for ministers and of vestments, ornaments, insignia, and so on, while they are conducting services is rapidly increasing. It is no uncommon thing to see a Protestant minister while conducting worship wearing a black gown with reversed collar, neck bands, a colorful academic hood, and a large, highly decorated cross suspended by an expensive chain around his neck. Ministers are being instructed in the meaning and use of the many articles of clothing worn by ministers in medieval times, and urged to make use of them with caution. The introductory chapter to *A Book of Worship for Free Churches* explains the use of clerical collars, black stocks, neck bands, the surplice, the stole with emblems and fringe in the proper colors of the season and festival, and the academic hood. The importance of the sermon and the other "didactic" elements of worship are now commonly played down, almost belittled by some, while the importance of the minister leading the people in "objective" worship is being played up. The pulpit with a "little man standing behind it as the master of ceremonies" is put in a secondary place, while the altar with the minister performing semipriestly functions is placed at the center of attention and interest. Thus the preacher is being rapidly replaced by the priest.

For some of the worship practices the leaders of this movement go back to the early reformers of the sixteenth century and bypass the developments in worship in the three centuries following. For other practices they bypass the reformers of all the centuries and return to the Church of the third and fourth centuries. Recent books on worship abound with open criticism of the worship practices of the various re-

---

[6] See *The Book of Common Worship* (Presbyterian), 1946 ed., pp. 11-19, 155-65.

[7] See *Monday Morning*, Sept. 18 and 25, 1950. This is a small weekly magazine published by the General Council of the Presbyterian Church in the U.S.A.

formers. It is said that they were not especially well versed in the history of worship, that they did not possess the facilities for appraising worship forms discriminatingly, and that they erred greatly in supposing they had restored worship to its New Testament, or subapostolic, purity. The classical age of worship, we are told, was the two or three centuries immediately following the apostolic days when the practices, actions, procedures, materials, and the exact manner of their use and their position in the liturgy settled into traditions.

It is insisted that to that period and to those traditions the reformers should have returned. As it is, they mutilated the liturgy and created a barren, severe, truncated, impoverished worship unworthy of Christianity. It is now our duty to restore it to its ancient glory. The reader is encouraged to check those sections of Maxwell's *An Outline of Christian Worship*, where the author criticizes the liturgies of the several reformers. He speaks of the "lamentable impoverishment" of the liturgy by the reformers. Such expressions as "indefensible innovation," "unfortunate departure," "unnecessary departure from a tradition," "needless innovation," and the need of "fidelity to primitive use" abound in the list of his strictures. That is, for his standard of worship he goes back beyond and behind the Reformation.

The exact period to which return should be made is not always indicated. Maxwell is not specific about this, but by putting together all that he says, we can reasonably conclude by the "traditional" and the "primitive" practices he means those of the third and fourth centuries. Like many other writers who take the order of worship of that period as a standard he appears to assume that the type of liturgy found in the fourth century prevailed not only throughout the centuries preceding the fourth but also in the New Testament Church itself. As we saw in our study of the first few centuries, the evidence now extant does not justify such a position, but rather proves that by the fourth century the Christian Church had already departed somewhat seriously from New Testament Christianity in general and from New Testament worship in particular.

Additional evidence that bears on this problem has been given recently by Dix in his monumental work *The Shape of the Liturgy*, pages 208 and following. The book of nearly a thousand pages is written to prove two things: (1) that it is not possible to penetrate through the fifth, fourth, and third centuries to an original uniformity of worship prac-

161

tices which can be called "traditional" and which may be taken as a standard or model for modern worship; and (2) that what was fixed and immutable everywhere in those centuries and as far back as the New Testament was the action in the Lord's Supper. This action he calls the "outline" or "shape" of the liturgy. Hence the title of his book, *The Shape of the Liturgy*, the principal purpose of which is to prove that from the beginning of Christianity the Lord's Supper was observed by a fourfold action first mentioned in the New Testament itself. Thus a noted scholar after exhaustive research concludes that uniform liturgical forms cannot be found in the ancient Church. Yet it is on the basis of that very belief that the leaders of the liturgical revival bypass the reformers and go back to the primitive Church for what they call "traditional" patterns for Christian worship practices.

C. Conclusion

As I conclude this final chapter of my historical review, let this be said: In the light of recent research it hardly seems fair to intimate that the reformers were not very well informed as to the history of worship. On the one hand they may not have known, as is claimed, precisely where such items as, for example, the *Gloria* and the *Nunc Dimittis* were "traditionally" used. On the other hand they may have known this but decided for themselves whether and where to use the same items. If the latter should be the case, and there is no reason why we may not so believe, they were building their rite upon some principle other than the principle of long or traditional usage. It seems to me that the reformers were seeking to develop a cultus for their day that was in harmony with prophetic, evangelical Christianity as they understood it. In which case the principle on which they made a decision whether or not to incorporate this or that in the rite was whether it was in harmony with, whether it fitted the nature of, that Christianity.

In my judgment this is the only proper basis on which evangelical Christians should make such decisions. When, for example, Maxwell takes the reformers severally to task for not doing a "creative" job with the liturgy, he ought to state what kind of liturgy the reformers should have undertaken to "create" considering the tenets of their faith. This he does not do, and unfortunately this generally is too seldom done. Evangelical Christians cannot wisely defer much longer the task of defining the reasons why they advocate a certain type of worship for free churches. It is not sufficient to accept a practice merely because of its age, or because it was once the practice of the Church in some distant period, or because one himself desires it. When a worship practice is adopted by evangelical Christians, it should be because it is in harmony with the basic principles of the type of Christianity they represent.

As we look back from the present time to the New Testament, several pointed questions arise. Within approximately 350 years after the days of Jesus the Church he established had departed from the simple, spiritual, evangelical worship which was originally used. When the Reformation had reached its climax, which I have roughly estimated at the middle of the nineteenth century, the Christian Church had reshaped its worship to conform again to the New Testament type. Within less than 350 years after the beginning of the Reformation, or about 1850, the Church again embarked upon a liturgical reform comparable to the reform that led to the medieval Church. Is history going into reverse? Is it repeating itself? Has the evangelical fervor of the reformers cooled off? Has it lost its force to where its power over the minds and hearts of men is on the point of vanishing? Must liturgical worship again replace evangelical worship?

We turn now to the second main part of this study, where we will endeavor to discover whether or not the questions just asked must inevitably be answered in the affirmative or whether it is possible to develop an orderly, dignified worship that befits the nature of evangelical Christianity without altering that nature and without quenching the Spirit (cf. I Thess. 5:19).

Part II

Developing an Evangelical Cultus in the
Light of This Historical Background

7

The Nature of an Evangelical Cultus

THE word "evangelical" is derived from the word "evangel," which is the same as the word "gospel" and means literally "glad tidings" or "good news." Evangelical, then, means "agreeable to" or "in the spirit of" the New Testament gospel. Evangelical Christians are those who regard themselves as "gospel" Christians. The term was used by some Protestant groups almost from the outset of the Reformation and is widely used today to describe Christians of the Reformation tradition in certain parts of Europe and of the Americas. Not a few Protestants wish the term could be substituted for the word "Protestant" because the latter word has lost its original meaning of "testifying for" (pro and testari) something and has come to mean objecting to something. It is a suitable term for setting forth the positive tenets of those who profess to follow New Testament Christianity.

Evangelical worship means worship agreeable to the gospel as it is found in the New Testament. This does not necessarily imply worship that conforms precisely in every detail to the worship of the New Testament Church, even though, as we have seen, this is what it has meant to a number of reformed groups. Rather it is to be understood as worship that is in harmony with the revelation of the character and purpose of God found in the gospel. That revelation began with the birth of Jesus and ended when the Christian Church was established and firmly convinced of Christ's abiding presence and continuing power in the person of the Holy Spirit. That is, evangelical worship is based squarely upon the total teaching of the New Testament about God. Unfortunately all Christians do not agree concerning that teaching. This accounts for the fact that though all Christian communions profess to worship the same God, all do not worship him in the same manner. Different methods of worship grow out of different ways of conceiving of God. Although the Christian groups who regard themselves as evangelical would have marked differences about a number of other matters, they would be in substantial agreement, at least in general outline, about the kind of God revealed in the New Testament.

The character of God is quite explicitly described in the records. To begin with, they tell us that God was incarnated in Christ, so that when we see Christ, hear what he said, and observe what he did, we know what God is like. The author of Hebrews said Christ was the "effulgence of [God's] glory" and the "very image of his substance" (1:3; cf. II Cor. 4:4). John said, "The Word became flesh, and dwelt among us" (1:14). Jesus himself said, "He that hath seen me hath seen the Father" (John 14:9). That is, God is like Christ. He treats people, looks at life, and thinks about things as Christ did. He is as righteous, as pure, as loving, as Christ. He wants the kind of fellowship with people that Jesus had. He came down to the level of human beings to make them realize their worth to him, to draw them near to himself. But he did something else of tremendous significance. On his own initiative he performed an act of redemption in the death of Christ, thus indicating his tremendous love for human beings and his yearning for their salvation and fellowship. This voluntary act of his forgiving love removed every barrier between him and his children, except the barriers they themselves erect. He has made access to him simple, easy, natural, human. Now all men may enter into the holy place (Heb. 10:12) and draw near to the "throne of grace" with boldness (Heb. 4:6) and without any intermediaries other than Christ.

But this was not all. The self-revelation of God was not complete when Christ died to effect salvation. Christ conquered death, arose from the dead, convinced his followers by a number of spiritual manifestations that he was alive, promised that God would soon usher in a new era in which he would be vividly and consciously present with his children in the person and power of the Holy Spirit, then ascended into heaven. Without any attempt at fine theological distinctions the New Testament writers speak of the omnipresence of God, the living presence of the resurrected Christ, and the continuous fellowship of the Holy Spirit as one and the same thing. The work of the Holy Spirit was the

168

most significant single fact about the experience of New Testament Christians with God. Christ continued to be with them and to do his redemptive work among them through the Holy Spirit. The Spirit guided and shaped their lives, opened new doors, started them on new and daring adventures, baptized them with amazingly new powers, re-generated their hearts, and transformed them into new men in Christ. The test of whether they were full-fledged Christians was whether they had received the Holy Spirit, whether they had experienced the presence and power of the eternally living, loving, ever-present, ever-redeeming God. A conception of God cannot be regarded as being fully evangelical if these ideas associated with the Holy Spirit are left out.

The records are also quite clear as to what was God's purpose by this complete, voluntary, dynamic revelation of himself. His purpose was moral. He wanted to aid men in becoming creatures who would embody in their personalities the moral qualities of his own nature. God is a spirit, the Father of our Spirits, a Person in the sense that we are persons. Human beings are the "children" of God (I John 3:1). God's desire for them, like the desire of earthly fathers for their children, is that they shall grow up mentally, morally, and emotionally. Jesus said, "Ye therefore shall be perfect, as your heavenly Father is perfect" (Matt. 5:48). The word "perfect" in the original Greek is teleios, which means literally "wanting nothing necessary to completeness." It is used through-out the New Testament to indicate "full-grown" persons.[1] In many modern versions the word in its several forms is frequently translated "mature" and "maturity." That is, God wants his children to become mature characters. Paul even went so far as to express the daring thought that God's whole creative and redemptive purpose will be achieved when through Christ men become "sons of God," mature, fully grown, fully responsible moral beings (Rom. 8:19 ff.).

Nor can there be any doubt about what the New Testament reveals concerning the sort of relationship God wants established between him-self and mankind. He wants it to be as natural as that between earthly fathers and children. Although he surrounds them with every possible assistance toward maturity, he waits for them to grow up. He does not coerce their wills. He wants them to become self-respecting, self-reliant, self-directing personalities. He is immediately accessible to them.

[1] Check I Cor. 2:6; 14:20; II Cor. 13:9, 11; Phil. 3:15; Eph. 4:13; Col. 1:28; 4:12; Heb. 6:1; Jas. 1:4.

They may approach him directly at any time and place as one human being approaches another in conversation and fellowship without the need of formalities and intermediaries, but only as spirit to Spirit, mind to Mind, heart to Heart. Whenever and wherever an individual human soul approaches God in humility and penitence, lifts up his voice in sincere petition, turns to God in faith, there God is to hear, to receive, to help, to save.

New Testament worship took place within an atmosphere saturated with these great convictions about God and his relation to men that grew directly out of his self-revelation, his redemptive acts in Jesus, and his workings through the Holy Spirit. It was conditioned by these convictions. Worship may be called evangelical when it takes place in the same framework of ideas, when it is carried out in conformity with those convictions. The word "cultus" means the system—rites or procedures—by which a deity is worshiped. We may properly speak of an *evangelical cultus* to indicate that type of worship which embodies and expresses the characteristic beliefs of New Testament Christians about the character of God, about what he expects of men and how he deals with them, and about how he is to be approached by them. Let us now try to determine the kind of worship that befits the nature of evangelical Christianity. It should be understood that what follows is to be thought of not as definitive but only as descriptive, that there is no particular significance to the sequence of the terms used, and that they are not mutually exclusive.

A. Mature Worship

The first and obvious thing to be said is that mature people should worship God in a mature manner. That is precisely what the New Testament says. It states specifically that God desires and is pleased with mature, rather than with primitive, childish, pagan worship. As indicated earlier in this study, the early Christians abandoned the ancient sacrificial, ceremonial, and legal systems and approached God directly without the mediation of any such external acts and ceremonies. Paul spoke of the old methods of approach to God as rudimentary (cf. Col. 2:8; Gal. 4:3). When he discovered many in the churches of Galatia going back to those practices after once having given them up, he asked, "Now that ye have come to know God, or rather to be known by God, how turn ye back again to the weak and beggarly rudiments, whereunto

170

ye desire to be in bondage over again?" (Gal. 4:9). He said to the Corinthians, "Be not children in mind: . . . but in mind be men" (I Cor. 14:20). The word translated "men" is that same word *teleios*, which means full-grown or mature. Paul is urging them to think like grownups instead of like children. It is difficult therefore to conceive of worship being New Testament in form if it makes use of primitive, elementary, and childish approaches rather than mature approaches to God.

B. Spiritual Worship

The term "spiritual" is here used in the New Testament sense of the meeting of spirit with Spirit. Wilhelm Pauck describes the nature of the religious experience as "inwardness, thought, spirit." [2] A vital worship experience takes place within the mind or the consciousness of the worshiper. Jesus many times asked his hearers to *think* things through for themselves. Paul urged his readers to adopt a new attitude of *mind* (Eph. 4:23), to have the same attitude of *mind* that characterized Jesus (Phil. 2:5), and to become transformed persons by the "renewing" of their *minds* if they wished to present a "spiritual worship" acceptable to God (Rom. 12:1-2). Worship, as Karl Heim insists, is a "transaction between God and my conscience . . . a clean spiritual act . . . accomplished in complete lucidity of mind." [3] It is what a thinking man does as he approaches another thinking being called God. We find in the New Testament such expressions as the "mind of the Lord" (Rom. 11:34), the "mind of Christ" (I Cor. 2:16), and the "mind of the Spirit" (Rom. 8:27). Worship in its highest form takes place when the worshipers think about God and with God through the "mind of Christ." Evangelical worship, then, involves the full use of the mental faculties. It is definitely designed to bring human minds and God's mind into closer understanding and accord, to produce a "fellowship of kindred minds."

C. Didactic Worship

It follows from what has just been said that evangelical worship should be didactic. The word "didactic" means "instructive" or "intended to teach." It comes from a Greek word meaning "teach" which is found in almost the exact form in the Greek New Testament in the past tense,

[2] *The Heritage of the Reformation*, p. 120.
[3] *Spirit and Truth*, pp. 95 ff.

as the word *didaktos* meaning "taught." Didactic worship is worship intended to teach, to change peoples' minds through the instrumentality of human speech. It strives to put Christian content into minds. Its avowed purpose is to break through with the truth of the gospel into the thought-making and judgment-making citadel of the soul. Instruction in the form of teaching and preaching is therefore an indispensable element of such worship because it is a method of transferring the truth of the gospel from the written Word to the active mind of the worshipers.

This is so universally recognized that it would be unnecessary to stress it had it not so often been said in recent years that worship should not be didactic. One writer says we worship to "please and glorify God, not to effect any particular change in the worshiper." [4] Precisely how does a worshiper "please and glorify God"? we may ask. By "vain repetitions" of words, forms, rituals, and ceremonies with the mind in a semiblackout? Or with some sort of stirring of inner thoughts in the direction of the truth that results from the impingement of the spirit of God? The same author in another place is especially insistent that "music should not be employed for a didactic purpose, either doctrinal or ethical," but that the congregation can "sing it without any particular attention to words or music in detail." [5] That statement either does not say what was intended by the writer or else should not be taken seriously. Singing without any particular attention to either words or music presumably would be making a noise with the mind completely shut off. That would resemble what Paul described in the fourteenth chapter of I Corinthians as "speaking in tongues." It appears that people in Corinth spoke, prayed, and sang "in tongues." "Tongues" seemed to have been a jumble of sounds that somewhat resembled human speech and provided a certain amount of emotional release to the one uttering them but that were unintelligible alike to the utterer and to the hearers. Paul labeled this "speaking into the air" (vs. 9), because it was in no way related to the "understanding." That is, it had no didactic value. In contrast to this he said everything done in worship should "be done unto edifying"; that men at worship should not be "children in mind: . . . but in mind be men"; that when they sing and pray, it ought to be not only with the spirit but "with the understanding also"; and that in worship it is far better to speak "five words"

---

[4] Devan, *op. cit.*, p. 6. Used by permission of Mrs. Winifrede R. Devan.

[5] *Ibid.*, pp. 152-53.

with the "understanding" intended to "instruct others" than "ten thousand words in a tongue," or in sounds that carry no mental content. The reader is asked to note the words "edifying," "mind," "understanding," and "instruct," all of which are didactic in nature. Evangelical worship always requires a didactic element.

Another idea to consider in this connection, and that is found in the current literature on worship, is that worship should be objective, not subjective. The late J. B. Pratt defined objective worship as the "attempt to influence God and please Him, or at least somehow to get into actual touch with Him." Subjective worship, on the other hand, he defined as the "effort to influence the mental state of the worshipper." [6] Pursuing the same general theme Devan says that for the purpose of study and clear thinking we must think of worship as a "thing-in-itself" and try to isolate it "as the chemist isolates the element he wishes to study from the various combinations into which it has entered. . . . When at last we have got our worship isolated in a 'pure' state, we find that it is inevitably objective—that is to say, it is directed by man toward his deity as an objective reality outside of or beyond his personal self." [7] Most assuredly God is an objective reality; otherwise when men worship, they are talking to themselves or practicing a form of self-suggestion. Worship should certainly be directed to God. But that is far from meaning that it should be severed, even temporarily, from what goes on within the worshipers. The only place men can get into actual touch with God is in their minds or spirits.

It is seriously to be questioned whether it is possible to isolate worship in a "pure state as a chemist isolates the element he wishes to study" or to think of it as a "thing-in-itself." It cannot be solely objective because what takes place inside the worshiper is part of the very act or process of worshiping. It is hardly possible to believe that God is indifferent to the quality of the thoughts in the inmost soul. What is going on in the mind determines whether worship is childish or mature, pagan or Christian. The word "worship" originally was composed of two words "worth" and "ship" and means literally reverence paid to worth. Such reverence involves a value judgment in the worshiper's mind. The individual turns toward God because he longs with all his mind, heart, and soul to have fellowship with such a great, divine Person. This

[6] *Eternal Values in Religion*, p. 28. Copyright 1950 by The Macmillan Co. and used by their permission.
[7] *Op. cit.*, p. 5

total act is both objective and subjective. There is no way to separate the two, and God himself is pleased as much with the judgments of worth in the heart as in the act of reverence itself; in fact, he is displeased with the latter if it is divorced from the former. Evangelical worship must always possess an aspect of subjectivity in order to be pleasing to God.

D. Personal Worship

Another word that should be considered in this immediate connection is the word "personal." It is used here in the same sense in which Luther used it when he insisted upon the personal character of faith. He was accustomed to say that every person must do his own believing as he will have to do his own dying. To say that every man is saved by his personal faith, however, is not equivalent to saying that faith is purely subjectivistic. The individual believer does not achieve faith by his own efforts. Rather his faith is created in his heart by the presence of the Holy Spirit. Paul said, "By grace have ye been saved through faith; and that not of yourselves, it is the gift of God; not of works, that no man should glory" (Eph. 2:8-9). By this he seems to have meant that the whole process of salvation—including both the grace and the faith—is a "gift" of God, not a "work" of man.

In a similar manner it can be said that worship is personal. When a person worships, he does not conjure up the presence of God by the exercise of faith. His faith is called forth by the operation of the Holy Spirit. The experience of the presence of God in worship, then, is a spiritual miracle, but a miracle that takes place in the secrecy of the believer's own soul. In the last analysis every believer is alone with God although he is surrounded by his fellow worshipers. If the worship experience is genuine, each one must be able to say, "God is my God. His grace has come upon me." That is, each one personally has his own encounter with God.

It is sometimes said that this destroys the corporate aspect of public worship, that it reduces worship to sheer individualism. That charge is not new. Since the days of Luther, Christians of the reformed tradition have had to defend themselves against it. They have done so by calling attention to the fact that the New Testament teaches that no experience of God can be genuine unless it has its social aspects. The

174

reality of a Christian experience is tested by whether it transforms us into a member of a "fellowship of self-giving love." John said, "We know that we have passed out of death into life, because we love the brethren. . . . Every one that loveth is begotten of God, and knoweth God. He that loveth not knoweth not God; for God is love." (I John 3:14; 4:7-8.) One must experience God for himself, but he must needs do so in social terms. The experience of the individual is verified, validated, and completed as it expresses the grace and love of God in a fellowship of loving service. It would be true of both private and public worship to say it cannot by its very nature be purely individualistic.

On the other hand, it is pertinent and profitable to ask precisely what happens to individuals when they worship together in public. Surely no one could be found to defend the proposition that they yield up their individuality completely to the group, so that the group does their thinking for them and experiences God for them. Each individual in the group is stimulated by the presence of others of like mind, like interests, like aspirations, and like needs. The worship seeks to bring the whole group into harmony with God along the same general or common lines. For this reason it involves what the group as a whole needs rather than what a particular individual needs. But it cannot achieve its general purpose unless it does something to the particular individuals composing the group. Corporate worship that achieves a purely group consciousness, or group emotions, but fails to achieve something definitely personal with individuals, ends with the act of worship and dissipates into a vague, ineffectual, nonproductive experience. All evangelical worship achieves its ultimate group purposes by being directed to specific accomplishments within each worshiper personally.

E. Pneumatic Worship

The word "pneumatic" comes from the word *pneuma*, which is the Greek word in the New Testament for "spirit." It is used here to describe the workings of the Holy Spirit in the lives of the early Christians. As already noted, the coming of the Holy Spirit into their lives was a *sine qua non* ("the thing without which") of being a Christian and therefore the indispensable condition of worship itself. When the worship of the Apostolic Church was under consideration in Chapter 3, we noted that this led to excessive emotional outbursts known as "speaking in tongues" and to so many spontaneous contributions by individual worshipers that they had to be curbed. But it also produced a fervor that affected the quality of everything that took place in worship. It was what has often been called "heartfelt" or "experimental" religion. Christians knew by the way they felt that they had experienced the presence of God's Spirit. The coming of the Spirit led to conscious changes in their hearts, which they variously called conversion, regeneration, the second birth, and becoming new creatures. It is these dynamic features of New Testament worship more than any others that Christians have in mind when they call themselves evangelical. They would insist that worship cannot properly be labeled evangelical if these features of fervor, spontaneity, and conscious feeling of the presence of God are missing.

F. Evangelistic Worship

The word "evangelistic" is used in the popular sense of deliberate effort to bring about decisions and persuade to action. The early Christians taught and preached for various purposes. Sometimes it was to tell of the events of the gospel as a crier or herald proclaimed the news. In this case they tried to convince their hearers that Jesus was the promised Messiah (Acts 5:40) and told the story of his ministry, especially of his teaching, of his death, and of his resurrection (Acts 28:31). At other times they expounded the meaning of those events (Acts 28:23). At still other times they endeavored to persuade people to act upon the truths embodied in those events. So we read that they attempted to persuade them to accept the things concerning the kingdom of God (Acts 19:8), to repent of their sins (Acts 2:38; 3:19; 17:30), to turn from their idolatry (Acts 19:26), to turn to God (Acts 28:20), to become Christians (Acts 26:28), to bring forth good works (Acts 26:20), to live by the grace of God (Acts 13:43). They were not so much presented with the truth as *confronted* with it, forced to come to a *personal encounter* with it and with God, to make commitments, come to decisions, and exert their wills. They were exhorted to live the Christian life, to apply the gospel to their personal and group problems, to accept the disciplines of the gospel, to test its cleansing or therapeutic powers, and to produce the fruits of the Spirit in their lives. To be truly evangelical, worship must be permeated with motives and purposes to persuade, must utilize materials designed to move to decisions and actions. That is, it must be evangelistic.

G. ETHICAL WORSHIP

We have so long taken for granted that worship is not acceptable to God unless it is bound up with ethics, that we have supposed it would be unnecessary in our time to discuss the matter in any detail. It is therefore somewhat arresting, if not actually shocking, to discover that many writers are sharply distinguishing worship from ethics and that the process of again separating religion and morality has begun. This easily may indicate that Christianity is entering another era when the fight must again be made to keep the two together.

For example, Pratt says:

Morality is concerned with conduct, especially toward one's fellow men: religion consists in one's attitude toward the Determiner of Destiny. Morality is social: religion cosmic; morality, active, religion largely contemplative. Now, worship is first of all a matter of religion. It is religion in act. Various aids to the moral life may be its by-products; but these are incidental to its central purpose. In fact, in so far as one's thought is occupied with questions of moral and practical life, one cannot realize what worship in its fullest sense can be. For it is precisely freedom from the limitations and fixities and strains of the practical life that worship seeks to bring. It is not one's human relations but one's ontological setting that worship especially fixates.[8]

Taking a similar position, Devan says that worship must be "divorced from both moral and utilitarian considerations. . . . If we would grasp worship in its real essence, we must for the time being remove from it all consideration of advantages to be derived by the worshiping man— even moral ones." [9] This sharp separation of worship from morality, even though made for the purpose of academic discussion, is dangerous. It puts asunder what the New Testament believes God intended to be forever joined together.

As we saw in the early chapters of this study, the distinguishing characteristic of prophetic religion in general and of Christianity in particular is the teaching that one's attitude toward God is wrapped up in the same bundle with his attitude toward his fellow men. The term "ethical mysticism," used by Ernest F. Scott to define Christianity, is equally suitable to describe New Testament worship. Such worship is a mystical belief in and experience of God coupled with—integrally and inextricably bound up with—ethical thinking and living. This is abundantly verified by many passages. Jesus said, "If therefore thou art

[8] *Op. cit.*, p. 47. Copyright 1950 by The Macmillan Co. and used by their permission.
[9] *Op. cit.*, pp. 5-6. Used by permission of Mrs. Winifrede R. Devan.

offering thy gift at the altar, and there rememberest that thy brother hath aught against thee, leave there thy gift before the altar, and go thy way, first be reconciled to thy brother, and then come and offer thy gift" (Matt. 5:23-24). This is quite different from saying, "In so far as one's thought is occupied with questions of moral and practical life, one cannot realize what worship in its fullest sense can be." Jesus also said, "Not every one that saith unto me, Lord, Lord, shall enter into the kingdom of heaven; but he that doeth the will of my Father who is in heaven" (Matt. 7:21). This is far from saying, "It is not one's human relations but one's ontological setting that worship especially fixates."

Since, as previously indicated, the effort has been made to isolate worship in a "pure" state entirely detached from all moral considerations, it is interesting to note that the New Testament also uses the word "pure" in connection with worship. Jesus said, "Blessed are the *pure* in heart: for they shall see God" (Matt. 5:8). In his letter to Timothy, Paul spoke of those "that call on the Lord out of a *pure heart*" (II Tim. 2:22). The word "pure" in the original distinctly carries ethical connotations. It means "free from corrupt desire, from sin and guilt, from every admixture of what is false; sincere, blameless, genuine." What these passages mean, then, is that only those who possess ethical qualities are qualified to conceive God, to see him, or to experience his presence. Worship as the "contemplation of God" wholly apart from thoughts of morality is the very type of worship which both the prophets and Jesus condemned as unacceptable to God.

God does not seek, is not pleased with, and is not influenced by contemplation and adulation as such, however dramatic and even spectacular they may be. Dissociated from what people are and from the way they live, such worship is an abomination to him. Worshipers do not succeed in "contacting" God if they approach him in nonethical terms and forms. Worship is evangelical when the worship takes place in an ethical setting. God is experienced fully when experienced ethically. The ethical element of worship is not incidental or secondary, or a mere by-product. It is structurally bound up with its very nature.

Separate Christian worship from ethics even to a slight degree, plant that idea of separation firmly in the minds of Christians, and give it a few centuries to produce its full fruitage, and you are certain to come out with some form of semipagan Christianity. From the history of religions we learn all too well the tragic social conditions that result when worship is divorced from ethics. The best insurance we can carry against such results in our western civilization is to keep worship "pure" in the New Testament sense, namely, maintain it in an environment shot through and through with ethical concepts and purposes.

H. Common Worship

The word "common" is here used in the sense of belonging to the community at large. In the New Testament Church worship was *common* in several significant ways. At the outset no one exercised a function in worship comparable to that of a priest in other religions, not even as a person specially delegated to lead in the worship. As shown previously, Paul described worship in which individual worshipers brought their share of the food for the agape and made their various individual contributions voluntarily and spontaneously. No one was authorized to perform functions which each person did not have both the right and the privilege of performing for himself. When by experience they discovered they could function properly only if they had leaders, these were elected, set aside for a particular task, inducted into office by an ordination ceremony, and given a title. This procedure did not distinguish them from ordinary people nor convey special grace or power or even authority as individuals, but simply authorized them to perform duties delegated to them by the whole group. Their leaders never became intermediaries between them and God. Each person had the freedom and the duty of approaching God directly for himself. He came to God through faith alone, not through another person and not through an ecclesiastical institution. The purpose of the worship was for the worshipers to stimulate one another to approach God in the secrecy of their own souls.

Out of these fundamental convictions came one of the distinctive tenets of evangelical Christianity, the doctrine of the universal priesthood of believers. This meant not only that each person came to God personally without the necessity of an intermediary, but that each person assumed his share of the responsibility of serving the needs of his brothers, of serving God in his own station in life, and of helping to make the world Christ's kingdom. Thus all Christians belonged to the same holy order, the Christian ministry. From this general doctrine there emerged two other beliefs distinctive of New Testament Chris-

179

tianity, that all vocations should be Christian and that God is a daily companion in the common life.

When the early Christians came together to worship, it was not to dispossess their minds of the problems of practical life and to contemplate God as an ontological, supramundane being, but to bring their problems to a God who was intimately interested in their daily life. They came seeking to find assurance that their God, though infinitely great and holy, was deeply concerned about their finite existence, and to remind themselves afresh that he was near and both able and eager to give them strength and grace for the problems of Christian living. They brought their anxieties and cares and cast them upon the heart of God because he had invited them to do so by what he had said to them and done for them in the revelation of himself and of his love, solicitude, and care in the gospel. In the presence of such a God they renewed their faith, poured out their hearts, talked out and thought through their problems, and found their souls revived and nourished for their ordinary tasks. They went out from worship convinced that his grace was sufficient for all their needs and proceeded, ordinary human beings though they were, to tackle extraordinary jobs believing they could do all things through him who strengthened them. The contents of all the books of the New Testament from Acts to Revelation could be submitted as evidence to substantiate these facts. Those books literally radiate with the spirit of joy, peace, courage, hope, and other Christian graces which those early Christians manifested as they went about their task of transforming themselves, their group life and labors, the social order in which they lived, and the whole world into the likeness of Christ.

Worship is evangelical when it is designed to carry over into the common life. It is not something staged, so to speak, as a thing apart from the real drama of living, but is integrally a part of that drama.

> Religion's all or nothing: it's no mere smile
> O' contentment, sigh of aspiration sir—
> No quality O' the finelier-tempered clay
> Like its whiteness or its lightness: rather, stuff
> O' the very stuff, life of life, and self of self.[10]

People worship together to become aware of the presence of God so that they can go out saying to each other, "Immanuel," which means,

[10] Robert Browning in "Mr. Sludge, 'The Medium.'"

180

"God with us." *God with us* here and now on this earth, in all of life, not merely in the place of worship on a specified day, but everywhere and always. Worship is the apprehension of the mystical, contemporary comradeship of God in common life.

I. CONCLUSION

It should be admitted frankly that evangelical worship makes a severe demand on the higher powers of human nature. It asks men to think, to worship, with their minds as well as with their hearts; to conceive of God in moral terms; to give the Spirit of God a chance to move their wills in the direction of their moral judgments; to put the emotions engendered in worship to work in their characters, in their ordinary human relations, and in their human institutions. It puts a heavy obligation upon all the deeper, higher, finer elements of human personality. Some insist that it is too high for human beings to attain. Of this more will be said in the concluding chapter of this study. Just now we want to face the fact that unless worship is of this high type, avowedly and unashamedly of this high type, it is not truly evangelical.

We turn next to the problem of implementing this doctrine of worship with respect to the various elements going into a worship service.

8

The Cultus and the Lord's Supper:
Its Interpretation

WE turn now to the question of applying the generalizations concerning evangelical worship to the actual task of planning that worship in detail.

It should be explained before proceeding further that no consideration is given to the sacrament of baptism. This is for two reasons. First, baptism is observed once in a lifetime by each Christian and is therefore not a regular or continuing experience like that of the Lord's Supper. Second, no important principles of worship are involved in baptism that require a treatment separate from the Lord's Supper.

The first problem confronting us is to determine what place the Lord's Supper should occupy in evangelical worship. To solve that problem, we must first seek to discover the proper interpretation of the Supper. Controversies over that have been raging for centuries and will undoubtedly continue. We shall not try to settle the controversies but to indicate along broad lines the interpretation which is most nearly consonant with the major beliefs of evangelical Christians. Prior consideration is given to this because one's interpretation of the Lord's Supper affects so vitally his ideas concerning the architectural arrangement of the sanctuary, the use of symbols and other elements of worship, and the order of service itself. Once a decision is made concerning the proper function of the Supper in worship, many other important questions involved in worship are also decided.

182

A. The Word and the Sacraments

The Word and the sacraments are placed in a co-ordinate position with each other in the definitions of the Church found in the creedal statements of most Protestant bodies. With some variation in wording the true Church is said to be where the Word is rightly preached and the sacraments are rightly administered. In a similar manner worship is described as being properly carried on where the Word and the sacrament of the Lord's Supper are both given their rightful place. Placing the Word and the sacrament together in this manner implies that the two are separate and distinct and that each apart from the other makes its own peculiar contribution to worship. But this is not the case. For its proper understanding and use in Christian worship the sacrament is dependent wholly upon the word of God. The sacrament proclaims no message of its own distinct from the gospel message itself. And it can proclaim that message only to people who have been prepared by the proper presentation of the historical facts of the gospel revelation to understand it. That is, the sacrament has no word to speak *sui generis*, in and of itself. Calvin said, "The office of the sacraments is precisely the same as that of the Word of God, which is to offer and present Christ to us, and in Him the treasures of the heavenly grace." [1]

If someone out of the ancient primitive past who had never heard of Christianity or of any of its worship practices were to attend a Communion service for the first time, he would undoubtedly interpret what he saw and heard in crude, superstitious, pagan terms. He would suppose the worshipers were having some sort of meal with their god, or were offering him some material gifts as a sacrifice, or were partaking in some crass way of a deity's flesh and blood—all for some presumably magical purposes. The only way he could possibly understand what was going on would be to go through a course of thorough instruction in the meaning of the facts of the gospel as found in the New Testament. If Christians themselves observe the Supper without continuously tying their minds to those same facts and their proper interpretation, they even now run the risk of interpreting it in the manner of pagans. Before Christians can celebrate the Supper in a suitable manner therefore, they must be conditioned to do so by proper indoctrination through the use of the Word of God.

[1] *Institutes of the Christian Religion*, IV, XIV, 17.

The only thing that kept the sacrament from being completely paganized during the conflict of Christianity with the mystery religions and during the dark medieval times was that it was definitely anchored in the historical facts as found in the written word. That is the only thing that can ever prevent it from being paganized. This is one of the main theses of the significant study of the sacrament by Bishop Brilioth of Sweden entitled *Eucharistic Faith and Practice, Evangelical and Catholic.* He argues at great length and with convincing force that the only way to safeguard the Eucharist from being paganized and degraded to sub-Christian levels is to anchor it in history through the liturgy of the Word. When he says it should be anchored in history, he means that it should always be linked with the historic act of Christ's death and with all the other historical elements which are found in the instruction, the preaching, and the general use of the Scriptures in the other parts of the worship service.[2] Can it not rightly be claimed therefore that in New Testament or evangelical worship the sacrament is subordinate to, because dependent upon, the preaching and the teaching of the Word of God?

B. Sacramental Bread and Wine

There are a number of indications that a crisis is shaping up in Protestantism over the sacramental problem that may prove to be as serious for the present-day Church as the same problem was for the Roman Church of Reformation times. One of the decisive battles of the Reformation was fought over the proper interpretation of the sacraments. Speaking in general, the reformers discarded the whole sacramental system of the Roman Church. Specifically they regarded the claim of that church to be able to turn the bread and the wine in the Supper into the objective, physical, visible, and tangible body and blood of Christ as a form of magic or superstitution or even pagan idolatry. For this crassly physical interpretation they substituted what they believed to be a nonphysical or spiritual interpretation. But of late years the whole sacramental principle is being so rapidly and widely reincorporated into Protestant thinking that Protestants must soon decide whether the early reformers were right or wrong in their opposition to the sacramental idea.

Let us endeavor to understand precisely what the term "sacramental"

[2] *Op. cit.*, pp. 69, 281.

means in current usage. In his book entitled A Sacramental Universe, Archibald Allan Bowman maintains that the universe in which we live is both physical and spiritual, and that the things we experience by our senses, and which we speak of as material or physical, or do may contain spiritual meanings beyond those which come to us through the mere senses. It is this plus-meaning, over and beyond what we sense, that is meant by the term "sacramental" when applied to the objects used in worship. Perhaps the most extensive treatment of the sacramental idea as it relates to worship is found in Paul Tillich's book The Protestant Era, ch. vii. He starts with the basic idea, similar to that of Bowman, of a "vitalistic interpretation of nature." He says that "even in the structure of the atom there is something primordial, a Gestalt, an intrinsic power" (p. 100). Building on that, he arrives at the position that natural objects used as "holy" objects in worship "become bearers of transcendent power and meaning" (p. 102), that they become "laden with divine power" (p. 108). That is, they become sacramental objects, objects that possess a meaning beyond the ability of the physical senses to detect. When applied to the elements in the Supper, this means God in some mysterious, mystical, or "sacramental" manner dwells in them and through them imparts himself, his grace, his power, to the worshiper.

Tillich deplores the fact that the sacramental element has so largely disappeared from Protestantism, attributes the secularization of Protestantism to the weakening of this element within its structure, and boldly asserts that it must be reincorporated in the Protestant cultus to prevent the further weakening and ultimate dissolution of the historical or visible church.[3]

The sacramental principle is found wherever holy objects are used in worship. In primitive nature religions it took the form of magic or of the actual worship of the objects which were supposed to possess or to convey mysterious power. The Roman Catholic Church carried the idea from the elements in the Mass to other objects they call "sacramentals." A recent Roman Catholic publication[4] contains a long, well-formulated explanation of how and why the Roman Church makes use of sacramentals and of what spiritual "favors" flow from their proper use. The sacramentals so treated are as follows: the sign of

[3] Tillich, op. cit., pp. 94, 112.

[4] John F. Sullivan, The Externals of the Catholic Church, rev. John C. O'Leary, 1951, pp. 217 ff.

the cross, the cross and the crucifix, holy water, vestments, the stations of the cross, the holy oils, candles, the rosary, scapulars, the *Agnus Dei*, palm branches, incense, church bells, religious medals, ashes, and Christian symbols. Some of these same objects are coming back into use in Protestant worship mostly in the name of religious symbolism or of liturgical art. And what is so significant, they are being spoken of as sacramental objects.

In an article in the *Union Seminary Quarterly Review*, entitled "Some Reflections on Liturgical Art," Mar., 1953, Cyril C. Richardson of Union Seminary expresses deep concern about the implications of the last-mentioned trend. He sets forth the meaning of the sacramental principle, shows how it stems from the general idea of a sacramental universe and of material things being able to express a hidden meaning beyond what can be sensed, then shows how the principle works out in the revived use of liturgical art in Protestantism. By liturgical art he means objects of art used in worship, regarded as holy and considered of sacramental value. He asserts that the current use of such art faces Protestants with a challenge which forces them to make a "radical decision which may reverse essential elements in Protestantism" and that they must choose "either to return to the iconoclasm of the prophet, and to say that liturgical art is impossible . . . or else . . . to admit the Catholic principle that these hidden depths [of sacramental objects] can be gateways to the Divine." He closes his article by raising, but not answering, the crucial question "Should Protestantism embrace such art, and will it endanger the divine transcendence and the prophetic basis of our message?"

Can it be that the crisis in Protestantism of which we have heard so much in recent decades is going to focus in its cultus? Has the crisis in fact been passed? Has the turning point already come, and is Protestantism now on its way back to Catholicism? Tillich says that unless Protestantism puts the sacramental principle back into its cultus it is doomed.[5] I would like to say that if Protestantism reincorporates that principle into its cultus, it will cease to be Protestant and will revert to some form of medieval sacramentalism. Evangelical Christians of whatever name must reconsider thoroughly their interpretation of the Lord's Supper to save its essentially spiritual nature and to prevent Christianity from again becoming paganized.

[5] *Op. cit.*, p. 94.

All who discuss the problem of using sacramental objects in worship recognize how easily this could lead us back to paganism, even those who advocate their use. None is willing to see Protestantism revert to paganism in any form or to any degree. Hence all are seeking ways of preventing this from happening. Richardson, in the article referred to above, says the way to prevent objects used in Christian worship from becoming pagan is to bring them "within the realm of the church." He says:

[The Church must insist that] only within the Christian context can objects be holy. For when one penetrates beneath the outward mask of things to catch a glimpse of their mysterious and hidden essence, one finds a distorted or demonic element. All creation is under Satan's temporary rule. Hence to be seen as they are in God, things have to be viewed eschatologically, from the point of view of the redemption of all creation. Only in this way are we prevented from worshipping a false God or many Gods. The mysterious essence behind a cube is Satanic as well as divine. It must be exorcised before it can become a part of liturgical art. It has to be baptized into the church.[6]

Tillich expresses it similarly by saying that purely natural objects can become Christian sacraments only in so far as they participate in the "history of salvation" and are thereby "liberated from [the] demonic elements and thus made eligible for a sacrament." [7] Just how the demonic is exorcised from natural objects is not clearly indicated. Presumably this is accomplished by their being blessed by the Church or by being brought within its traditions.

This is a precarious argument because it works both ways. It is precisely the same argument in principle as that of the Roman Catholic Church to justify its use of such objects and as that of pagans to justify their use of the same. Holy objects are made holy to every group using them by being blessed by their "church" or by its duly authorized representatives, by being baptized into their body by some sort of ceremony, or by being incorporated into or correlated with the traditions, practices, and beliefs of their particular group. If you admit the validity of sacramentals, how can you assign to Protestants the exclusive prerogative of declaring what objects are Christian and what are pagan? Start with the idea that the person ministering in God's name and under the authority of the Church can consecrate an ordinary object and thereby transform it into something holy or sacramental with a mysteri-

[6] Op. cit., p. 26. Used by permission of publisher and author.
[7] Op. cit., p. 110.

ous and mystical meaning different from what it has when used as an ordinary object, and the door is opened wide for the development of something bordering on magic and superstition. This proposal does not meet the real issue in the problem.

Another proposal is that the use of the bread and the wine in the sacrament must not be regarded as a species of natural sacramentalism. That is, the use of two objects by Jesus does not justify attributing sacramental qualities to all natural objects used in worship. This is Tillich's primary method of preventing Protestantism from relapsing into a "pre-prophetic or pre-Protestant attitude" toward sacramentalism. He says, "The intrinsic power of nature as such does not create a sacrament. . . . For a Christian the idea of a purely natural sacrament is unacceptable. . . . There can be no sacramental object apart from the faith that grasps it." [8] By the last statement he means the historic faith, the historic setting in which the object originally became sacramental. There are other phases of his argument too complicated to mention in this connection and unnecessary for our present purposes. He calls attention to the fact that neither bread nor wine is an original natural object. Both are produced artificially by man's manipulation of natural forces. It can also be said that in itself neither had any natural connection with the death of Christ. Christ simply took two types of food used at a traditional fellowship meal and more or less arbitrarily used them for the specific definite purpose of symbolizing his death and the partaking of its spiritual benefits. The fact that Jesus made use of these two elements cannot legitimately be used as an argument to justify the wholesale use of all sorts of objects as sensible mediums to God or as sensible channels of his grace. Nor can it be argued that the sacramental use of natural objects in worship by primitive peoples justifies the sacramental use of wine and bread in the Supper. The two things are not to be identified. The Supper is tied to a specific historical setting and to precise and peculiar theological concepts. This is why the Church has always insisted the Supper must be accompanied by the distinctive words and ideas which made Christianity what it is.

Again, it is essential to treat the language used by Jesus as figurative if the Supper is to be preserved as a spiritual, rather than a physical, experience. And this the Church has consistently endeavored to do from the start, although it has not always succeeded in doing it clearly

[8] *Ibid.*, p. 110.

because of the complicated arguments used. When the simple figures of speech used by Jesus are given a mysterious and mystical meaning, it leads to a number of difficulties and errors. The expressions "broken body" and "poured-out blood" are figures of speech for dying; they simply signify death. Eating Christ's body and drinking his blood are sheer pagan ideas if taken literally. The expressions are figures of speech to convey the idea of receiving or appropriating the spiritual benefits of Christ's redeeming sacrifices. As Zwingli expressed it, "To eat the body of Christ spiritually is nothing else than to trust in spirit and heart upon the mercy and goodness of God through Christ." [9] Cranmer put it this way, "[When] we spiritually eat the flesh of Christ, and drink his blood, then we dwell in Christ and Christ in us, we be one with Christ, and Christ with us." [10]

Tillich (pp. 96 ff.) says, "The meaning of the Lord's Supper as a sacrament is that it is the sacramental appropriation of the exalted body of Christ." The eating of his real body is out of the question because it is obviously not accessible to us, and anyway Christ now has only a transcendent body in heaven. That "spiritual body" in heaven is accessible to us through the "organic substances" substituted by Christ for his real body. "That is, in place of the body we have the elements that nourish the body" (p. 97). This takes as literal what was meant to be only figurative and thereby distorts the meaning of the sacrament and reduces it to a semipagan level.

Christ did not mean to say that his body, earthly or heavenly, physical or spiritual, would or could be eaten in any literal sense. He meant to say only that just as we eat physical food to nourish our body, just so we can receive the great benefits flowing from his death for the nourishment of our spirits. The benefits of his death, though not visible to the senses, are just as real as though they were. Though not corporeally present, they are nevertheless actually there. This is what the carefully guarded and worked-out wording of the confessions try to say. In Article XXVIII of the Anglican Articles of Religion it is stated thus:

The Supper of the Lord is . . . a Sacrament of our Redemption by Christ's death: insomuch that to such as rightly, worthily, and with faith, receive the same, the Bread which we break is a partaking of the Body of Christ; and likewise the Cup of Blessing is a partaking of the Blood of Christ. . . . The Body

[9] Richardson, Zwingli and Cranmer on the Eucharist, p. 29.
[10] Ibid., p. 28.

of Christ is given, taken, and eaten, in the Supper, only after an heavenly and spiritual manner. And the mean whereby the Body of Christ is received and eaten in the Supper is Faith.

The *Westminster Confession of Faith*, chapter XXIX, section VII, says:

Worthy receivers, outwardly partaking of the visible elements in this sacrament, do then also inwardly by faith, really and indeed, yet not carnally and corporally, but spiritually, receive and feed upon Christ crucified, and all benefits of his death: the body and blood of Christ being then not corporally or carnally in, with, or under the bread and wine; yet as really, but spiritually, present to the faith of believers in that ordinance, as the elements themselves are, to their outward senses.

Through all their teachings, written and spoken, about the meaning of the Supper evangelical Christians should make clear, in categories and in terms familiar in our day and that cannot be misunderstood, that the words of Jesus are not to be taken literally but figuratively.

Also the experience in the Supper should be interpreted in *personal* terms. The grace that comes into the soul is not a substance, a medicine, a thing, a quiddity, something to be dispensed or even conveyed, but the gracious love of God through his personal presence. When it is said that the Spirit of God comes into our hearts, that too must be thought of as personal, not as physical: he comes directly to our spirits. The Spirit does not have to be mediated to us. Or as Zwingli stated it, "A channel or vehicle is not necessary to the Spirit, for He Himself is the virtue and energy whereby all things are borne and has no need of being borne." [11] The faith by which the benefits of Christ's sacrifice are received is created immediately by the Spirit not by the bread and wine. "Faith is fed by spirit, not by flesh," said Zwingli.[12] This does not exclude the idea that God *makes use* of the elements to arouse faith. They then become the *occasion* for the exercise of his grace.

[Cranmer believed in the] instrumental connexion between the sacrament and the working of God's grace. It is the same relation, he contends, which entails in baptism and in preaching. Christ and the Holy Spirit, "being present in their mighty and sanctifying power, virtue and grace," in the hearts

[11] *Ibid.*, p. 12.
[12] *Loc. cit.*

of believers, use the voice of the speaker or the water of baptism or the bread and wine of the Supper, as "instruments" to "work by." [13]

But nevertheless the experience of the believer with God is personal and spiritual, not physical.

In this connection a word should be said about the use of the term "epiclesis." By the *Catholic Encyclopedia* it is defined as the prayer "in which the celebrant prays that God may send down His Holy Spirit to change this bread and wine into the Body and Blood of His Son." That sort of prayer is entirely out of harmony with evangelical beliefs. The Holy Spirit comes upon people, not upon things, although he may use things as his instruments. Oesterley says that originally the epiclesis was a prayer for the coming of the Spirit upon the worshipers, not upon the elements; that as early as the second century there is no mention of the Spirit coming upon the elements but only upon communicants. [14] But because of the technical meaning assigned to it for so many centuries, the word ought to be eliminated from the ecclesiastical vocabulary of evangelicals. And the wording of the Communion prayer should strictly reflect evangelical beliefs in this particular.

A controversy has gone on for years over the moment when the bread and the wine are properly consecrated. One school says it happens when the formula of the institution has been completed and another school that it happens when the epiclesis is finished. Gregory Dix maintains that when a properly authorized and ordained person has completed the previous action and finished the prayer, the Eucharistic consecration occurs. This discussion has no particular significance for those who believe in evangelical worship simply because there is nothing in the gospel records concerning such matters, and because they do not believe the elements can be changed or charged with mysterious powers by anything the celebrant does. A material thing, whether a building, or an altar, or money, or bread and wine, cannot be changed from an ordinary object to a holy or sacramental object by a mere act of prayer. It still remains what it was. It can be used for the purposes of worship, but that does not give it a mystical meaning beyond what it had previously. This ought to be made clear in all explanations of the Supper to prevent the elements from being thought of and treated superstitiously.

[13] *Ibid.*, p. 34.
[14] *Op. cit.*, pp. 228-30.

When interpreting the sacrament of baptism, Luther insisted that God does not give any extraordinary power to the water; it is "still water in substance no better than that which the cow drinks. . . . For if the Word of God is separated from it, the water is no different from that which the servant girl uses in cooking or in preparing a bath. . . . Not that the water in itself is nobler than any other water, but that the Word comes upon it." [15] It is a pity that Luther did not say the same thing about the elements in the Lord's Supper. Had he not insisted upon retaining some aspects of medieval sacramentalism in his interpretation of the Supper, Protestantism might have been saved considerable misunderstanding and grief resulting from bitter controversies over the Supper. To preserve the evangelical interpretation of the Supper, it ought to be said that the bread and the wine in themselves are at no time different from similar articles put to ordinary use. As Luther said, it is the Word that counts. It is the meaning represented by the elements in the gospel and the faith that results from their use under the inspiration of the Holy Spirit that make the difference.

Considerable to-do is being made in some Protestant circles about the proper way to dispose of the elements left over after the Communion service is completed. The rubrics in some books of forms suggest that "reverent disposition" of the same shall be made by the minister and other ordained officials. The very use of the expression "reverent disposition" suggests the Roman Catholic attitude toward the holy bread (host). The extremes to which Catholics are taught to go to preserve the host from contamination by treating it as ordinary bread is by Protestants considered an obnoxious form of superstitious awe. Such notions are completely out of harmony with evangelical doctrines. They lead directly back to the semi-idolatry of the past. We need to be reminded again and again of what Bucer said in a letter to Cranmer about this very thing:

Some make for themselves the superstition that they consider it unlawful, if anything of the bread and wine of the communion remain over when it is finished, to allow it to become to common use; as if there were in this bread and wine of itself anything of divinity or even sanctity outside the use at communion. And so men must be taught that . . . outside that use of the communion which the Lord instituted, the bread and wine, even if they have been placed on the table of the Lord, *have nothing in them of sanctity* more

[15] Karl Heim, *Spirit and Truth*, p. 179.

than have other bread and wine. . . . These things it is fitting that the people be taught as in word so also in deed, as diligently as may be.[16]

By way of a summary of this point it may be said that evangelical Christians could wisely simplify their teaching about the Supper so that it would not be necessary to hedge it about with a variety of explicit definitions of a philosophical nature, and with limitations and explanations that are calculated to confuse the mind of the average worshiper. Unless one is skilled in semantics and logic and is well informed about philosophical terms, it is well-nigh impossible for him to engage in the complicated process of theological and philosophical reasoning necessary to distinguish some Protestant explanations of the Sacrament from those of Catholics or to distinguish either from paganism. Since in practically all the creeds faith and the operation of the Holy Spirit are regarded as absolutely essential, these two experiences should be interpreted as spiritual experiences frankly and clearly as they are in the New Testament. They should be relieved of all physical and semiphysical meanings. Only thus can the Supper be prevented from constantly running the risk of being thought of in pagan terms by ordinary worshipers untrained as logicians and theologians.

C. Sacramental Action

In current discussions of the sacraments much emphasis is placed upon the *sacramental* nature of the action. One writer says:

The sacramental value is . . . not in the symbolism, not in the water "set apart," not in the bread or the wine consecrated upon the holy table, not in the words of the institution, not in the person who administers the sacraments, but in the complete sacramental act, which is one and through which the Holy Spirit, and he alone, seals to believing recipients the blessings of the new covenant.[17]

Gregory Dix makes the action in the Eucharist its *sine qua non*. In his judgment a valid and effectual observance of the Eucharist is one in which the actions of Jesus when instituting the Supper are reproduced in the same manner and sequence by the bishop authorized to perform the same.[18] Over the centuries many groups have undertaken to imitate Christ's actions meticulously and have considered this quite important

[16] *Scripta Anglicana, Censura,* iv. Works, p. 464.
[17] Hugh T. Kerr, *The Christian Sacraments,* p. 24.
[18] *Op. cit.,* pp. 49, 153, 238-39, 244-45, 268-69, 270-72.

for a proper observance of the Supper. They used unleavened bread and fermented wine, broke instead of sliced the loaf, passed the common cup from hand to hand, used the exact words of the institution, and did all this in the same sequence as Jesus did. The celebrant communed first because apparently Jesus sipped the cup before passing it to the others. Since the meal ended with the singing of a hymn, the modern observance must so conclude. Since the meal was held by them sitting around a table, the elements must be taken by the people sitting in groups around the table, not in their pews, not kneeling at a rail, and not standing. In the belief that Jesus washed the disciples' feet in connection with the meal, some groups have observed this as an ordinance at the observance of the Supper. So far as is known, no group in modern times has insisted upon partaking of the elements in the same reclining position as that of Jesus and his disciples.

The actions as listed in the several accounts of the Supper cannot be precisely correlated with one another in every detail. Neither Christ nor the New Testament writers say anything about the action being necessary for an effectual celebration. To call the action sacramental as though in itself it carries a special mystical or holy meaning is to run the danger of paganizing the Supper at still another point, namely, to make the ritual or ceremonial a bit of magic. It is all but impossible for some people to believe that Christ intended his movements to be interpreted in this manner or to be imitated with such careful attention to minute details. At its best that attitude makes "vain repetitions" out of the movements, and at its worst it turns them into a superstition. That the Supper was intended to be repeated and for a purpose is quite clear. Its symbolism can best be carried out by observing it in the same simple manner with the same general actions which Christ used at its institution. There are valid reasons for standardizing the general procedures in the observance of the Supper, especially for a particular denomination. But to make a sort of fetish out of the action is to reduce to a low level what should be a high moment of spiritual worship. What happens to the worshipers is due not to the exact reproduction of the external actions of Christ but to the spirit in which they participate, the meditations of their hearts, their prayers, their faith, and the presence and power of the Holy Spirit.

In this connection something needs to be said about the theology of the action in the Supper. Evangelical Christians should take care

194

to avoid expressing through the action or procedures in connection with the observance of the Supper a theology that is out of harmony with that spoken from the pulpit and proclaimed in written creeds. The few simple actions of Jesus in the institution of the Supper (four or seven in number according to one's analysis of the records) may wisely be taken as a pattern for our procedures. But it is quite easy to go through those actions in such manner as to make them mean what we know from a study of the New Testament neither Jesus nor the early Christians intended them to mean.

Take, for example, the question now being discussed in some Protestant circles as to what is the proper order in which communicants should be served. It is not clear from the accounts of the institution of the Supper whether Jesus partook of both elements before passing them to his disciples. If he followed the procedure customary at meals of that sort, he undoubtedly sipped the wine before passing it to the others; for it is almost certain that the one presiding at a kiddush partook of the wine first. On the basis of the gospel of Jesus we can with some assurance affirm, however, that by so doing he did not mean to set himself apart into a different category from his disciples as though as the one presiding he should be given preference in the matter. To have implied these things by his action on that occasion would have been contradictory to the whole tenor of both his teaching and his deeds throughout his ministry. Yet as early as the fourth century A.D., the custom of the minister communicating first was being interpreted as his privilege by virtue of his high office. If a bishop was one of the officiants, he communicated before the other ministers as an indication of his superior rank. After the clergymen communicated, the elements were offered to the elders and last to the people, not so much to imitate Jesus but to set the ministers above the people.

To eliminate this distinction and to incorporate in the Supper the spirit of Christ's teaching and example concerning the greatness of humble service, the custom arose in time (but just when it first began is not definitely known) of the elements being given to the people first, to the elders next, and to the minister last. That procedure has been followed for a long period of time by many modern Christian groups. This order of communicating places the minister and officers in a humble position that befits those trying to serve in the spirit of their Master. Recently, however, there has developed a movement of some proportions to restore among modern Protestants the order of communicating which existed in the ancient Church of the fourth and following centuries. Which procedure is proper? That question cannot be answered properly merely by determining which was the ancient practice, but by deciding which is more in harmony with the intention of Jesus and with the tenets of the evangelical faith.

All the actions connected with the Supper should be similarly scrutinized and appraised to make sure they do not teach something contrary to distinctive Protestant doctrines. Lifting the elements, not merely to offer them to the people, but as though they are a material sacrifice to God; keeping the minister aloof from the people as though he is of a different order from the laity; guarding the table from the common people as though it is a holier place than the nave where they sit; placing the table far away from and elevating it high above the people so that it is necessary for them to approach it by a series of steps on several levels as though what takes place around the table is awesome, mysterious, and too sacred to be brought into intimate contact with common folk—these and other actions tending to set the Supper apart as a sacerdotal act to be performed by persons of a higher order than ordinary people should be carefully avoided and the effort made scrupulously to insure that the symbolic action of the Supper will not convey meanings contradictory to beliefs proclaimed as basic by evangelicals. This then is a fundamental principle of evangelical worship: the theology of actions should harmonize with the theology of words. In the long run the former theology will prove to be as important a factor as the latter in the preservation of Christianity in its New Testament form.

D. The Sacramental Presence

The word "sacramental" is applied not only to the elements and to the actions in the Supper but to the presence of Christ. When so applied, it means that Christ is present in the elements—his body and his blood—in a special, mysterious manner different from his presence at other times and places. How is that to be distinguished from the Roman view of his actual physical, sensible presence and from the mysterious, localized physical presence of deity in pagan worship? The answer must be that it cannot be so distinguished; in principle and in essence these are the same concepts. This has been frankly acknowledged by Brilioth, whose book on the Eucharist [19] was referred to earlier in this chapter. Believing that the idea of "mystery" contains "high religious value; it is an expression for the awfulness of the holy, the *tremendum*, which belongs to all deep religion" (p. 65); he simply retains it in his interpretation of the presence of Christ in the elements, and then endeavors to safeguard it from becoming sheer paganism.

He distinguishes two types or modes of "presence," one that he finds in the Gospel of John and labels a "mystical sacramentalism," and the other that he finds in the other Gospels and loosely labels "Synoptic mystery type." The Johannine mystery is localized in the bread and the wine of the Supper and is to be thought of as quasi-physical. The Synoptic mystery is diffused throughout the service and is to be thought of as personal. He admits that this localization of the mysterious presence in the elements "runs a special risk of degradation to something like a pagan level" (p. 58), that it "shows a dangerous tendency to occupy almost the whole field of view," and that it thus tends to crowd out the personal or the other mode of Christ's presence (p. 287). Therefore the Eucharist must always be accompanied by or tied to the liturgy of the Word, which is "characterised by the sense of the Master's presence rather throughout the service than locally in the elements, by the interpretation of communion as the expression of fellowship, and by an emphasis on the historical aspect of the rite," and where the "Presence is thought of as personal" and where the "ethical demand remains real" (p. 69).

There is no justification whatever for distinguishing two types or modes of Christ's presence or for localizing his presence at one spot in the building and diffusing his presence in another part of the same building. This compartmentalizes the worship service and divides it into two separate and distinct parts that are of a different quality and nature from each other. This procedure endeavors to carry both pagan and Christian ideas in the mind alongside each other. Such a divided mind and a divided worship cannot stand any more than a house divided against itself can stand. What is often spoken of as different degrees of God's presence with us is attributable to the limitations of language. When we speak of God being nearer to us in a place of worship than in our homes, nearer in prayer than in work, nearer in the Supper than in ordinary worship, we do not mean that God is actually *more* present or present in a different way at one place or time than another, but

[19] *Op. cit.*

that we are more aware of his presence. The presence of Christ in the Supper is not different from his presence in the other parts of the service. But the nature of the Supper is such that our thoughts and our moods may make us more receptive to his presence than at some other times. We realize or apprehend his presence in a different manner. But His presence is the same in every part of the service, a spiritual presence "in our midst" and in our hearts. As Bishop Moule said, "Our Lord is present not on the table but at it," in fellowship with us.

To localize God anywhere is a dangerous thing. To localize him in an object, no matter what the nature of that object, is a species of magic. If it is dangerous then to speak of Christ's presence in the elements as something semiphysical, and if it is difficult to safeguard this idea from paganism, why utilize the concept at all? Why not unify both parts of the service around the one idea of Christ's personal and spiritual presence? If that were done, we would have the true evangelical interpretation of Christ's presence, namely, that he is present in person or in spirit wherever a believer is able under the inspiration of the Holy Spirit to apprehend his presence and to receive his grace by faith. This by no means robs worship of the element of mystery. God, the spirit of man, life, the universe, prayer, and the mystical communion of God and man, the workings of the Spirit in our hearts, the death of Christ—all these are mysteries. To say that all mystery, all sense of the awfulness of the holy, is eliminated from the sacrament by calling Christ's presence "spiritual" is simply a misrepresentation. To say that Christ is personally and spiritually rather than physically present takes away none of the reality or vividness or mystery of the experience.

It has been claimed in recent years that Zwingli and Cranmer were the only early reformers who carried their Protestant principles to their logical conclusions in this phase of the interpretation of the Supper. Cyril C. Richardson pointed this out in his study of Zwingli and Cranmer referred to already several times. In his *Spirit and Truth* Karl Heim[20] shows that a residue of medieval sacramentalism was left in Luther's view of the Supper because he was unwilling to go as far in its spiritual interpretation as he was in the spiritual interpretation of the sacrament of baptism. Wilhelm Pauck says that both the Lutheran and the Anglican conceptions of the sacraments "preserved certain features of Catholic

[20] Pp. 179-80.

sacramentalism." [21] A careful study of the interpretation of the sacraments in the major Reformed confessionals will reveal a deposit of Catholic sacramentalism at many places. All sorts of verbal difficulties were encountered and several kinds of philosophical arguments engaged in to avoid making their statements sound like medieval magic. Is it not possible or even probable that the ease and rapidity with which Catholic sacramentalism is coming back into Protestant thought and practice are due to the failure of the early reformers to break completely with the quasi-physical Roman view of the sacraments and to come out as boldly as did Zwingli and Cranmer in favor of the spiritual interpretation? Does not the critical situation now prevailing in Protestant worship necessitate a complete break with Roman concepts of the Supper and an adoption of the thorough evangelical interpretation of Zwingli? In my judgment both these questions ought to be answered in the affirmative.

The interpretation of the Supper in a spiritual rather than in a semiphysical manner would not be as radical a step as it might appear, because in practice, if not in theory, the observance of the Supper by most evangelical groups in the United States has been of the spiritual type. It would be necessary, however, to eliminate from, or prevent the injection into, the liturgy of the Supper a number of medieval practices and versicles which once definitely carried the idea of the physical presence of Christ. In medieval days the elements were *elevated* immediately after the epiclesis, for at that moment the miracle of transubstantiation was supposed to take place, the elevation being made so that all could behold and adore the Christ who had appeared. The elevation was accompanied by the *Benedictus qui venit* (cf. Matt. 21:9), as follows:

> Hosanna to the Son of David.
> Blessed is He that cometh in the Name of the Lord.
> God is the Lord, and hath appeared unto us.
> Hosanna in the highest!

These words meant that at that moment Christ had appeared, had become visible, had come again "in the name of the Lord," and was to be properly welcomed. Because of these associations the elevation of the

---

[21] *The Heritage of the Reformation*, pp. 305-6. It is to be remembered that Cranmer's view of the sacrament was not accepted in full by the Anglicans.

cup is out of place in an evangelical service as is also the singing of the Benedictus in connection with that act. Both the Benedictus and the Agnus Dei ("Lamb of God") were expunged from the liturgy of the Communion by the English reformers because in the medieval Church these were used to welcome and adore the real presence of Christ in the elements. To revive their use in their traditional places in the liturgy, as advocated and practiced by many, is to run the risk of also restoring a theology associated with them which is contradictory to evangelical beliefs.

E. The Supper as a Sacrifice

Another problem connected with the interpretation of the Lord's Supper is whether or not it should be regarded as a sacrifice to God. This aspect of the Supper has been considered from time to time in this study. It has been shown that there is nothing in the New Testament records to justify its being interpreted as a sacrifice in any sense. But in due time by a series of steps which are not necessary to be restated, the Supper began to be spoken of as a sacrifice to God. Cyprian, for example, said that the "passion of the Lord is the sacrifice which we offer." Augustine spoke of the body of Christ as the "Christian sacrifice." In some of the prayers of the early centuries occur such statements as, "Here we offer unto thee thy gifts of bread and wine," "Send down thy Holy Spirit upon this oblation (sacrifice) of thy church," "Accept this our sacrifice of praise and thanksgiving," and, "We offer and present unto Thee ourselves . . . as living sacrifices." The Roman Church finally came to interpret the Mass as a reoffering of the sacrifice of Christ to God for the "quick and the dead."

All the reformers rejected the idea of the Supper as an *objective* sacrifice. That rejection is registered strongly in Article XXXI of the Anglican creed in these words: "The sacrifices of Masses, in the which it was commonly said, that the Priest did offer Christ for the quick and the dead, to have remission of pain or guilt, were blasphemous fables, and dangerous deceits." The language of the *Westminster Confession of Faith* is equally strong:

In this sacrament Christ is not offered up to his Father, nor any real sacrifice made at all for remission of sins of the quick or dead, but only a commemoration of that one offering up of himself, by himself, upon the cross, once for all, and a spiritual oblation of all possible praise unto God for the same, so that

200

the Popish sacrifice of the mass, as they call it, is most abominably injurious to Christ's one only sacrifice, the alone propitiation for all the sins of the elect.[22]

But both Luther and Calvin accepted the medieval view that the Supper was a *subjective* sacrifice, that is, an offering of thanksgiving and praise and an oblation of self. Zwingli seems not to have concerned himself with this meaning of the Supper in either sense. But such expressions as, "Here we offer unto Thee thy gifts of bread," "Accept this our sacrifice of praise and thanksgiving," "We offer and present unto thee ourselves . . . a living sacrifice, and "memorial sacrifice" appeared in the Eucharistic prayer in many of the liturgies.

No special attention was paid to this aspect of the Supper during the period when the worship of most of the Protestant groups was non-liturgical and when the Communion prayer was largely extempore or free prayer. But in recent years, due to the restoration of the wording of the Communion prayer as it was found in the older liturgies, much discussion has been provoked about whether and in what sense if at all the Supper should be regarded as an offering or sacrifice to God. As the ancient forms have been reintroduced into the liturgies, the tendency has been more and more in the direction of the medieval idea of the Supper being a subjective offering accompanied by an oblation of self. Some extreme liturgists, such as Gregory Dix, would restore the idea of it as an objective reoffering of the sacrifice of Christ to God. He says, "What the Body and Blood of Christ were on Calvary . . that they are now in the eucharist. . . . What the church does with them in the eucharist must be in some sense what He did with them, namely an offering." [23] Some less extreme liturgists urge Protestants to embody in their thought of the Supper those ideas of the Eucharistic sacrifice which are so dear to the Anglo-Catholics and to those of the Eastern Orthodox faith and which may assist in bringing about an ecumenical worship.

To begin with, it is very difficult to keep the idea of sacrifice subjective in nature if it is to be associated with material bread and wine. Again this is recognized by Brilioth with his usual frankness. As in dealing with other phases of the interpretation of the Supper, he labors long and diligently to keep a certain point of view which he values highly

[22] See ch. XXIX, Section II.
[23] Op. cit., pp. 242, 245. Used by permission of A. & C. Black, Ltd.

without involving it in pagan conceptions. He admits that "there is in the eucharist no sacrifice in the ordinary sense: there is no material immolation to be accepted by God, no oblation to propitiate his wrath." [24] But he is of the opinion nevertheless that there are so many valid and valuable Christian insights in the idea of sacrifice that he thinks the Supper can be considered a sacrifice without dragging it down to the level of paganism. He makes the same noble effort to hold on to an idea that is dangerous and at the same time hedge it about in such a way as to prevent it from leading us astray as in his treatment of the other phases of the Supper. His solution involves the main thesis of his book that the Eucharist can be understood in its fullness only if considered from five different viewpoints as follows: (1) thanksgiving; (2) Communion-fellowship; (3) commemoration (the historical side); (4) sacrifice, including the act of memorial and the church's self-oblation; (5) mystery.[25] The corruption of the Supper, he believes, stems primarily from isolating one of these aspects from the others and developing it without regard to them. "The effective defence [against the danger of degradation to the pagan level] is therefore the maintenance of all the aspects in their completeness and harmony." [26] So the way to prevent the aspect of sacrifice from being degraded is to keep it tied to the other four phases.[27]

Having said all this, he is likewise quite insistent that the only sense in which the Supper can be regarded as a sacrifice is that of "self-devotion" of the individual to Christ: "Any doctrine of a material presentation made by man to God must involve the paganising of the church's worship. The only conception of sacrifice which is beyond all criticism is that of the self-devotion of man himself to God; such is the one sacrifice of Christ, and such is the self-oblation of the humble communicant through him." [28] "The deepest religious meaning of the oblation of material gifts is seen in their symbolical significance, as representing that oblation of self which is a necessary part of all living faith. The Christian has in truth but one gift which he can give to God, namely

[24] Op. cit., p. 43. Used by permission of the author and the London Society for Promoting Christian Knowledge.

[25] Loc. cit.

[26] Ibid., p. 48.

[27] Ibid., p. 281.

[28] Ibid., p. 138.

himself; and the eucharist could not be the central act of Christian worship if it did not include and express this idea." [29]

It is not necessary to interpret the Supper as itself a sacrifice and run all the risks incident thereto, in order to retain in the Christian tradition the values found in the idea of self-sacrifice, spiritual sacrifice, and living sacrifice, on the part of the individual and of the Church as a whole. When observed, the Supper ought to provoke the mood of sacrifice in all its New Testament meanings. When Christians remember the death of Christ, they might well offer thanksgiving and praise to God and dedicate themselves and their material possessions as instruments for the service of God. But we should distinguish sharply between *meanings* of the Lord's Supper and the *moods* it provokes. It is not a sacrifice offered by the people, but a remembrance of Christ's sacrifice. Why not say this frankly and let the matter rest there, leaving the moods generated by its observance to take their course? This would safeguard it from all the abuses which have grown up around it and will continue to gather around it despite all efforts to the contrary, when it is considered a sacrifice. The idea of self-sacrifice is certainly bound up with our Christian gospel. But to interpret the elements of the Supper as an offering to God on the part of those who partake of it conveys pagan ideas of material sacrifices and does so almost inevitably. The whole idea of the elements themselves being offered to God in any sense should be eliminated from the observance of the Supper. It is not consistent with evangelical Christianity. If the Protestant bodies would take this position unequivocally and embody it in their practices, it would be another effective factor in preventing corrupting paganistic ideas from becoming again associated with it. And it would help to keep the Supper evangelical.

F. Summary and Conclusion

For their conception of the Lord's Supper evangelical Christians go back to the simple, but profound, theology of the New Testament Church. The Supper is a memorial of Jesus, a reminder of his life and labors, of his death, of his spiritual presence with his followers, of the fellowship of believers with him and with one another, of their great debt of gratitude to God, and of their obligations to serve as "living sacrifices." It is a sign of the grace of Christ and of the need of his

[29] *Ibid.*, p. 283.

redemptive love, and a seal of these things provided the worshiper can apprehend them by faith. It symbolizes Christ's presence, but that presence is apprehended directly, immediately, and mystically by faith, in a spiritual and not in a physical or even semiphysical experience. The proper and practically only successful method of safeguarding it from being paganized and of keeping it evangelical is to eliminate from it all ideas leading in the direction of magic, of mechanical grace, of medieval sacerdotalism, and of material sacrifices, and to think of it purely as a spiritual experience.

9

The Cultus and the Lord's Supper:
Its Observance

WE turn now from a consideration of the interpretation of the Supper to a consideration of a number of practical problems involved in its observance.

A. FIXED EUCHARISTIC PRAYER

I have already dealt with two parts of the Eucharistic prayer, the epiclesis and the oblation (anamnesis). Evangelical beliefs require that the epiclesis be so worded as to ask for the Holy Spirit's coming not upon the elements but upon the worshipers, and that the oblation be so worded as to indicate that the worshipers are offering themselves to God as evidence of thanksgiving and praise, not offering the elements as a sacrifice. We are concerned now with the prayer as a whole. It is customary to insist that from the earliest times this prayer has had a definite structure and wording and that it should be continued in its traditional fixed form. As already said, Dix has shown rather conclusively in an exhaustive study of the prayer that both the structure and the wording of this prayer for the first few centuries were in a fluid state and that the effort of the "traditionalists" to locate anywhere in those early centuries a model of the prayer for all future ages is doomed to failure.[1]

However, it is clear that gradually the prayer assumed a fairly fixed general pattern sometime in the early medieval period, and that it consisted of four traditional parts: the thanksgiving, the oblation (anam-

[1] *Op. cit.*, pp. 156-232.

nesis) or offering the elements, the prayer for the coming of the Holy Spirit (epiclesis), and the offering of self. This pattern was by no means uniformly followed in the reformed liturgies. For example, the prayer of consecration in the Anglican liturgy of 1662 contains only two parts: a prayer that in receiving the elements the participants may be partakers of Christ's body and blood and the words of institution. Since Wesley's liturgy prepared for American Methodists followed this pattern, the consecration prayer in the Methodist liturgy has since then had these two elements only. But the consecration prayer in the Protestant Episcopal liturgy included, in addition to those two elements, the traditional oblation, the epiclesis (called "invocation"), and the sacrifice of praise and thanksgiving. The liturgies of the Lutherans and Moravians do not have an epiclesis. Like the Methodists they consider the words of the institution the supreme act of consecration. Orders of service for the Communion which have come into use in recent years, for example, in the Scottish *Book of Common Order* and in the Presbyterian (U.S.A.) *Book of Common Worship*, have returned to the ancient pattern with the four traditional parts, the words of the institution being used previous to the consecration prayer proper.

We are not concerned here with the details of any of these parts of the Eucharistic prayer. They may well be the *general* elements of such a prayer, provided the wording is always safeguarded against paganistic ideas. But to insist, as is now so consistently done, that both the general form and the particular wording of each part shall be fixed and used at every observance of the Supper in precisely the same manner, defeats one of the important purposes of the Supper, namely, that the Supper shall provide for the special spiritual needs of a particular household of faith. The worshipers assemble as a fellowship, and together they gather around the table to partake of a symbolic meal and to ask God to nourish their souls with the spiritual sustenance signified by the bread and the wine. The Eucharistic prayer fails in one of its most important functions if it does not in some way incorporate petitions in which the minister in behalf of the fellowship of believers brings before God the common needs of the people as those needs are known to him at that particular time—their sins, sorrows, social hopes and dreams, family and personal and community tensions, fears, doubts, frustrations, and other problems.

206

B. *Sina Qua Non* OF COMPLETE WORSHIP EXPERIENCE?

In the Anglican creed the visible Church of Christ is defined as a "congregation of faithful men, in the which the pure Word of God is preached, and the Sacraments be duly ministered according to Christ's ordinance, in all those things that of necessity are requisite to the same." [2] A definition in this or in similar language is found in the Methodist creed and in other creedal statements of Protestants. That the observance of the sacraments and the preaching of the Word are essential marks of a true Christian church is taken for granted by all evangelical Christians. But there is a difference of opinion as to whether this implies that the sacrament of the Lord's Supper must be observed in connection with every weekly service of worship and whether that is necessary in order to constitute a valid and complete service of Christian worship. The differences of opinion at this point arose at the very beginning of the Reformation. Luther and Calvin both tried to make the Supper the norm of the regular weekly service. But Zwingli, convinced that the Supper was not necessary for every worship service, was in favor of less frequent Communion. When John Wesley prepared his liturgy for use by the Methodist Societies of America, he advised that the Lord's Supper be administered every Lord's Day. The "General Rules" of The Methodist Church prescribe frequent Communion. From the start the Disciples Church has observed Communion every Sunday. But in common practice, if not in theory, practically all Protestant churches, except the Disciples, have observed Communion less frequently than weekly.

The failure of the reformers to restore the Supper as the norm of worship everywhere is sometimes attributed to local reasons here and there—for example, to the political situation at Geneva in the days of Calvin when the city authorities forbade the weekly observances and to the shortage of ministers in Scotland in the early part of the Reformation. But more often the reasons assigned are three.

The first reason assigned is the "lamentable ignorance" of the reformers concerning the history of Christian worship. It is stated that if all the reformers had been as well informed concerning history at this point as were Calvin and Luther, they would have been in favor of the weekly Supper. In Chapter 2 I stated it is questionable whether

[2] See "Articles of Religion," Art. XIX.

Jesus intended the Supper to be observed as a regular rite. It is by no means certain that either in the New Testament times or in the next two centuries thereafter was the Lord's Supper the central act of every Christian worship service, as we saw in Chapters 3 and 4. As indicated in Chapter 4, Gregory Dix shows that the two parts of the service, which he calls the "synaxis" and the "Eucharist," were often held separately until well into the fourth century.

The second reason assigned is that the reformers and the people were simply following the pre-Reformation custom of communicating infrequently. By the time of the Reformation the entire service of the Mass revolved around the Communion, but the people actually communed only a few times, frequently only once a year. By this time the complexity of the Mass together with the crowding out of other acts of worship by the one act of the Supper caused the people to demand a simpler type of worship service without the Eucharist, or else provoked the priests to provide it because of the practical necessities of the situation. It may be argued with considerable justification that in so doing they were providing for a neglected Christian need, not emasculating worship.

The third reason assigned is the excessive zeal of the reformers for change. This weakness, characteristic of all revolutionary movements, it is said, caused the reformers to go to extremes that impoverished worship by eliminating the Supper as the weekly norm. So they say it is now their duty to restore what the overzealous reformers unwisely discarded. It may be asked whether the reformers did violence to both the facts of history and the intention of Jesus by not restoring the Supper to a central place in weekly corporate Christian worship, or whether they too, wittingly or unwittingly, were getting back to basic Christian principles.

In view of what was said in the historical part of this study concerning the meaning of the Lord's Supper, and in the light of what was said in Chapter 6 concerning the type of cultus required by the nature of evangelical Christianity, let us proceed to face pointedly and candidly whether the Supper should be regarded as the norm for all corporate worship or as merely one way, but an important way, for evangelical Christians to worship. As a point to begin we may face two statements, one by Brenner and the other by Brilioth, which are typical of many present-day writers. Brenner says, speaking of the early Church, "All the other services of prayer or preaching were primarily preparatory to the Eucharist or served as post-communion services," [3] the implication being that our services should have a similar purpose. Brilioth says a service of worship without the Supper means the "loss of the classical form of the Christian service; common prayer loses its natural focus, Christian worship misses the central expression of the beauty of holiness. . . . The exposition of the word by the preacher, too often the exposition of his subjective opinions, takes the place of the objective word of the sacrament";[4] and again that the "eucharist [is] robbed of one of its essential elements, the balance of the service" is upset, and "a narrow conception of the eucharistic sacrifice" receives "disproportionate emphasis." [5]

I agree that the Eucharist is robbed of something essential if it is observed wholly apart from preaching and the other elements of the liturgy of the Word. But I cannot agree that other parts of the service are impoverished if they take place apart from the Supper. It is not true that all elements receive their focus in or gain their significance from being associated with the Supper. To make it appear so is to set the Supper up as an intermediary, yea, a barrier, between God and man, something that Jesus surely never intended it to be. We do not need to come before God with the Lord's Supper any more than with sacrifices, but only with "broken and contrite hearts." Dix and others insist we must think of the Supper as something distinctive in itself; otherwise it is a mere duplication of the service of the Word. It is not something different in essence from the other parts of the service, but something different in method. It does the same thing in another way. The whole gospel is not in the death of Christ, as important as that death is. The living presence of the resurrected Christ is also tremendously important. There are other ways of giving thanks and praise and other occasions when it is both natural and fitting to offer oneself to God other than through the Communion.

There are other ways of sensing his presence. The presence of Christ in the Supper is no different in principle or reality from his presence in a prayer that is differently constructed from the Eucharistic prayer, or in the sermon, or in the congregational singing, or in the reading of the Word, or in a litany, or in the responsive reading. The offering of one's self at the time of the Supper is no different in essence from the offering

[3] Op. cit., p. 74. Copyright 1944 by The Macmillan Co. and used by their permission.
[4] Op. cit., p. 274.
[5] Ibid., p. 279.

of one's self symbolized by the gift of money, or when one publicly professes Christ in the presence of the congregation, or when he commits himself to Christ as the result of the influence of a sermon. The great services of worship at Easter when we celebrate the Resurrection, at Christmas when we celebrate the Incarnation, at Pentecost when the coming of the Holy Spirit is commemorated, at the beginning of the new year when new life in Christ is the theme, on Reformation Sunday when freedom in Christ is stressed, on Sunday after Sunday when the application of the gospel to individual and group life is uppermost—on all these days, when the Supper is not observed, Christ is just as near, the services as sacred and as suffused with his presence and with the spirit of thanksgiving and self-dedication—or may be—as in the Communion service. And this is as Christ intended it, or so we dare to believe. The Supper is one way to say some things, and an important way, but it is not the only way. Neither can it offer everything needful for our many-sided common human life, nor set forth all phases of the manifold grace of Christ. In short, the Lord's Supper is not the *sine qua non* of a complete and valid Christian worship service.

C. Order of Service for Communion

The order for the observance of the Supper should not be that of the regular morning service with the Communion added as a sort of appendage or as something to be celebrated after the main service has been concluded. It should be specially arranged for the purpose. The service should be a unit, a complete whole. It should not be divided into two parts, either in conception or in execution. The old twofold division into the liturgy of the Word and the liturgy of the Upper Room has no significance for the present-day church. The part of the service preceding the Communion should be designed to prepare for and lead up to the Communion. The call to worship, the hymns and anthems, the scripture readings, the responses, the prayers, and the sermon should all bear directly upon the central Christian truths associated with the Supper. If the service is to achieve its special purposes, it must be prepared and prepared for with great care. This lays upon the minister a heavy responsibility which, alas! too few ministers are willing to assume.

The service should not be too long or too complicated. Here perhaps as nowhere else in worship the attention curve of the people of our generation should be carefully and consistently kept in mind. (The entire service might wisely be about the same length as the usual morning service.) The prayers preceding Communion should be brief and not too many, partly so as not to prolong the service and partly because of the long prayer of consecration in connection with the Communion proper. The pastoral prayer should be omitted from the pre-Communion service. The sermon should be brief. Care should be taken to insure that the moods of the service are in complete harmony with that of the Supper itself. Humility, repentance, confession, self-examination, and commitment should be the predominant and prevailing moods throughout. The theme for different observances may be varied but should always be related to the central and constant theme. When themes for special occasions, such as the new year, Independence Day, and Universal Communion Sunday, are chosen, the material selected should be in keeping with the theme and the occasion. The whole service should be saturated with the Word of God. The great affirmations and blessed promises concerning God's grace, his forgiving love, his faithfulness, his nearness, the comforting and cleansing presence of the Holy Spirit, should be woven into the prayers, versicles, and responses used throughout the service.

The order for the actual Supper should be relatively simple, partly to harmonize with the general simplicity of evangelical worship and partly to give it a chance to make its own special contribution to worship, which is to proclaim the gospel through action. For the first few centuries the celebration of Communion consisted of the simple actions indicated in the New Testament without elaborate music, ecclesiastical vestments, liturgical ornaments, or other symbols. It was the elaboration of the liturgy of the Supper, the piling up of item upon item, ceremonial upon ceremonial, that brought about a major portion of the abuses in pre-Reformation worship. To avoid the revival of these abuses, the liturgy should be brief and the action simple. Standing at this point, kneeling at another, facing the altar here, facing the people there, and other complicated actions suggested by many in our day should be avoided, not merely because of the medieval ideas suggested, but because they divert attention from the main purpose. It is unwise to utilize too many versicles and responses, either spoken or sung, while the Communion service proper is in progress. The service should be conducted with dignity and solemnity and with as much silence as possible so that the people will have opportunity to meditate and pray without distractions. "Rightly

211

used, the silence of a great congregation whilst communicating may be one of the most uplifting and inspiring influences that flow from the observance of the Sacrament. It has the inestimable advantage of providing a time when the voice of man being hushed, Christ is left free to speak His own word to the soul that waits upon Him." [6]

In the New Testament records four main actions are indicated: (1) Jesus "took" bread and wine, which roughly corresponds to the modern "bringing in" of the elements; (2) he gave "thanks" and "blessed" the elements, which corresponds to the prayer of thanksgiving and consecration; (3) he "brake" the bread, which is called "fraction." It is to be noted that he broke pieces off a single loaf, which was later used by Paul to symbolize the unity of the partakers (I Cor. 10:17); (4) and he "gave" the elements to his disciples, which is called the "delivery." Considerable argument has gone on in recent years as to whether these four actions only should be repeated, the bread and the wine being passed simultaneously or in quick succession, or whether Paul's order found in I Cor. 11, which may be divided into seven steps, should be followed closely. Unless one believes there is some virtue or necessity in going through the precise steps which Jesus himself took, it is difficult to see how it makes any particular difference whether, for example, the bread and the wine are passed simultaneously or whether they are passed separately, whether the people partake by coming to the table and being served or whether they are served in their pews. Suffice it to say that the order ordinarily used in modern churches, which in general outline may be traced back many centuries and which may wisely be the outline for every Communion, is as follows:

1. The invitation to the Supper.
2. The words of the institution.
3. The prayer of thanksgiving and consecration, often followed by the Lord's Prayer.
4. The fraction in symbolic imitation of Jesus.
5. The delivery, usually in two parts.
6. A post-communion prayer.
7. A hymn, because it is said, "And when they had sung a hymn, they went out" (Matt. 26:30).
8. The apostolic benediction. (The benediction in Heb. 13:20-21 is also peculiarly appropriate for the Communion.)

[6] O. B. Milligan, The Ministry of Worship, p. 113.

The Communion prayer is one of the great pastoral opportunities and responsibilities of the minister. It should be prepared with great care and with much thought and prayer. Its form might wisely be that of the traditional Eucharistic prayer. Its themes should certainly include those of that ancient prayer, namely, thanksgiving, invocation for the coming of the Spirit, and self-dedication. In preparing for it the minister should saturate his mind with the language and the thoughts of the prayers found in books of order, not only because they express the traditions of centuries, but because they exemplify the quality of language and of ideas that should characterize the prayer. But he should not treat those prayers as fixed, not to be altered and for which there is no substitute. All those prayers were once contemporary and are neither sacred nor unchangeable. Any evangelical minister is at liberty to use them or not as he chooses, but he is derelict in his duty as a pastor if he does not phrase the content of the Communion prayer to fit the needs of his contemporaries. Only he knows the needs of the people over whom he has been placed as pastor. Though in his preparation he should be aided by ancient prayers even to the extent of utilizing their words and phrases, he should formulate his prayers to meet the particular needs of the people at the particular times, seasons, and special occasions when the Supper is being observed.

D. PRIVATE COMMUNIONS

The tendency recently has been to increase the number of Communion observances with the sick, the invalids, and the dying. Many now suggest private Communions before weddings, with a family before a member leaves the family circle, when fathers and mothers are concerned about their families, and for individuals and small groups in times of tragedy, and sorrow and death, and disaster, and in hospitals and prisons. This is one more bit of evidence to show that Protestants little by little are restoring medieval practices from which so many of the abuses in worship in that era stemmed. Private Masses were one of the grave abuses which provoked the Reformation. If, as we teach, the Lord's Supper is a corporate function or a function of the church family, and if it is a fellowship of believers, then a private Communion is an incongruity. The practice of the minister and some of the officials of the church taking portions of the elements left over from the regular Communion service and on the same day holding Communion with those members of the

213

church who are unable to be present because of invalidism or some other infirmity is a custom of long standing. It is rightly regarded as the inclusion of absentees in the corporate fellowship of the occasion. The Reformation churches in general were very specific in their warnings to ministers and members against private Communions, against reserving the elements for any future religious use, and against giving the Communion to any not then present in the congregation, except as indicated above. This was for the purpose of preventing the elements being thought of as having any magical virtue in themselves. Evangelical Christians should be especially careful not to hold, or to give others the impression that they hold, the idea that the Communion shortly before death either assures or hastens the partaker's entrance into heaven or affects his eternal standing in the eyes of God.

E. SUMMARY AND CONCLUSION

The observance of the Lord's Supper, entered into in the right spirit, greatly enhances the importance of what it symbolizes, because it is both an object lesson and a dramatic action. It brings home the work of Christ to the believer in an impressive manner. God uses the whole observance to stimulate believers and to challenge them or, to use Zwingli's phrase, to "prop us up." But it is contrary to the purpose of Christ in establishing it to make it the end and aim of all public worship, to concentrate the energies and abilities of the leaders of worship upon a liturgy that revolves solely about it, and to focus the attention of the people upon it in a manner that makes it appear that Christ came into the world mainly to establish a worship rite. To do these things sets up, in effect, another form to take the place of the legalistic, ceremonial, and sacrificial forms which Jesus opposed and abolished because he fulfilled them. The procedures in the observance of the Supper should be in harmony with the simple procedures of Christ and of the New Testament Church. Its observance should not crowd out or overshadow other elements and purposes of Christian worship. It should not be treated as though it contains the whole of the gospel and as though the primary function of the Christian Church is to observe it and to persuade others to observe it. If the Christian Church would observe the Supper in accordance with the intentions and purposes and in the spirit of its

214

Master, who instituted it, a major step would be taken in the direction of keeping the cultus of Christianity and therefore keeping that Christianity itself thoroughly evangelical in nature.[7]

[7] Those who wish to pursue further the subject of the evangelical meaning of the Lord's Supper are referred to the following: (1) Henry Sloane Coffin, *The Public Worship of God*, pp. 141 ff.; (2) E. S. Freeman, *The Lord's Supper in Protestantism*, chs. vi, vii; (3) Harold E. Fey, *The Lord's Supper: Seven Meanings*; (4) Hugh T. Kerr, *The Christian Sacraments*; (5) Robert Hastings Nichols, *Primer for Protestants*, pp. 21-22; (6) J. R. P. Sclater, *The Public Worship of God*, pp. 145 ff.

10

The Cultus and Symbolism

A. LIMITATIONS OF SYMBOLISM FOR EVANGELICAL WORSHIP

THE use of symbols has developed in every sphere of human life—in the home, in the association of the sexes, in government, in sports, in the professions and crafts, in education, in every department of military life, and of course in religion. People use objects of many kinds as symbols to express their sentiments and their deepest convictions. They communicate with one another quite as effectively, and sometimes more rapidly, through symbolic acts, such as smiles, gestures, and handshakes, as through words. Visible objects and perceptible actions used as symbols therefore both express and stimulate thoughts and emotions. Hence they may perform a necessary and useful function in worship. But nevertheless their usefulness in evangelical worship has distinct limitations because of the very nature of that worship.

There is common agreement among scholars that, generally speaking, the degree to which people employ symbols in worship depends upon the degree of their intellectual development. The most extensive use of symbols is found among ignorant and primitive peoples. The more literate people become and the more facilities they develop for communicating through words, the less they either desire or require symbols in worship. We are told that the mystery religions, with their prominent use of symbolism, made their strongest appeal in ancient Greece "where survivals of primitive religion were rife," [1] but made very little appeal to the minds of the more cultivated Greeks. In his study of church archi-

[1] Hastings, op. cit., XII, 139.

216

tecture J. R. Scotford says, "As a rule, the poorer and more ignorant the people, the more eloquent the appeal which the church makes to them through their eyes." [2] When the bishop of Marseilles expressed to Pope Gregory the Great his objection to pictorial decorations in a particular church, the pope replied in a letter (ca. A.D. 600) that pictures were used so that those who were ignorant of letters might by looking at the walls read what they were unable to read in books. Gregory Dix bases his plea for the extensive use of symbols in Christian worship partly upon the belief that they are necessary to the "immense numerical majority of uneducated people" to whom Christianity can never be either a spiritual philosophy or a pure theology.[3] Nearly every Protestant writer of recent years who has advocated the revival of the use of symbolism in worship does so partly for the same reason, namely, that he does not believe ordinary people can rise to the demands spiritual Christianity makes upon the higher elements of human nature. When Christianity undertakes to appeal to the senses instead of to the intellect, it runs the risk of ceasing to be primarily a spiritual religion.

It is sometimes said quite casually that evangelical Christians are more at home with verbal symbols than with material or visible symbols as though it were merely a matter of preference with them. This of course does not accurately represent their attitude. They do not prefer verbal to visible symbols; rather the nature of evangelical Christianity makes it necessary for preference to be given to verbal symbols. Evangelical Christianity is a mature religion. It is based upon historical facts which are found written in historical documents called the Word of God. It cannot be understood or practiced or perpetuated properly except through the extensive employment of words. Didactic elements must predominate in evangelical worship if it is to be preserved in its true form.

The history of Christianity shows that as the symbolism in worship increases, interest in preaching and other didactic elements decrease. At every step in the development of sacramental and symbolic priestly worship in the medieval Church, preaching declined until in the days shortly before the Reformation it was quite occasional and incidental. It was the recognition of these facts that caused P. T. Forsyth to say, "You cannot quench the preacher without kindling the priest." [4] It could also be said

[2] *The Church Beautiful*, p. 158.
[3] *Op. cit.*, p. 432.
[4] *Positive Preaching and the Modern Mind*, p. 110.

with equal truth that you cannot kindle the priest without quenching the preacher. The medieval Church became what it was largely because the didactic elements of worship were subordinated to the sacramental elements, because verbal symbols gave way to visible symbols. It is sometimes said that the reformers discarded symbolism because of the natural tendency of all reform movements to go too far. But this is too easy an explanation of their actions. Granted that they went to an extreme, their concern was to restore evangelical Christianity to its original type and to hand it down in its true form to future generations. It was not a question primarily of narrowness or prejudice or excessive zeal on their part, but of trying to guard spiritual religion from the dangers inherent in symbolism. Faced with the necessity of deciding between making the major appeal in worship either to the mind or to the senses, they chose the former, their decision being prompted by what they believed to be necessary to safeguard the nature of New Testament religion.

Some of the specific reasons for their decision may be considered briefly. *First, symbols are always in danger of being taken for the things symbolized.* There is an old saying, "Where the symbol is, the fact lurks just behind." When Jereboam set up in the northern kingdom a rival sanctuary to Jerusalem, he made two calves of gold and set them up in shrines, one at Bethel and the other at Dan, to symbolize the God of Israel. Before long these symbols became themselves the objects of worship (cf. I Kings 12:25 ff.; II Kings 17:16). Icons in the Eastern Orthodox Church and statues of Mary and of the saints in the Roman Church became idols to the great masses of the people. Symbols originally introduced as aids to worship became objects of worship. *Second, once symbols lose their meaning, they tend to become mere superstitions.* After all, the meaning of many symbols is more or less arbitrarily read into them by a process similar to the allegorizing of scripture. Often there is no obvious connection between the object and the metaphorical meaning assigned it. Even after the arbitrary meanings of symbols have been explained, they still do not necessarily suggest those same meanings to others. So it comes about that the meaning is easily lost, and the symbol is perpetuated as something to be venerated merely because of its age. One often wonders how many symbols used in worship, which have lost their meaning in transmission and are continued only because they have come down from the past, are little more than pious superstitions.

Third, symbols may convey no ethical suggestions. The lore of symbolism is a fascinating study. It absorbs the interests, the time, and the energy of its devotees and exhausts their emotions, often leaving little time or energy, or even desire, to think of the practical applications of the thing with which they are dealing. In 1534 Cranmer published a book which assigned symbolic meanings to the articles comprising the vestments of ministers as follows:

The amice signifies the veil or cloth with which our Saviour's eyes were bound during his subjection to the mockery of His foes. The alb typifies the robe in which Herod arrayed Him. The girdle is the cord of the scourging, and the stole the robes by which He was bound to the pillar for that torture. The maniple speaks of the bonds which fastened the sacred hands of the Redeemer. The chasuble symbolizes the purple robe with which Pontius Pilate invested him.[5]

It is quite easy for one to meditate upon the various parts of Christ's dress without any thought of the meaning of Christ's gospel. There is no end to this sort of allegorizing of the various parts of the church structure, of its furnishings, and of the objects used in worship. This type of mental ingenuity can become fascinating in itself and even satisfying to the imagination without provoking any ethical implications or impulses. The danger is that the worshiper will suppose that the satisfying contemplation of such matters actually constitutes genuine worship. The religion that Karl Marx labeled the "opiate of the people" lulled them to sleep with beautiful symbols and fascinating ceremonials that carried no suggestions for brotherly living. Medieval worship crowded the minds of the people to the point of supersaturation with symbolism which left them with little opportunity or impulse to meditate upon the social implications of the faith being symbolized. Thus the mere use of symbolic objects may provoke no thought of the true nature of God, make no ethical demands, carry no social implications, and leave the conscience of the worshiper undisturbed.

Fourth, symbols may be entirely detached from personal fellowship with God. It is possible for worshipers to become absorbed in the symbolic meanings of impersonal things—the number of candles, wreaths of grapes and sheaves of wheat, the three steps leading from the nave into the chancel, the eight sides of the baptismal font, the *Chi Rho* and the fleur-de-lis, the triangle and the trephoil, the pelican and the rooster, the

[5] Tyack, *op. cit.*, pp. 125-26.

olive branch and the anchor, to name only a few of the symbols now being suggested for use in modern churches by the proponents of symbolism—without having the experience of a personal relation to God. Worship is the play of Mind upon mind, Judgment upon judgment, Conscience upon conscience, Spirit upon spirit, not the play of the human mind upon mere objects or things. That is why worship is incomplete without those elements which stimulate the worshiper to approach the personality of God through the higher qualities of his own personality. And that is why representatives of spiritual religion have always sought to make worship a simple, direct, personal approach to God with the minimum amount of mediating forms, ceremonies, and symbols.

Fifth, in the final analysis the real value of symbols depends upon the contents of the mind. J. B. Pratt says, "Not only are verbal or auditory symbols needed for the communication of thought: some form of symbol seems necessary for thought itself if it is to reach its maximum of clearness and efficiency. Our private conceptual thinking has constantly to make use of verbal and visual imagery." [6] But note! It is the mind making use of the imagery, not the imagery substituting for the mind. The purpose of symbols is to release the imagination, to start the mind to work on the thing symbolized. Symbols can mean therefore only what minds are prepared to make them mean. It has been said:

How long will it take to say in words what is said by the two bits of stick tied crosswise and set on the soldier's grave? How else could you say it to the passer-by and touch every heart? That symbol creates its own atmosphere. It appeals to imagination and to association. It unites. It brings together in time and space—what it means to one it has meant to so many in all the ages—what it means to us it means to men of the one faith the world over. And it has the power of allusion, bringing before the mind on the moment a world of recollection, and places the soul in contact with its beliefs and hopes. It has the short way to the heart. The two sticks on the grave have infinite implications —of sacrifice, redemption, peace, promise for the body—"still united to Christ": could any inscription say as much, or say it and be felt as all men feel this? [7]

But those two sticks say those things only to a mind thoroughly saturated with Christian concepts. To a pagan mind or to an ignorant, uniformed mind they would—and could—say nothing of the sort. They can pro-

[6] *Eternal Values in Religion*, pp. 134-35. Copyright 1950 by The Macmillan Co. and used by their permission.

[7] H. J. Wotherspoon, *Religious Values in the Sacraments*, p. 17. Used by permission of T. & T. Clark.

voke only such thoughts—such recollections, such associations, such implications—as are already in the mind. The preparation of the mind for the use of symbols is therefore a prior consideration. Christian interpretations must be potentially present in the mind if the symbols act as a suggestion to stimulate and release Christian thoughts and impulses. It is extremely important that the minds of worshipers be of the right Christian quality, filled with the right Christian content, to make proper Christian use of symbols. This is why so many have insisted that the use of symbols in themselves is not only limited in value but potentially dangerous. Their use must be preceded, accompanied, and controlled by Christian instruction.

For all these reasons the usefulness of symbols in spiritual and therefore in evangelical worship is definitely limited. In all spiritual worship visible symbols must necessarily be subordinate to verbal symbols; didactic elements must occupy the place of major importance.

B. Distinctions Between Religious and Liturgical Symbols

A distinction is sometimes made between general religious symbols and liturgical symbols. It is a valid distinction if not pressed too far. Religious symbols are those that have only an indirect bearing upon worship. Liturgical symbols are those that come more or less actively into the picture while the congregation is at worship. Many symbols may be thought of as *structural*. They are embodied in the building for general effect. The first requirement of a church building is that it shall look churchly, that it shall give the impression of being a place of worship, not a lecture hall, a library, a school, or some other public building. To give that impression, it is necessary to make use of symbols traditionally associated or historically connected with Christian churches—such symbols as the spire, the bell, stained-glass windows, pointed arches, high-beamed ceilings, pews, a table, and the pulpit. From this viewpoint it is the *total* effect that is to be sought. The churchliness of a building is due primarily to its general proportions and the fitness or orderly arrangement of its beauty, not necessarily to the number and variety of its separate symbols.

Some symbols may be thought of as *decorative*. Many objects in a church, like bric-a-brac in a home, serve merely to create atmosphere. They suggest a place of worship like curtains, draperies, paintings, vases, lamps, candlesticks, and the like make one feel that he is in a home. To the worshiper they have no special significance, convey no particular con-

221

cepts, carry no figurative meaning. They simply help create a mood conducive to worship. Aristotle, speaking of the Eleusinian mysteries, observed that the "initiated learned nothing precisely; but that they received impressions, were put into a suitable frame of mind." [8] Numerous people associate worship with the kind of building and the kind of furnishings they have been accustomed to since childhood. Such a setting puts them in the mood for worship. The desire for the use of the same symbols from generation to generation does not necessarily mean that the symbols themselves have any spiritual significance but only that people like to worship in a traditional or familiar setting.

Some symbols may be thought of as *historical*. They link the present to the past and may suggest whatever values flow from the feeling that one is in the line of a long and noble succession. These symbols are of many kinds. In fact a large proportion of symbols are of this nature. They may be placed on the outside of the building, in the floor, on the ceilings and walls, in the windows, on the beams, or on the pieces of furniture. They may consist of crosses, figures, monograms, seals, or objects, each of which at some time in the past, near or remote, was used by Christians as symbols, or which symbolize what Christians of a particular period or place stood for. Sometimes a window or several windows contain groups of these symbols which set forth in sequence a number of historical episodes. Sometimes they have a special connection with the history of the particular denomination with which a local church is connected.

It is not expected that many of the symbols just mentioned will actually be used by worshipers to provoke their thoughts or to convey a message to their minds. Most of them are too far away from the observer to be identified or are too unfamiliar to him to be recognized for what they stand. The detailed meaning of such symbols rarely impinges upon the religious consciousness of the worshipers. They can be understood only when closely inspected and carefully explained under the tutelage of a pamphlet put out by the architect or of a guide who has been thoroughly instructed about their historical significance. Symbols that require long explanations have already largely failed in their purpose as symbols. "Mind and symbol should meet in lightning flash of mystical knowledge and feeling."[9] Unless the mind of the worshiper quickly perceives in a symbol a meaning which stimulates his own mind and leads

[8] Hastings, *op. cit.* XII, p. 139.
[9] Clarence Seidenspinner, *Form and Freedom in Worship,* p. 15.

his thoughts godward, it is of little direct assistance in worship. That is, it is not a *real* or *live* symbol. Many of the symbols now being advocated for use in Protestant worship are a "dead language." They have lost their ancient meanings, and these cannot be resurrected except through a long, difficult, and complicated process of education which would be wearisome and valueless to modern folk. It is not to be supposed that the modern Church will take the time and trouble to instruct each worshiper in the history of all the symbols which face him from the time he approaches the building until he takes his seat in his pew, so that as a part of the worship itself he will pause before each symbol long enough to contemplate its mystical meaning.

A worshiping congregation can be surrounded with an atmosphere conducive to the spirit of worship without it being necessary to read an allegorical meaning into each color, each figure in the windows, each carving upon the furniture, each decoration upon the wall, each part of the attire of the minister. To overcrowd the service in its surroundings with symbols focuses attention upon particular spots, areas, and articles in the building rather than upon the soul's mystical response to God. It appears that some church architects and building committees have an urge to place somewhere in a single sanctuary every symbol that was once used by any Christian group in the past. Some places of worship I have known have ten or more forms of the cross out of the fifty or more forms available. This overuse of symbols is distracting. An elaborate system of symbols, calling attention to themselves, occupying the center of attention, kept prominently before the eyes of the worshipers, placed so that whatever direction the worshipers' eyes may move they will fall upon another symbol, is unwise. This is calculated to divert the minds of the people from the main purpose of worship, which is to come into personal fellowship with God.

A church should proclaim its purpose through the use of a very few symbols featured in a dramatic fashion. If this is done effectively there is no need of repeating ecclesiastical motifs all over the building. . . . One strong impression is worth a multitude of weaker ones. . . . A cross should be a cross, and there should be only one. . . . Something carved into wood can be appreciated only upon close inspection—and there is always danger that a confusion of detail may confuse the picture.[10]

[10] From John R. Scotford, "Design for Worship," in *Presbyterian Life*, Oct. 1, 1949.

In evangelical worship, then, symbols should be used with *simplicity, economy,* and *restraint.*

C. Symbolism of the "Sanctuary"

The word "sanctuary" is used here in its restricted meaning to refer to the front of the building where the worship centers. The arrangement of this center is expected to symbolize the basic beliefs of a congregation and is decidedly the most important part of its symbols. The guiding principle in this arrangement is "Form follows function." The determining factor in the choice is not which arrangement is the oldest, or which is now the most popular, or which has more advantages or disadvantages than others, or which appeals most to the most people, but which best embodies the beliefs of the worshiping group and which performs best the functions that group wishes it to perform. If, for example, we believe that Ralph Adams Cram, the noted church architect, was right when he said a church "is the house set apart where the mysteries of the Christian faith are to be symbolized," we will come out with one type of arrangement. But if we believe the church is a house set apart primarily for the proclamation of the Word of God, we will come out with another type. In short, the center around which evangelical worship takes place should be designed to embody and express evangelical beliefs.

There are two general types of arrangement, which may be called pulpit-centered and table-centered. Let us now examine them to determine which, if either, is better suited to carry out the purposes and perform the functions of evangelical worship.

The Pulpit-centered Arrangement. The principle governing this arrangement is that the house of worship should be designed to emphasize the major importance of the preaching and the teaching of the Word of God. At the front of the church is a raised platform at the center of which is a pulpit. On the pulpit is an open Bible. The Communion table is immediately in front of and below the pulpit on the floor level of the people. The platform may be reached from the floor by steps at either end or both ends. Back of the pulpit against the wall are seats for those officiating at the service. These seats may be chairs or may be built into the wall itself. In some churches the wall is the end of the room. In which case the organ console and choir are usually on the floor level to one side of the platform, or else in the balcony in the rear. In most churches the wall is a partition, or half wall, which divides the semicircu-

224

lar apse from the nave. In the apse and somewhat elevated above the platform are the choir loft, the organ console and pipes, and back of the pipes the organ itself. In some buildings there is space above the organ on the back wall of the apse for a decorative object of some sort, such as a stained-glass window, a cross, a hanging, or a carving. It is upon this object that the eye of the worshiper finally comes to rest as he looks up the center aisle of the church.

This arrangement definitely expresses certain fundamental evangelical beliefs. The pulpit at the center with the open Bible on it indicates that the written Word of God is the center and source of our faith, that the didactic elements of worship occupy a primary place, and that the spoken and written word belong together. To some the position of the table indicates the sacrament is subordinate to preaching, but that is not the primary purpose of this arrangement. The table is on the level of the congregation, or "in the midst of the people," to signify the evangelical doctrine of the universal priesthood of all believers. The minister comes down to the level of the people to conduct the Communion service. He stands behind the table (the basilican position) while doing so. Symbolically gathered around the table in front of him are the officers and members of the church to signify that the Supper is a fellowship of believers. The platform is within the nave of the church. The apse is usually so shallow that it appears to be an integral part of the nave. The space between the platform and the pews is narrow. All these details are designed to make for intimacy between the minister and the people and to enable the service to proceed as a single unit. This plan provides satisfactorily for common worship. The compactness of the arrangement makes for group fellowship, for good visibility and acoustics, and for all forms of congregational participation, especially for congregational singing under the leadership of the choir.

One of the objections to this arrangement is that it prevents differentiation between the several parts of the service. That is quite true and is so intended. Another objection is that the choir and organ pipes are not worshipful symbols as a resting place for the eyes of the worshipers. This is often obviated, at least in part, by making the choir invisible when not in action or by placing above the choir and organ a cross or stained-glass window or some other object as the final focal point of attention. The problem may be obviated entirely by placing the choir and organ console elsewhere, by eliminating the organ pipes and chamber and placing them to one side, or by replacing the pipes with an organ grill with graceful lines and figures supporting and framing a cross in the center. In effect this closes off the organ chamber entirely and becomes the east wall of the apse. In one church I know of there hangs behind the grill just above the ministers' seats, as though the grill were laid against it, a soft blue cloth with tiny crosses and other symbols on it, showing through the interlacing of the grill. This provides a touch of color that blends with the other colors of the interior and adds to the worshipfulness of the entire front of the church. And it is as beautiful and as effective as an expensive reredos could possibly be.

Another criticism of this plan is that it is man-centered instead of God-centered. This is a misleading and careless statement. God is not visible in any sanctuary, no matter how it is arranged. All sanctuaries are planned to make God the center of the worship. All the statement can mean is that some *object* other than the pulpit or the organ is more satisfactory for the center of attention and for symbolizing God. Specifically it does not mean that worship under some other plan is carried on without the presence of a man. In actual fact the man who leads in worship must of necessity occupy the center of attention when he is in action regardless of the architectural arrangement of the church. Finally, it is held that this plan is not very worshipful or beautiful. That depends largely upon whether somebody has gone to the trouble and expense of making it worshipful and beautiful, and to a lesser extent upon the judgment of the worshiper. By the use of high-beamed ceilings, wood paneling in the proper places, stained-glass windows, hidden choir, organ grill, lighting fixtures, beautifully finished and shaped pulpit, the table and the object on it, the baptismal font, candlesticks, flowers, the cross and other simple symbols, the bookmark, and the use of colors in the interior decorating, such a sanctuary may be worshipful and beautiful and provide all the surroundings essential to complete and satisfactory worship. These facts are attested by numerous churches with pulpit-centered arrangements.

The Table-centered Arrangement. This arrangement calls for the Communion table to be placed in the center of the platform at or near the east wall of the apse. The platform is reached from the nave by wide central steps, often arranged in series on different levels, so that the table is elevated considerably above the floor level of the congregation. The pulpit is placed at the front of the platform at one end and the reading desk (lectern) at the other, both projecting into the nave. Ordinarily the plan calls for an apse of some depth. As in the pulpit-centered plan, the choir stalls are in the apse, but are divided and arranged on either side facing in. Thus the place of worship is sharply divided into two separate areas, one for the action taking place within the apse and centering around the table, the other for the action taking place in the nave and centering around the pulpit and lectern. When the worshiper enters this type of building, he has an unobstructed view up a long center aisle from the door to the table. His eyes finally come to rest upon the table or upon whatever object may be on the wall behind or above the table. As in the other plan, that object may be a cross, a hanging, a stained-glass window, or something comparable to a reredos.

Preference in late years has been given to the table-centered sanctuary, and the current tendency is to minimize and sometimes actually to belittle the pulpit-centered arrangement. The reasons given for preferring the table-centered plan may now be summarized briefly as follows: The Communion table is more appropriate as a symbolic focus for the eye than the pulpit and the organ pipes. The arrangement is more convenient and manageable. It assigns appropriate places for each function of the service. It provides for more dramatic action. The broad and deep area between the front pews and the steps leading into the chancel serves well for weddings, funerals, and other unusual events in worship. The long vista as the worshiper enters the building comes at last to rest not upon the pulpit and the man behind it, nor upon the organ and choir, but upon the table, or altar, which ever it is to be called, and upon the cross, or reredos, above it. The table and the cross symbolize the presence of God, focus the attention of the worshiper on God, and make God the "object of worship," instead of the human leaders of worship.

Everything seems to have been cleared away to make room for God. Minister, singers, preaching station, organ—all are as it were pushed one side or the other to make a clear path to the cross. The human leaders of worship, and the appurtenances of worship are assigned places of secondary important. No one can mistake the object of worship. A chancel carries with it an automatic atmosphere of reverence which has an effect both on the congregation and on the leaders of worship themselves. No minister ever carries himself as carelessly in a chancel as he may on a pulpit platform.[11]

[11] Devan, *op. cit.*, p. 134. Used by permission of Mrs. Winifrede R. Devan. It is his reasons for the choice of the divided plan that have here been summarized because they are complete and typical.

This arrangement is usually spoken of as the "divided chancel." The word "chancel" is derived from a Latin word meaning "lattices" or "crossbars," which were used in medieval times to fence off this area for the exclusive use of the priests in the conduct of the Mass. A substantial number of Protestant churches in recent years have put up something that suggests lattices to separate this part of the church from the nave where the common people are seated. In every case the plan calls for an imaginary line to separate the two areas from each other. It can be categorically stated that the word "chancel" in its technical meanings should be eliminated from the ecclesiastical vocabulary of evangelical Christians. Any suggestion by architectural planning or by treatment that this area of the church is holier than the other areas, or that it is reserved for clergymen and forbidden to laymen, is contrary to evangelical doctrines.

As previously stated, it is not possible to get rid of the human leaders of worship. When they are in action, they are no more conspicuous in one arrangement than in the other. Nor can it be said that God is any more present or any more the "object of worship" in one arrangement than in the other. And it is a matter of judgment and observation whether one set of objects better suggests God than another and whether one plan automatically carries with it an atmosphere of reverence while the other by implication lends itself more easily to careless or irreverent attitudes. But some rather pointed things can and should be said about certain features of the divided plan which are or easily may become detrimental to evangelical worship.

The arrangement:

1. Puts the sermon and the Word in a secondary place to the sacrament.

2. Divides the church into two areas and the service into two parts, thus tending to destroy the unity of both the sanctuary and the worship service.

3. Tends to localize the presence of God and implies that one spot in the church is more sacred than the others and that something different goes on at a holy table which does not and cannot go on at the pulpit and at the lectern.

4. Suggests sacerdotalism and exalts the priestly above the prophetic functions of the minister.

5. Differentiates sharply between the ministry and the laity and tends

to negate the equality, the sainthood, and the priesthood of all believers.

6. Hinders common worship by weakening the intimacy of the relation between minister and people, by putting the pulpit at a bad angle for speaking and the people at a bad angle for listening comfort, by making congregational singing more difficult, and by affecting adversely the contribution that the choir makes to worship.

7. Diminishes acoustical effects and reduces still more the naturalness and intimacy of the service if the building is long and narrow and the depth of the chancel is augmented by a divided choir.

8. Separates scripture and sermon architecturally, thus symbolizing an untruth according to evangelical belief.

9. By making the table an altar restores to Protestant thought a doctrine which has been repudiated since the beginnings of the Reformation.

All things considered therefore, we may conclude that it is exceedingly difficult to keep the symbolism of a table-centered sanctuary evangelical.

If the table is really a table and treated as such, some of these dangers may be minimized. The table in evangelical worship should be shaped like a table and unmistakably look like a table. It should be spoken of as the "Communion table," the "Lord's table," or the "table of the Lord." It should be treated as a table. This means that if placed at the back center of the platform, it should be away from the wall. It should have seats back of it for ministers and sufficient room about it for the seating of the representatives of the congregation when Communion is being observed, if this practice is traditional in a particular denomination. The minister should always administer the Communion from behind the table, facing the people. The people, or their representatives, should be privileged to come to the table to receive the elements. The ushers should be permitted to bring the offering plates to the table and hand them to the minister. The minister's regular seat when conducting services other than the Communion service should be behind the table. He should conduct certain parts of the ordinary worship service, certainly the pastoral prayer, while standing back of the table. The apse should be shallow enough to permit him to move easily and smoothly from his seat behind the table to the lectern and the pulpit. This procedure was strongly advocated by Calvin and is now widely proposed for the table-centered sanctuary. The symbolic actions involved in this procedure focus the attention of both minister and people upon the idea of fellowship represented by the table and help to prevent medieval theology concerning the

Supper from infiltrating into the worship. By such procedures the minister can avoid suggesting that he goes to a particular area from which the people are barred and to an "altar" to perform sacerdotal functions in their behalf.

The widespread use of the terms "altar" and "altar table" for the table in Protestant circles and the enthusiasm with which the idea of the altar is accepted and advocated by Protestant writers and ministers are amazing. One wonders if they have forgotten the real issues of the Reformation and the "rock from which they were hewn." Their indifference to the consequences—their refusal even to face the possible consequences—of this practice are alarming. At one stroke this procedure wipes out the most important single advance of the reformers, namely, the rejection of the sacerdotal system of the Roman Church centering in the altar. That system was repudiated by the reformers without exception. They pulled the altars from the wall, turned them into tables, and restored the Communion to the people, to whom it belongs. To retransform the table into a high altar, separated from and elevated above the people and the Word of God, is a complete betrayal of the evangelical faith. To make the table in the shape of an altar, to fasten it against the east wall of the apse, to take up a position facing it, to bow to it as if it were an altar, to decorate it like an altar—these actions introduce into worship theological ideas incongruous with the evangelical faith.

The lengths to which this process of restoring the altar has already gone were cited in Chapter 5, where attention was called to the rapid development of altar guilds and to the increasing amount of time, energy, talents, and skill that are going into the adornment and care, yea, the semiadulation, of altars in Protestant circles. Where all this is going to lead ultimately is certain; it has turned Protestantism straight back toward the kind of church from which it emerged through the Reformation. The only uncertainty is how long it will take to complete the process. In view of the rapidity with which the idea of the altar has been reintroduced into Protestant churches in the last few decades, one can safely hazard the prediction that the time is shorter than we think. When it is recognized that there are some desirable values to be found in a table-centered sanctuary, the important question still arises: Can we afford to take the long-range risks involved just to secure those values?

Ironically an opposite trend is taking place in Roman Catholic architectural circles. Clarence Seidenspinner tells of churches designed by

THE CULTUS AND SYMBOLISM

Barry Byrnes for Roman Catholics in which the chancel is projected into the nave of the church so that the parts of the congregation on the side aisles sit on either side of the platform. "Since the altar is thus brought forward into the nave, there being no apse, it is easier for the congregation to have a sense of being participants in the mass." He also tells of the effort in France to make worship in Catholic churches communal. To accomplish this, the altar is actually moved entirely out of the chancel and placed in the main aisle of the nave, where it is surrounded by worshipers.[12] Thus while Protestants are taking the table away from the people, the Roman Catholics are bringing the altar back to them. The Roman Catholics are putting the altar in the midst of the people, and the Protestants are detaching their table from the people. The Roman Catholics are seeking deliberately to create a more intimate fellowship in worship, while the Protestants, wittingly or unwittingly, are destroying the intimacy of their worship. It should be said quite candidly and emphatically that at this point Protestants have taken over a medieval Catholic principle while Catholics have taken over a major Protestant principle.

A large share of the responsibility for the return to the altar in Protestant architecture must be laid squarely upon building committees and pastors of churches who are ordinarily important and influential members of such committees. These committees are not performing their primary function of deciding on the general type of sanctuary demanded by the tenets of their faith before engaging the services of an architect. As is well known, the trend among church architects in recent years is to give preference to the divided chancel with the table in the form and position of an altar. If a building committee do not know their own minds and have no convictions about how an evangelical sanctuary ought to be arranged, if they are doing careless or fuzzy thinking, or even no thinking at all, about their problems, the architect is likely to suggest the arrangement now in vogue among his fellow architects instead of one that harmonizes best with evangelical principles and functions. It is the responsibility of building committees to know how a sanctuary for evangelical worship should be arranged and why and to make known their wishes to the architect when preliminary discussions begin. They should employ an architect only if he understands their needs and is willing to carry out their wishes. It is a serious dereliction of duty and the

[12] See *The Pulpit*, May, 1952, p. 28.

betrayal of a great trust if as custodians of evangelical Christianity they fail to exercise their function.

D. OTHER LITURGICAL SYMBOLS

Cyril C. Richardson says:

Man needs to worship not only with his mind but with his whole being; and all his primary capacities such as tasting, seeing, touching, smelling, as well as hearing, speaking and singing, must be involved. For our keenest awarenesses spring from levels of life deeper than the intellectual; and these are aroused far more profoundly by performing sacred actions, than merely by listening. It is by feeling and doing as well as by thinking that worship becomes most alive.[13]

That statement provides a brief summary of the several types of symbols that might possibly be used in evangelical worship. Let us group the symbols he lists under several headings, for purposes of study, with the understanding that there is some overlapping.

Symbols for the senses. Symbols for the eye included the cross, lights, colors, pictures, sculpture, flowers, textiles and hangings, organ pipes and grills, woodwork, the pulpit and lectern, the Bible, the bookmarks, the baptismal font, the windows, and the frescoes, mosaics, and murals on walls and ceilings with all the figures, objects, insignia, and other decorations found therein and thereon. Symbols for the ear include music and singing, scriptures, prayers, and creeds, all of which will be dealt with in some detail in the next chapter. Some of the symbols for the eye have already been considered. Here I wish to deal primarily with those not already considered and with the symbols for touch, taste, and smelling.

The basic symbols for the eye in an evangelical church should be the cross, the table, the pulpit (and lectern), the Bible, and something symbolizing music. As to the last item mentioned, something symbolizing music, it may be said here, somewhat incidentally, that if organ pipes are not suitable for this purpose, something else should be found that serves the purpose as well. The cross, next to the pulpit and the table, is the most important single symbol to be used in Christian worship. It should always be empty to symbolize the evangelical belief in a living, resurrected Christ. If relatively small, it can properly be placed on the Communion table when desired. However, a cross of some size can more properly be placed or hung at an appropriate place on the east wall where

[13] "Toward an Ecumenical Worship," in *Christendom,* Autumn, 1947, p. 450.

it can become a focal point of attention for the eyes of the congregation.

The tendency recently has been to crowd the Communion table with objects—the cross, two candlesticks, two vases, the offering plates, and some sort of covering. Close by, possibly at each end of the table, also may often be found two seven-branched candelabra. This overcrowding and surrounding the table with objects is equivalent to decorating an altar. In fact, manuals for altar guilds often suggest that the proper ornaments for the altar, when not being used for the Communion, are the cross, two candlesticks for single candles, two vases, and two candelabra. It is now widely held that the table, when not in use at the Supper, should be left unadorned with covering or articles of any kind except the offering plates and one other object. That other object may be a cross, a chalice, or a suitable vase of flowers used somewhat in rotation, but never more than one at a time. A cloth of any kind, especially if it covers the table and carries elaborate designs, is likely to suggest an altar cloth. The table should be permitted to symbolize unhampered what it stands for in evangelical Christianity. Candlesticks and candelabra should not be in close proximity to each other and had better be used apart from the table itself. Ordinarily flowers should be placed on the floor level of the congregation well toward the ends of the platform or if on the platform itself, well toward the ends. The principles of simplicity, economy, and restraint, mentioned above, should operate in the use of symbols on and near the table. Too many symbols immediately before the eyes of worshipers are likely to be more diverting than helpful.

The Bible should rest upon the pulpit (or lectern) and should have a bookmark of suitable colors and design. Not a few Protestant churches are resuming an old custom of having someone—the custodian if desired or, better still, an officer of the church appointed for the purpose—bring in the Bible, place it on the pulpit, open it at the desired place, and arrange the bookmark properly, as the signal for the morning worship service to begin. This provides a bit of dramatic action which calls attention to the significance of the Word of God in evangelical worship. This of course is similar to the dramatic bringing in of the scroll of the Law in the Jewish synagogue service. Aside from the Bible and its bookmark the pulpit should go unadorned in order that it too may carry its own important symbolic meaning. Insignia have little meaning except upon close examination and when they are explained. They are often in old English or other classical or ancient letters and figures that are undecipherable by ordinary worshipers. For this reason they should be used with great caution and then mostly for atmosphere rather than as real symbols. As real symbols they are of little value, and as meaningless designs they are likely to be distracting.

It is seriously to be questioned whether evangelicals can wisely use pictures in their places of worship, except occasional subdued figures used as symbolic decorations in the windows or ceilings. Elaborate paintings of any type, especially those with life-size figures of the apostles or of some other Christian "saints" with haloes around their heads, are too closely associated with medieval Christianity and too easily suggest the idea of the veneration of sacramental objects. The same is true of sculptured figures. Pictures, small sculptured figures, elaborate tapestries or other hangings, and other works of art are suitable for homes, educational buildings, art galleries, and private meditation, but not for places of public worship.

In churches that practice immersion as the mode of baptism the baptistry is usually not visible when the sacrament of baptism is not being observed. But in churches that practice sprinkling or pouring as the mode the baptismal font is always visible and may be thought of as a symbol. For this purpose it ought to be at the front, not at the back, of the sanctuary. It is now frequently suggested that the baptismal font be placed at the entrance of the building because baptism is the act by which one enters into the fellowship of the church. To place it there reduces its value as a symbol and minimizes the importance of the sacrament. It should be placed near the front of the church in full view of the congregation so that as a symbol it will have opportunity to speak, and when baptism takes place, one's reception into the household of faith becomes for him and for the congregation an act of central importance not something to be half hidden from view.

It is doubtful also whether evangelicals can wisely go very far in trying to worship God with the senses of taste, touch, and smelling. These three senses are much more closely connected with the purely physical, or shall we say animal, aspects of human life than are the senses of sight and hearing. Of course human beings cannot see or hear God in a physical sense any more than they can touch or smell or taste him in a physical sense. But to speak of seeing and hearing God in a *spiritual* sense is a much more mature idea and carries with it less suggestion of the animal than to speak of smelling, tasting, or touching God in a spiritual sense.

234

Or to state it another way: The former runs less risk than the latter of reducing worship to a purely physical experience. The Lord's Supper is a symbolic meal, to be sure, but the sense of taste is there very mildly brought into play. The early Christians attempted to have a more elaborate—probably a full—meal in the form of the agape. The results were doubtful, it not somewhat disastrous, as should have been expected under the circumstances.

The use of incense, which originated from many motives, including the need for fumigating poorly ventilated houses of worship, has provoked pleasant physical sensations after the manner of perfumes for personal use. The primitive man supposed that incense provoked a similar sensation in God, as he also imagined God was pleased, as hungry men are, by the "odor of a sweet smell" from cooking food (sacrifices). Flowers, if fragrant, may give a pleasant sensation. The early Church used the sense of touch in the "kiss of peace" and in the "right hands of fellowship" (Gal. 2:9). Modern Christians exercise this sense in the handshake. Among some pagan folk the sense of touch was carried as far as the sex acts and led to temple prostitutes and phallic worship. It is difficult to imagine precisely how Protestants can use symbols involving these three senses without in time leading to primitive and pagan ideas. The history of worship should surely warn us to guard scrupulously against running the risk of reintroducing, even in a modest way, into Christian worship crude and physical ideas which have been the source of so many corruptions and abuses, and sometimes scandals.

Symbolic Action. Action or bodily movement during worship can serve a number of valuable purposes. It may provide a needed physical stimulus. The very exertion of standing makes for physical alertness, and this in turn makes for mental alertness. It is equivalent to the seventh-inning stretch at a ball game or to rising or taking a few deep breaths in the middle of a lengthy after-dinner program. It prevents physical drowsiness, wandering of mind, and nervous fatigue. A service of worship, as we shall see in the next chapter, should embody the principle of alternation in moods and movements. Variety prevents monotony. Processionals and recessionals by the choir, standing while singing or reciting the creed, should be definitely planned for with the very practical purposes in view of stimulating body and mind and preventing monotony.

But actions also have a psychological effect. There is an old saying that "we sit to hear, kneel to pray, rise to praise." The bodily action in each case undoubtedly provokes an appropriate mental attitude. Again, convictions are strengthened when put into action. We do not really believe things until we feel them, and we feel them more deeply when we express them in action. Standing while reciting a creed makes it both sound and feel more like a real conviction. Walking to the front of the church and making public confession of one's faith before the congregation both prove and strengthen that confession. It gives a person added courage when he is willing to "stand up and be counted," to let his fellow men know where he stands on important issues. That is one reason why baptisms are performed and why members are received into the church and take church vows before the congregation. People enter into these events, become participants in what is going on, by virtue of the action involved.

There is something to be said for going to the front of the church to participate in the observance of Communion, as was the custom in the ancient Church, rather than having the elements brought to the pews. It is customary in some churches to have the people come to the table and present their annual pledges to the budgets of the church, because that very act gives the pledge a more *personal* meaning. The acts of singing, of saying the "amen," of taking part in a litany or in a responsive reading or in a printed prayer, make worshipers participants instead of spectators. These values have undoubtedly been long overlooked and neglected by Protestants. But to what extent these actions need to be "symbolic" is an open question. Standing while singing enables one to sing more lustily and perhaps more meaningfully, but that does not necessitate calling the standing a symbolic act. Possibly one is more likely actually to pray if he kneels or bows. The act of kneeling or bowing is also an indication of humility. But it is doubtful whether when praying one needs to be conscious of going through a symbolic act; it is far better if the act is the natural expression of a sincere mood within.

The reformers largely discarded the elaborate processionals, pageants, and ceremonials of the medieval Church because they had evolved into scenic spectacles which were more pomp and display than actual worship. Someone has said that some Protestants seem to think God can hear but cannot see what the worshipers are doing, because they are willing to sing and pray but unwilling to engage in ceremonial actions. Evangelicals are reluctant to engage in dramatic ceremonial because these things tend to become a theatrical performance—something staged rather

236

than something sincerely entered into. They are more like public parades in which the main intention is to present a spectacle, to make a dramatic effect, to exhibit colorful decorations, or even to outdo others in the costliest and most elaborate costumes.

Dramatic ceremonials, like symbolism in general, are fascinating and alluring, especially when they involve precise rules of ecclesiastical etiquette. Because of their fascination they are difficult to keep under control once they start; they tend to become the main center of attraction and interest. They often accompany and assist in causing decay in spiritual religion. The history of religion "shows that the decay of spiritual fervor and force in the church is usually accompanied by a craving for elaboration in forms and punctilious ceremonial in detail." [14] For these reasons symbolic action bordering on pageantry in public worship is out of place in evangelical worship. Action in worship should be confined to those simple movements designed primarily to offer worshipers opportunity to participate sincerely and meaningfully in the various parts of the service.

Symbols for the Mind. Here we come to verbal symbols, the most important symbols used in evangelical worship, symbols involving the heart and the soul and the mind of the worshipers. Of course words may be read by the worshipers, in which case they become both verbal and visual symbols. The reading of prayers and responsive readings and reading in unison all have their special values. But the major use of verbal symbols is in the preaching of the Word of God by the minister. In the act of preaching the whole personality of a man becomes a symbol through which the personalities of the hearers are stimulated to worship God.

One of the arresting—even amazing—aspects of the modern liturgical movement is the effort to eliminate the human personality as completely as possible from public worship. This effort is often observed in a type of worship service becoming somewhat popular among young people. No human being is visible at any time during the service except of course the members of the congregation. The other appurtenances of worship, however, are there. The pulpit and the chairs and, as the case may be, the lectern are there; but they are empty. (In one service I attended the pulpit was completely covered with a dark cloth in order to accentuate the absence of the preacher.) The cross with a hanging behind it is at the center of the back wall and is brought into more prominence by a strong

[14] John Macpherson, *Presbyterianism*, p. 29.

spotlight thrown upon it. The leadership comes either from people hidden from view in the rear of the church or from recordings. Special and incidental music comes from recordings, but the congregation joins in singing hymns. The idea is to keep human beings entirely out of sight in order better to center attention upon God. As stated previously, many writers advocate the divided chancel because supposedly it puts the personality of the minister in the background and God in the foreground.

One is prompted to ask: Where is God in the worship service? In an object or in the hearts of men? Is a "disembodied" voice more worshipful than the voice of a visible person? Is God symbolized better by inanimate objects than by living men? Surely God is more like a human personality than like any material thing, even if that thing be a cross. A man with mind, conscience, judgment, and will; a man who can love, and embody virtues in his character, and be sensitive to moral values, and be moved with passion for social ideals; a man dedicated to truth and goodness, whose personality is aglow with the Spirit of God, is the only *living* symbol of God and the highest symbol of God known. No "thing," no sensation of sight or sound or touch or smelling, would have any conscious significance were it not for the mind that comprehends it and the soul that responds to it. All emotions aroused by other symbols would in themselves be purely physical, more or less animalistic, were it not for the mind of man.

God as a personality can be conceived nowhere else on the created earth except by the mind of a human personality. Actually it is not possible to eliminate the human element from worship; it comes into play in one way or another, directly or indirectly. But from the evangelical viewpoint it is dangerous to try to do so. It takes the higher powers of one human personality to stir the higher powers of other personalities to their noblest expression. It takes words to proclaim and explain the Word. It takes a mind to stimulate other minds to think about the great truths of the gospel. It takes a conscience to stir consciences, ethical judgments and social passions to stimulate those same things in others. Evangelical worship is made and kept spiritual, prevented from degenerating into mere formalism or into something akin to pagan superstition, by one human mind using words to symbolize to other human minds what God is, what are his purposes, and what he requires of us. Symbols of the mind must therefore always occupy the place of major importance in evangelical worship.

238

Vestments. The word "vestments" comes to us out of medieval times and refers to special articles, clothing, or insignia worn by priests when conducting Mass. A few basic garments were worn by all priests, and others were worn to indicate the hierarchical rank of the wearer. When properly dressed for the purpose, the bishop wore some twelve or more different articles. Many of these vestments were highly colored, elaborately decorated, and expensively jeweled. Generally speaking, vestments were discarded by the reformers, although this was not uniformly the case, especially in the early years of the reformation. Their reasons for this were: (1) these articles were associated with priestcraft; (2) they set the priest off into a different and higher order from the laymen; (3) they implied he was engaged in functions of a different quality and value from those of the other worshipers; (4) because of their symbolic and allegorical meanings they tended to be looked upon as *holy* objects in some superstitious manner; and (5) they continued alluring temptations toward ostentation and display. In their stead the reformers adopted the simple black gown worn by the scholars as the only special garment for ministers while conducting worship.

Since that time it has been customary in most evangelical churches for the minister either to wear no special article or to wear only the long, flowing black gown when conducting worship. But in recent years interest in vestments has been growing to the extent that they are now being widely suggested and cautiously worn here and there by Protestant ministers. The article being most often used at present is the academic hood, which hitherto has not been regarded as a vestment. The stole, ornamented with symbols of appropriate colors and regarded as the sign of ordination, is also worn about the neck by some ministers when they conduct Communion. Now that the use of vestments has been resumed again, no one knows how far the practice will go.

Like ceremonial and symbolism in general, vestments are fascinating and intriguing. They contain subtle and deceptive temptations for ministers. Interesting enough, some advocates of a worship arrangement designed to put the personality of the minister in a secondary place in worship are those most eager to reintroduce the use of vestments which are calculated to attract more attention to him. Ministers adorned with articles that are decorated with colors and designs containing hidden symbolic meanings and with insignia of their office are peculiarly susceptible to temptations of pomp and show. The academic hood, which introduces distinctions in academic achievements and awards and therefore in rank between ministers, is peculiarly unfitted for purely ministerial attire. It is often suggested for the purpose of adding a "touch of color" to the black gown. To wear it at all while conducting service is a questionable practice, but to wear it merely to "add a touch of color" tends toward display.

The simple, unadorned black gown, worn solely as a garment suitable for the occasion or for the purpose of removing from sight any parts of the minister's personal attire which are likely to attract attention to themselves, may serve a useful purpose. Anything more than that is likely to run the risk of suggesting to clergy and laity alike ideas that are out of harmony with evangelical beliefs. For the first few centuries the Christian Church was careful to insist that ministers when conducting services, including the Communion, should dress as ordinary men. This was for the purpose of making sure that ministers and people alike would be reminded continuously that all men stand on the same level in the eyes of God. The general principle underlying this practice harmonizes fully with New Testament doctrine. Any article worn by the minister and considered a vestment in the technical sense, or that suggests he is performing priestly functions, or that he is of a different order from others, or that his garments and actions are holy, or that introduces the distinctions in rank between ministers, or that leads to pomp or display, is out of place in evangelical worship.

E. Conclusion

The limitations placed upon the use of symbols in worship by the nature of evangelical Christianity necessitate a choice, before the service is planned, of the direction one wishes to go. Once that choice is made, the service must be weighted with means and materials calculated to carry the worshiper in that direction. The primary question always is where to put the emphasis in order to come out in the long run with a spiritual rather than with a semimaterial worship. Teaching people to worship in the evangelical sense is not merely nor mainly teaching them the metaphorical and mysterious meanings of objects but teaching them how to turn their minds and hearts Godward. Material symbols have a function to perform, but it is a secondary not a primary function. They play their part more or less indirectly. Their function is performed properly only if they are used with caution and restraint and primarily to produce the atmosphere or mood for worship. If they are too numerous or too conspicuous, they are likely to call attention to themselves, to confuse the minds of the people, and to divert them from the main purpose of worship.

That purpose is to help people to become aware of God's presence and to understand his nature and purposes, and to teach them how to translate their worship experiences into practical living. In achieving this purpose, verbal symbols are primary and do their work more directly. The ultimate aim of every worship service is to help each one find God personally for himself. Every man's heart is *his* altar. At that altar and at no other can he really come in touch with God. There he offers himself. There he acknowledges God's claim upon his life. There he worships God in spirit and in truth. It is upon that altar within the souls of men that evangelical worship focuses its main attention. If it achieves its purpose, it must of necessity give preference to verbal symbols. Human beings need as clean, as clear, as straight, a pathway to God as possible, without too many impedimentary and diversionary symbols. The procedures and the materials of worship used should be such as to lead them as directly as possible into a consciousness of his presence.

11

The Cultus and the Materials for Worship

T HE purpose of this chapter is to list the verbal forms that are available for evangelical worship and to consider the ways in which they may properly be used. These forms are abundant and varied, because Protestants are free to utilize materials from whatever source, ancient or modern, provided they embody for their own age and in the language of their generation the faith they profess. It is the privilege of Protestants "to create liturgical forms in which ancient and modern materials can both be used, and to give the worship service a growing edge by incorporating into it what is best and most challenging and inspiring in modern religious thought and literature." [1]

A. The Bible

From the beginning the Bible has occupied a primary place in the Protestant tradition. From it have come the texts and much of the materials for sermons. The reading of selections from the various parts of the Bible has been an important element in all public worship services. It has been the textbook for religious instruction, the book of private devotions and meditations, the source of benedictions and other prayers, and the inspiration and the basis of much of the best church music, including hymns, anthems, and solos. Hence it has always been placed in a prominent place in the house of worship to symbolize its central importance in Protestantism.

The first part of the service throughout the days when the service was

[1] Albert W. Palmer, *The Art of Conducting Public Worship*, p. 101.

242

divided into two parts was called the "liturgy of the Word." Since the regular morning service of Protestant churches omits the Communion service, the entire service now revolves around the various uses of the Bible. It is doubtful, however, whether many Protestant ministers make full use of the varied materials found in this book in the worship services planned by them. Let us now consider the several ways in which the Scriptures may be used in the service other than in the sermon.

The Call to Worship. This practically always consists of a passage or passages of scripture. The passages in the Bible provide materials for a variety of calls to worship for the many types of services held during the year. Many ministers have the habit of gathering them together and filing and classifying them for future use.

The Scripture Readings. Since the Bible is regarded as the Word of God, the source of authority for Protestants, and the infallible rule of faith and practice, and since they believe individuals have the right of private judgment and are privileged to interpret the Bible as they are led and aided by the Holy Spirit, the reading of selections from the Bible has occupied a regular place in the order of worship. Ordinarily the selections are read without any interpretative comment in order to let God speak his own message directly to the hearts of the individual worshipers through his Word. This reading of the Bible without comment has considerable exegetical and instructional value. More care and attention should be given to it. Very few Protestant denominations have adopted a lectionary which follows the course of the Christian year. Hence the responsibility for the selection of the passages to be read, the number and their source, rests upon the minister. In the early centuries, when the liturgy was being greatly elaborated, selections were read from each of the major divisions of the Scriptures in succession. Later the selections were reduced to three: from the Old Testament, from the Gospels, and from the Epistles. For centuries it was customary for the congregation to stand while the lesson from the Gospels was being read to stress its superior value to other portions of scripture. In recent years the custom has been to have two selections, one from the Old Testament and one from the New.

Responsive Readings. Ordinarily the Old Testament lesson is a responsive reading participated in by the minister and the congregation. For a long period of time the responsive readings were exclusively from the psalms. That portion of the hymnal devoted to these readings was

243

called the "Psalter." But of late years other portions of the Bible have been used for this purpose, so that the section of church hymnals devoted to these readings is now labeled "Responsive Readings." Responsive readings need not be confined to those in the hymnal. Ministers should choose their own passages for occasional special use in this manner. Usually the *Gloria Patri* is used after the responsive reading because originally it followed the reading of Psalms to provide the Trinitarian formula to that Old Testament lesson.

Biddings to Offerings. It is surprising how many ministers use the same words each Sunday to call for the offering, such as, "The offering will now be received," or "Let us now make our offering," instead of using different passages of scripture suitable for the purpose. Many such passages may be found in both the Old and the New Testaments. These should be collected together in considerable numbers and used as needed to suit the particular occasion. If used in rotation over long periods of weeks, they serve the purpose of familiarizing the congregation with passages they probably would not otherwise come to know. This procedure also constitutes valuable instruction on the subject of Christian stewardship.

Variables. Most of the variables used in the ancient Church were composed of verses of scripture. Some were sung and some spoken either in unison or responsively. While most of them still in use in modern church services were originally in the form of prayers known as versicles, to be mentioned later, that does not necessarily need to be the case. There is no reason why brief passages of scripture could not be used occasionally as biddings to prayer, or before the sermon, or as affirmations and responses at other places.

B. PRAYERS

Prayers have been the main method by which men have approached God in all ages, especially since prayer worship was substituted for sacrifice worship in the Jewish synagogue. For purposes of study they may be classified roughly under several headings.

Public Prayers Classified as to Content. Traditionally prayers have been classified as to general content as prayers of: (1) adoration, (2) thanksgiving, (3) confession, (4) petition, and (5) intercession. For generations all these were constituent parts of the general or pastoral prayer. In more recent years the tendency has been to separate these into smaller units and use them at different places. This is especially true of the prayer of confession, which is now customarily used alone and followed by an assurance of pardon. It is also true of the prayer of adoration, which is often confined to the invocation. In fact the invocation is now often spoken of as the "Adoring Invocation." The pastoral prayer then becomes a prayer primarily of thanksgiving, petition, and intercession.

Public Prayers Classified as to Form. *The collect.* This is a brief prayer carefully constructed according to a special form. It is a single complete sentence with five parts: (1) an invocation; (2) a relative clause—"Some truth about God which you wish to keep before your mind and that of the people"; (3) a petition; (4) a statement of the purpose of the petition; and (5) the conclusion, which is usually a doxology. It must express a single thought and be brief and compact. The prayer most often used as an illustration of a collect is the following prayer found in the old Gregorian sacramentary: "Almighty God, unto whom all hearts be open, all desires known, and from whom no secrets are hid; cleanse the thoughts of our hearts by the inspiration of thy Holy Spirit, that we may perfectly love thee, and worthily magnify thy holy name; through Christ our Lord. Amen." Collects are sometimes used singly and sometimes in groups as substitutes for the pastoral prayer.[2]

The bidding prayer. This is a combination of audible and silent prayer. The minister *bids* the people pray for certain things or tells them what to pray for, then waits while they pray silently in their own words. He usually begins by saying, "Let us pray for," then mentions the object of the prayer and what to pray for in a few words carefully prepared beforehand, then waits while the people offer their own prayer. Then he proceeds in the same way to tell them what else to pray for and waits for them to pray silently, and so on to the end of the prayer. Ordinarily he concludes the whole with a very brief prayer of his own. This type of prayer is especially useful in teaching people how to pray and in broadening the scope of their prayer interests.

Litanies. Litanies are responsive prayers, which may be thought of as extended versicles. The custom of using them is very old, dating from the earliest centuries when they were nearly always led by the deacon. The minister voices a prayer which leads up to and prepares for the *brief*

[2] One of the best treatments of the subject of collects may be found in Dearmer, *op. cit.*, pp. 149 ff.

response of the people which is little more than an arrow prayer. That prayer may be some such expression as "Lord, have mercy," or "From this deliver us, O Lord," or "We sinners do beseech thee, O Lord," or "Hear us, O Lord, hear us," according to the petition just uttered by the leader. The responses of the people should be varied a number of times in the same litany to avoid monotony and the risk of their becoming meaningless repetitions. A great deal of thought is now going into litanies of many kinds for many purposes, and they are available in printed form in books of prayers, books of common worship, and so on. They are especially well suited for congregational participation. They should be utilized more generally in public worship, and more ministers should arrange litanies of their own for occasional use.

Arrow prayers. These are brief single sentences, sometimes called "ejaculatory prayers," which may be interspersed at suitable places in the service.

Versicles. A versicle is a dialogue prayer used responsively. It is usually composed of actual passages of scripture or is in the language of scripture. Most of the traditional variables, so named because they were or were not used in the several rites according to choice, such as the *Salutation*, the *Sursum corda*, and the *Sanctus*, are versicles. Some are sung antiphonally. They may be inserted here and there in the service as may seem most fitting. Traditional versicles were originally composed to fit contemporary needs. Modern ministers miss an opportunity if they use only the traditional ones and fail to devise their own to fit the special needs of their contemporaries.

Responses. A response is usually in unison, not in the form of a dialogue, and may be either spoken or sung as is most appropriate. The Lord's Prayer is usually utilized as a response. Other traditional responses are the "Doxology" and the *Gloria.* There is no reason why ministers should confine themselves to the use of ancient responses of this type.

Public Prayers Classified as to Location in the Order of Service. The *invocation.* This usually appears near the opening of the service and is an expression of adoration to God and a petition for his blessing upon the people assembled for worship. The invocation should be brief and should be varied according to the season, the occasion, and the general purpose of the particular service. Because of the brevity of this prayer much care and thought should be given to its wording. A wise minister will make collections of such prayers from printed sources and of his own, not necessarily to be repeated in precisely the same form each time, but to avoid monotony and the repetition of the same words and phrases, and to cover the varied needs of the people.

Pastoral prayer. As stated above this was formerly called the general prayer because all types of prayer—adoration, thanksgiving, confession, petition, and intercession—were combined in this single prayer. It was customarily too long and easily became wearisome. A general prayer in this sense is now not often used. It has been replaced by what is called a pastoral prayer, a prayer in which the pastor brings before God weekly the special needs of individuals and groups in the congregation known to him because he is pastor, to offer intercessions in behalf of other groups throughout the world, and to express in behalf of pastor and people the general yearnings and hopes that should characterize Christians.

The offertory prayer. In connection with the morning offering a prayer is customarily used, sometimes before the offering is taken, but more often as a dedicatory prayer after it is placed upon the table. This prayer, like the invocation, should be brief and varied from time to time. Many ministers have found it advisable to prepare the offertory prayer so that it will harmonize with the passage of scripture used as a bidding to the offering, and to make a collection of such scriptures and prayers to be used in rotation over the year.

Framing prayers. These are ascriptions of praise or benedictions used before and after the sermon and the reading of the scripture. So it can be said that the reading of the scripture, for example, is "framed" with prayers.

The benediction. This is customarily used at the conclusion of the service, though there is no reason why a benediction should not be used at other places, for example, at the close of the reading of the Scriptures. The benedictions most frequently used are those found in the Scriptures—the so-called apostolic benediction found at the conclusion of Paul's second letter to the Corinthians (13:14), the prayer of Paul in Eph. 3:20-21, the prayer with which Jude concludes (vss. 24, 25), the priestly blessing of the Old Testament (Num. 6:24-26), being the most frequent passages used for this purpose. Other brief prayers found in the scripture are sometimes also used as benedictions. A number of other passages of scripture, with some adaptation, make suitable benedictions; and appropriate benedictions can be made out of combina-tions of several passages of scripture. And of course benedictions may be formed by the minister as he forms other prayers. It is a good policy to accumulate a variety of benedictions, to vary them deliberately from time to time, and to learn how to use those most apt for the occasion.

A recent custom is growing up in the churches of the minister going to the back of the sanctuary to pronounce the benediction, especially if it is the practice for the choir to have a recessional. The benediction should always be given from the pulpit or the platform; otherwise it loses an essential part of its symbolism, which is the pastor gathering the congregation under the shadow of his outstretched hand, or hands, while he asks God's final blessing upon them. There is a difference of opinion as to the exact manner of using the hands. The old synagogue custom was to use both hands outstretched. Some ministers use the right hand uplifted with all fingers and the thumb spread out, while others use it with the first and second fingers and the thumb only out-stretched to signify the Trinity. No important principle is here involved. The main thing Protestant ministers need to remember is that they are not priests and that they are not engaged in any sacerdotal act of blessing the people when they pronounce the benediction; they have no special access to the divine favor and no authority to dispense divine power, but are simply asking the continued favor of God upon the people. Some denominations insist that only duly ordained ministers are authorized to use the apostolic benediction, but that all others who use it must substitute the word "us" for the word "you," or better still, must be discouraged from using it at all. This attitude smacks of sacer-dotalism and is out of harmony with the true evangelical doctrine of the ministry. The apostolic benediction is not the exclusive property of the ordained ministry; in the eyes of God it would be just as mean-ingful and effective when used by a layman as when used by the clergy-man.

Public Prayers Classified as to Type. *Fixed* or *printed* prayers. There is no doubt that with the proper discipline and concentration one can really pray when reading a prayer or when listening while someone else reads it. But it is difficult to do as every worshiper knows from experience. And there is no doubt that such prayers may be profitably used in evangelical worship. In the historical section of this study it was shown that the Puritans, who for years tried to bring about certain changes in the

Anglican prayer book, made it clear that they believed in the use of printed prayers; but they wanted the privilege of using extempore prayers also. Some ancient prayers are classics and, when translated into the modern vernacular, are surprisingly fitting. Invocations, offertory prayers, benedictions, and versicles, and as for that, the prayers of confession, thanksgiving, petition, and intercession, can be wisely gathered and used in rotation as relatively fixed prayers. People sometimes worship better when forms are fairly familiar, as we shall see a little later. Fixed prayers provide for this need. Printed prayers of various kinds often help both minister and people express what many find it difficult to express for themselves.

Spontaneous prayers. These are prayers formulated on the spur of the moment, without any previous preparation ahead of time. Unfortunately it has sometimes been assumed that the leader of public prayer should trust to the promptings of the moment, or to what is most often called the leadings of the Spirit, for his prayers, otherwise they cannot be true prayers. All too frequently this results in another type of "fixed" prayer, prayers in which the same expressions and phrases and even words, carelessly and lightly put together, are used over and over from Sunday to Sunday until they become habitual; and the prayers move around in a cycle that is fixed as surely as if they were written down. It is this sort of prayer that has brought into disrepute what is known as extemporaneous prayer. The word "extemporaneous" literally means speaking without preparation, from the promptings of the moment, or impromptu. A spontaneous prayer, every word of which is invented on the spot while one is standing or on his knees, as the case may be, can certainly be a genuine prayer. But when a minister publicly leads the same congregation in prayer every week, spontaneous prayers can become as meaningless as the hasty repetition of printed prayers.

Free prayers. The word "free" is used to describe a type of prayer that is carefully prepared ahead of time but that is spoken freely when actually used in the service. It is difficult for the prayers of a person in one generation, however beautiful and well worded, to express adequately the needs of a person of another generation, partly because of the actual changes in the meaning of words, partly because of the changes in styles of expression, and partly because of the changing social conditions. It is even more difficult for a committee, however devout and capable, to compose prayers that will suffice for the public

249

services of churches of a whole denomination for decades, or perhaps centuries, to come. For this reason it is highly desirable that in every public service there shall be a place for prayers that express the needs of the people of that particular congregation, upon that particular oc-casion, in terminology and concepts that are relevant to contemporary life. Such prayers are of the very essence of living, vital worship. They are at the same time the highest and the most difficult form of public prayer. To lead the people in that type of prayer is one of the heaviest responsibilities of a pastor.

To prepare for this kind of prayer, the minister formulates clearly what he wishes to say, saturates his mind with the ideas and thoughts to be expressed and with the words best fitted to express them, and by meditating in the presence of God. But when he prays, he speaks with the kind of freedom as does the preacher who after thorough prepara-tion speaks without manuscript or notes. The *Directory for the Worship of God* adopted by the Presbyterian Church in the U. S. A. in 1788 concludes the chapter, giving directions to ministers about the use of this kind of public prayer, in the following significant words:

We think it necessary to observe, that although we do not approve, as is well known, of confining ministers to set or fixed forms of prayer for public wor-ship, yet it is the indispensable duty of every minister, previously to his enter-ing on his office, to prepare and qualify himself for this part of his duty, as well as for preaching. He ought, by a thorough acquaintance with the Holy Scriptures, by reading the best writers on the subject, by meditation, and by a life of communion with God in secret, to endeavor to acquire both the spirit and the gift of prayer. Not only so, but when he is to enter on particular acts of worship, he should endeavor to compose his spirit, and to digest his thoughts for prayer, that it may be performed with dignity and propriety, as well as to the profit of those who join in it; and that he may not disgrace that important service by mean, irregular, or extravagant effusions.[3]

Calvin believed in the minister using extemporaneous prayer preceding the scripture readings and the sermon but in having fixed prayers else-where. Of the latter he said: "I highly approve of it that there should be a certain form from which Ministers be not allowed to vary. That first, some provision be made to help the unskilfulness and simplicity of some; secondly, that the consent and harmony of the Churches one with another may appear; and lastly, that the capricious giddiness and

[3] Ch. V.

levity of such as effect innovations may be prevented." [4] Prayers need not necessarily be fixed to help the "unskilfulness and simplicity" of some and to avoid the "capricious giddiness and levity" of others. They need only to be carefully prepared. It is no proper excuse to say the task is hard, or that many are unequal to it, or that it is better to use the printed prayers of others than the poor prayers of one's own. Protestant ministers neglect a primary obligation if they fail to prepare for using "free" prayers that are genuine prayers relevant to the occasion, that fit the contemporary needs of people, and that are in the thought terms and language of their own day.

Some General Problems Connected with Public Prayer. Congregational participation. One of the important principles of Protestant worship is that there should be definite and genuine participation on the part of the congregation. This participation can be achieved so far as prayer is concerned by litanies, bidding prayers, prayers in unison, and by periods of silence when individuals may offer their own prayers. J. B. Pratt says:

We should ask ourselves very seriously whether we really believe there is any kind of genuine prayer except individual prayer. . . . The aim of liturgical prayer, properly understood, is not to tie down the mind to a form of ancient words, but to encourage the individual to make his own prayer. . . . I have heard earnest Protestants say, "I could pray if the minister would only keep quiet and let me." At worst the man who has come to worship finds himself indignant; at best he prays a little by himself with many interruptions. If he is docile he mentally follows the words that he cannot help hearing. A great many of us seem to have identified praying with following someone else's prayer. Every truly prayerful soul knows that the two things are poles apart. The highest praise that could possibly be given to a church would be to say that it is a good place to pray in. It is an astonishing fact, when one reflects upon it, that our entire Protestant service offers not a single opportunity for genuine individual prayer.[5]

Pratt was a layman, not a minister. Since this reflects the feeling of a thoughtful, devout layman, it ought to be taken to heart seriously by evangelical ministers. Somewhere in the service there should be a period of silence where prayers may be offered by the individual worshipers. This period is frequently provided immediately preceding the pastoral prayer, while the organ softly plays one stanza of a suitable hymn.

[4] W. D. Maxwell, Concerning Worship, pp. 50-51.
[5] Op. cit., pp. 20-23. Copyright 1950 by The Macmillan Co. and used by their permission.

251

Length. Sometime ago the *Reader's Digest* printed the following typographical error found in the column of a Massachusetts newspaper: "Reverend David B. Matthews presided and opened and opened and opened and opened the meeting with prayer." That might easily have been the result of the workings of the subconscious mind of the typesetter who had often been exhausted by the long prayers of his pastor. Pratt says, "If a perfectly frank and truthful vote could be taken among a large number of Christian laymen on the subject, I think 75 per cent would tell us that they regard the 'long prayer' . . . as something to be lived through, and at least 50 per cent, I believe, would confess that they face it, every Sunday morning, as a period of mild boredom." [6] We should often remind ourselves that Jesus said we will not be heard for our "much speaking" and that "vain repetitions" are characteristic of pagan worship. Better a few brief prayers that really express the petitions of the heart than one long prayer that frays the nerves and exhausts the patience of the congregation.

The language of prayer. One of the fundamental principles of public prayer seems often to be the most difficult to learn, and that is that prayer is not preaching, not exhorting the people, not informing or instructing God about what is going on in the world, but actually praying to God. When chaplains' prayers in Congress were being criticized for their political flavors about the middle of the last century, Senator Willard Saulsbury of Delaware offered the following resolution:

Resolved, That the Chaplain of the Senate be respectfully requested hereafter to pray to and supplicate Almighty God in our behalf, and not to lecture him, inform him what to do, or state to him, under pretense of prayer, his (the said Chaplain's) opinion in reference to His duty as the Almighty; and that the said Chaplain be further requested, as aforesaid, not, under the form of prayer, to lecture the Senate in relation to questions before the body.[7]

Prayer should not be designed to exhibit the minister's learning or eloquence. I once heard a prayer of twenty minutes' duration which consisted of an excellent exposition of the Lord's Prayer. It indicated that the minister was a scholarly expositor and may have informed God as to what Christ meant when he suggested the prayer, but it could hardly be called a real prayer addressed to God. Prayer should be in simple,

[6] *Ibid.*

[7] Anson Phelps Stokes, *Church and State in the United States,* III, 135-36. The date is not given in the source, but was apparently in the 1850's or 1860's.

252

direct, dignified language that is devotional, not didactic, and is free from florid, flamboyant, rhetorical phrases. And above all it should come from a sincere, humble heart.[8]

C. Music

A detailed history of the part music has played in religious worship is not necessary for the purposes of this study.[9]

Fundamental Principles. The basic principles to be kept in mind are: *Music is an adjunct to worship, never an end in itself.* One of its main functions is to produce the moods and stimulate the emotions conducive to the spirit of worship. If it falls short of doing this, or if it produces moods and emotions contrary to the spirit of worship, it fails. If it is detached from the purposes of worship and made a means for the improvement of the general musical taste of the congregation or for training musical artists and displaying their abilities, it loses its religious values.

Someone has said that music is "vague, mysterious, indefinable, intangible and evanescent." [10] It is all these things and more. For this reason there is a wide difference of opinion as to its actual effects, and even purposes, in worship. Some think it has a direct effect upon the involuntary muscles and the glands of the body and therefore upon the emotions. However it is to be explained, the average person knows that some types of music have a quieting effect upon his nerves and produce a meditative mood, while other types upset his nerves and produce a mood of irritation. Some types make him want to relax, and others make him want to become active. Some dogs howl when certain sound waves strike their ears, presumably because they are actually painful to the dog. Many worshipers testify that some church music makes them sympathetic with the dog that howls when the church bell is rung; it makes them twist and squirm in their seats and want to get up and leave the church. It is to be hoped that a definitive psychological study will some day appear showing the relationship, if any, between certain

[8] The reader who is interested in pursuing this subject further is referred to the following: (1) M. P. Talling, *Extempore Prayer*; (2) Coffin, *The Public Worship of God*, pp. 70 ff.; (3) John A. Kern, *The Ministry to the Congregation*, pp. 66 ff.; (4) J. R. P. Sclater, *The Public Worship of God*, pp. 55 ff.; (5) Palmer, *The Art of Conducting Public Worship*, pp. 116 ff.; (6) Maxwell, *An Outline of Christian Worship*, pp. 163 ff. and *Concerning Worship*, pp. 112 ff.

[9] The reader interested in this is referred to Devan's *Ascent to Zion*, ch. v, pp. 147 ff., which is the best brief history of religious music I know of.

[10] *Ibid.*, pp. 149-50.

types of religious music and certain types of religion. Be that as it may, the problem of church music resolves itself into a question of using such music in such ways, with such associations, as to produce the moods conducive to spiritual worship.

Music should be within the appreciation range of the worshipers. They should be able to understand and comprehend it, musically speaking, and respond to it spontaneously. It should fit their needs. They should be able to use it enthusiastically as an expression of their feelings. Otherwise it is meaningless, worthless, as a vehicle of worship.

Church music should be the medium for the development, the expression, and the transmission of the evangelical faith. In the evangelical service of worship only that music is to be used that is calculated to assist in achieving these ends. There are moods, emotions, and ideas associated with music that are in open conflict with evangelical beliefs. For this reason Protestant music should always be of a definite type. This is partly what is meant by saying it should be didactic in nature; that is, it should be fitted and intended to teach something specific. Paul told the early Christians that they ought to sing with the spirit and with the understanding also, which simply means that they ought to understand what they are singing. From the very beginning therefore music in the Christian tradition was subordinated to or controlled by the faith they professed. As has been stated already in this study, some insist that worship in general and music in particular should not have a didactic purpose of any kind. The use of music in an evangelical church can be justified ultimately only if it harmonizes with the spirit of the gospel and puts it to work in the minds and hearts of the worshipers.

Instrumental Music. Instruments have not always been used in Christian worship. In the days of Jesus the chief religious music was the singing of psalms. Apparently this was done antiphonally and, at least in the Temple, was accompanied by wind, string, and percussion instruments. But no musical instruments are mentioned in connection with worship in the New Testament. Apparently through the early centuries, certainly throughout the medieval period, the chants, recitatives, responses, and chorus music were unaccompanied by musical instruments. Calvin could not abide the use of instruments, with the result that metrical psalms were sung unaccompanied in the Reformed churches for almost two centuries. This aversion to the use of instruments was due partly to their association with pagan religions and with the licentious life of the pagan world about them, and partly to the distrust of the sensuous impressions aroused by music. Some modern churches refuse to use instruments in worship primarily because they are not mentioned in the New Testament. The organ, improved and used to accompany the singing of hymns in Germany, became the first instrument to be used by Christians. In time it became the standard instrument for use in Protestant worship. By a natural process of evolution it has become the symbol of music in the general arrangement of the sanctuary.

Other instruments are used occasionally, notably the piano because it is less expensive than the organ. But harps, violins, and some wind instruments are used here and there in isolated instances. There are a few Protestant churches that have developed orchestras for use in worship. They are not regarded as being especially conducive to the spirit of worship, but rather suggest public concerts. The organ is especially suitable for worship because of its soft, pleasing tones and its ability to imitate the human voice. The organ prelude while the people are gathering puts them rather quickly into the mood of worship, and the postlude after their dismissal leaves a lingering mood in their hearts. The music of the organ plays an important function in sustaining the entire service and in holding its parts together. This function is performed by the brief incidental music that makes transitions from one part of the service to another and fills the interludes while the late comers are being seated, by the quiet music in preparation for prayer, and by solos during the offering.

Vocal Music by the Choir. The choir has often been a useful adjunct to Protestant worship, in spite of the fact that Protestants seem continuously to have had difficulty deciding where the choir should be placed and precisely what functions it is supposed to perform. It has served the useful purpose of providing leadership in the singing of hymns, has been a powerful stimulus to desirable religious emotions, an effective method of transmitting the gospel truths, and a persuasive force in influencing Christian decisions and actions. Numerous worshipers in all sorts of Protestant churches could testify to the good influences upon them of the anthems by the choir as a whole and of the quartets, trios, duets, and solos by members of the choir. Responses by the choir, like incidental music of the organ, help to round out the service and weave the parts into a unified whole. Brief choir music is an especially worshipful way to bring separate parts of the service to a con-

255

clusion—for example, the prayer and the offering—and to conclude the service after the benediction. In some churches the choir assists effectively in the calls to worship, with introits, and in antiphonal singing, or in a combination of antiphonal singing and reading.

But unfortunately a considerable amount of music by choirs and choir members has a questionable worship value. Many numbers are rendered with such poor articulation that they are hardly understandable. Some tunes not only are not melodious but are jarring. Some of the music is so difficult that the average church choir is incapable of rendering it satisfactorily. Some of the parts are repeated over and over until they become irritating, throw the listener into a kind of suppressed rage, exhaust his emotions, and upset his nerves. Some numbers contain no important spiritual message. Some express adulation for the Virgin Mary or other medieval dogmas that are contrary to Protestant beliefs. Many anthems and solos are presented for the purpose of displaying the abilities of the singers instead of aiding in worship. In recent years it is the openly expressed purpose of some choir leaders to use choir music as a means of educating the congregation in musical appreciation and in the history of religious music of various periods.

The use of medieval music in the Latin tongue is being revived in many Protestant churches by many musical directors. Historians regard the Gregorian chants of the early period and the chorus music of the later medieval period as the grandest expression of sacred music in the history of Christianty. But it is complicated, highly technical, slow in movement, difficult to render effectively, lacking in lyrical appeal, and of interest only to those who have musical training sufficient to understand and appreciate it. Its whole purpose is un-Protestant; it was confined almost exclusively to the clergy, officially prescribed and controlled by the clergy for a purely sacerdotal function with which Protestants have no sympathy, and rendered in a foreign tongue. It is therefore wholly unsuitable as a medium for Protestant worship. Music that is little more than an exhibition, that carries moods and meanings contrary to Protestant beliefs, that conveys no particular evangelical message, and that is not in the vernacular has no place in evangelical worship.

Congregational Singing. In the New Testament Church worshipers made their own individual contributions. (I Cor. 14:26.) Some of these contributions were psalms, and some were teachings of one sort or another. It is believed some were also spontaneous songs of praise to Christ and to God, which are referred to by Paul in Eph. 5:19 and Col. 3:16 and which he urged them to use "singing with grace in your hearts unto God." These songs were in germ the beginning of Christian hymnody. In his letter to the Emperor Trajan (ca. 112) explaining the custom of Christians in Bithynia, Pliny the Younger said the Christians "sang a song to Christ as God responsively." But sometime after the middle of the fourth century all congregational participation in church music ceased and was not restored again until the Reformation. Throughout the thousand years or more preceding the Reformation the people were carefully excluded from all participation in the music. Among the evangelical sects that sprang up before the Reformation and that were partially responsible for it was a group of followers of John Huss in Bohemia, later known as Hussites. To them belongs the honor of putting out the first Protestant hymnbook in 1505 in Prague.

Luther encouraged and stimulated congregational singing in hymns and wrote words for some thirty or more, although he did not compose the music for any. During the lifetime of Luther some sixty hymnbooks were published. Being the most conservative of the Reformers and the most reluctant to make changes, he tried to preserve both chants and anthems, but largely failed in the effort. The chief, almost the sole, music in the worship of the Calvinistic churches was the singing of metrical psalms by the congregation. The Genevan *Psalter*, which was published in 1552, became the hymnbook and the standard of church music for the Reformed churches of Europe and of the United States and remained so for more than two hundred years. In the Anglican Church, which remained more like the medieval Church than any of the other churches of the period, the music was liturgical in nature and was intoned somewhat after the manner of the clerical music of the Roman Church.

The singing of hymns by the congregation in the modern sense did not begin until the eighteenth century during the Wesleyan revival. Hymns, written by Isaac Watts and John and Charles Wesley, were widely used. The revival that swept through the free churches of both continents stimulated the writing of new hymns and tunes, and began a development in hymnody that has not ceased to the present time. The result was that there now exists among the free churches, especially of the English-speaking world, a vast storehouse of gospel songs and

257

hymns of high order, which makes the last two centuries one of the outstanding periods in the history of Christianity from the viewpoint of the music of worship. There are some people who believe that the Reformation reached its highest point and reverted completely to the type of New Testament Christianity when congregational singing got into full sway. It is fascinating but futile to speculate on the form the Christian Church might have taken had it followed through in the early centuries of its existence on the path it started when "spiritual songs," sung to God "with grace in the heart," sprang up spontaneously in the churches established by Paul.

Hymn singing is an ideal method of congregational participation. It provides an unusual combination of several necessary worship procedures. To begin with, most hymns are prayers which are spoken audibly by the individual himself and as an act of the common worship of the group, thus affording both common action and individual expression. They combine the effects of music, poetry, and ideas. According to Pratt the emotional power of the verbal harmonies and rhythms of poetic form blended with the influence of the music and the intellectual power of ideas combine to make the hymn an unusually powerful mood and emotion.[11] Hymn singing is a method of etching the gospel on the minds and hearts of the worshipers. It is therefore one of the important mediums for the transmission of the evangelical faith and one of the most influential single devotional forces in evangelical worship.

For hymns to achieve their maximum effects, both the words and the music must be "singable" for the average worshiper. They must express the mind and the mood of the worshipers spontaneously; they must be easy for the people to take hold of and to take away with them, which is saying in effect that they ought to be in the vernacular of the people, musically speaking. If the hymns, as we popularly say, "go over the heads of the people," if they are too difficult to sing in harmony or in parts, without "catchy" melodies that provoke a response that starts them singing in the soul, they fail in their purpose. The effort to lift the musical level of hymns is laudable, but if made an end in itself, it can easily and quickly defeat the purpose of the hymns, which is to sing the gospel into the lives of the people. It is not necessary that all the hymns in worship be great hymns, worthy of being handed down

[11] Op. cit., pp. 17-18.

from generation to generation. Much serviceable music dies with the generation that produced it and found it satisfying.

Many of the gospel hymns, of the evangelistic type, are a form of folklore, with all the practical values found in Negro or cowboy spirituals over which musicians sometimes go into ecstasy. They are spirituals of a distinct type and that serve a distinct purpose for the generations that use them. The Protestant churches, if they wish to be the religion of the common folk, cannot afford to neglect the best of these spirituals, even though they may never qualify as classics. It also defeats one of the main purposes of music in worship to try to revive a type of music, like that of the medieval Church for example, that manifestly does not fit the needs nor serve the purposes of this generation, and to impose it on people to whom it means nothing and who cannot use it as an adequate vehicle of their own worship. It is not so important that people become acquainted with the type of music used in former days as to have a music that they can appreciate and understand, that serves their purposes and fits their needs, and that expresses adequately their spirit of worship.

D. The Sermon

Frequently someone, referring to the morning worship service, will speak of the worship and the sermon as though the sermon were something added to worship or something taking place after the worship was over. The sermon is not an intruder in worship; it is an integral part of the worship. The gospel is good news about events that occurred in history. To be heard, that news must be proclaimed. The only way the gospel can do its work in the lives of men is through the instrumentality of human speech. "Whoso said Christianity, said preaching." [12] Words are a form of energy. They are "ignition devices," as Fritz Kunkel called them. They are sound waves transmitted by the voice mechanism through a receiving instrument called the ear to the human brain. There they start a process called thinking. If they carry the Word of God, that process is a redemptive process. Speaking of his own preaching, Paul said, "We are ambassadors therefore on behalf of Christ, as though God were entreating by us" (II Cor. 5:20). God was making his appeal through the Word spoken by Paul. "The primary

[12] Herbert H. Farmer, *The Servant of the Word*, p. 19. Used by permission of Chas. Scribner's Sons.

task of the Christian preacher is to bring about a meeting between the Word of God and the mind of man." [13]

Preaching not merely is speaking words but is a deed—a redemptive deed. P. T. Forsyth put it this way: Preaching is a "part of the dynamic event wherein the living, redeeming God reproduces his act of redemption in a living encounter with men through the preacher." [14] He was probably the first person to speak of preaching as a "living encounter" between God and man. In recent years that idea has been taken up by many writers and promises to revive the New Testament idea of preaching and restore it to its rightful place in Christianity. One of the most incisive elaborations of this idea may be found in Herbert H. Farmer's *The Servant of the Word*. Developing the theme that preaching is an essential continuation of the "saving activity of God," he says:

> The necessity of preaching resides in the fact that when God saves a man through Christ He insists on a living, personal encounter with him here and now in the sphere of present personal relationships. Preaching is that divine, saving activity in history, which began two thousand years ago in the advent of Christ and in His personal relationships with men and women, and has continued throughout the ages in the sphere of redeemed personal relationships (which is the true Church), now focussing on me, confronting me, as a person indissolubly bound up with other persons at this present time. This focussing on me is not apart from what has gone before, nor can it be, for it is part of the continuous purpose throughout the years which began in Christ; hence preaching is telling me something. But it is not merely *telling* me something. It is God actively probing me, challenging my will, calling on me for decision, offering me His succour, through the only medium which the nature of His purpose permits Him to use, the medium of a personal relationship.[15]

Because preaching thus provokes or brings about a personal encounter between God and the hearer, it is often spoken of as the "sacrament of the Word." [16] When man comes into spiritual contact with God, that *is* communion; *it is* worship. Preaching is spiritual worship of the highest order because by means of it God comes directly to the minds and hearts and consciences of men. Through the preacher he stimulates

[13] See E. Jerome Johanson, "What It Means to Preach the Gospel," article in *Theology Today*, Oct., 1951. This article is a study of the teaching of the Swedish theologian Gustav Wingren, whose central idea is that preaching is a redemptive act.

[14] *Positive Preaching and the Modern Mind*, p. 22. Also cf. Donald G. Miller, "Words or a Deed," an article in *Interpretation*, April, 1952, where the same idea is further developed.

[15] Pp. 27-28.

[16] *Ibid.*, p. 28. Cf. Henry Sloane Coffin, *Communion Through Preaching*.

and challenges all the higher qualities of the soul. Hence preaching is indispensable to mature worship. It is preaching that primarily makes worship mature and keeps it so.'As people leave church, they are often heard to remark that they *enjoyed* the service. This may mean only that they had pleasant sensations as they sat in a building that was artistically and architecturally satisfying, as they listened to the music, as their eyes responded to the variegated colors of decorations, vestments, and stained-glass windows. So they left *feeling* better. The sermon if of the right quality forces them to be honest with themselves and with God as to whether they actually *are better* morally than when they entered. The sermon can do more than anything else to make and keep the worship a personal matter between the soul and God. It focuses attention upon the inner man, upon the moral judgment, the conscience, and the will. It endeavors to prevent the worshiper from trying to hide his real spiritual and moral needs from God or to substitute for them mere formal acts, or empty words, or pleasing emotions./ For the perpetuation of evangelical Christianity it is therefore essential that the sermon always be an organic and central part of the worship service. It keeps worship from dissipating into mere feeling.

E. Other Materials

Other materials for worship include the use of silence, the offering, and symbolic action, which have already been dealt with in the previous chapter. Some New Testament passages seem to indicate that a public confession of faith or creed was used in connection with baptism. Very early in the history of the church baptism must have been observed, certainly at times, in connection with public worship. Creeds have therefore been used as an element of Christian worship for many centuries. The Apostles' Creed or the whole or parts of other ancient creeds that are suitable for our generation, The social creeds of the churches or modern affirmations of Christian faith of other types, can be used upon proper occasions with good effects. Reading matter of a devotional nature—poems, prose, prayers, and so on—should be provided regularly in the weekly bulletin and the people given pauses and brief periods of silence here and there where these may be read and used as the basis of private meditation. Announcements during a worship service are now mostly decried as the obtrusion of an alien or distracting element. This need not necessarily be so. A congregation is supposed to be a church family, a household of faith, a brotherhood. They have their mutual interests and common activities, which if properly mentioned, may add warmth and a needed human touch to common worship.

F. Conclusion

Such are the varied kinds of verbal materials available for use in evangelical worship. This worship is enriched by the employment of these materials primarily rather than by increasing the number of visible forms. Visible symbols in themselves do little more than provide the setting and create the mood for worship. Beyond a certain point they add little to a vital, meaningful spiritual experience of God. Throughout the history of Christianity the craving for elaborate outward forms and symbols has always been accompanied by a corresponding decay of spiritual force and power within. The former has usually been an indication of the latter. When and where something really significant is taking place within the souls of worshipers, they neither need nor desire many visible forms with which to approach God. Precisely what do we refer to when we speak of people having a rich worship experience? We mean that God becomes real and comes alive to them; that their hearts are strangely warmed within them; that their highest thoughts are aroused, their consciences pricked, their noblest social impulses stirred; that their sins are consciously forgiven, the burden of guilt removed, and they know themselves to be in a loving fellowship with God, God's Spirit bearing witness with their spirits that they are the sons of God; that their fears are allayed and their doubts resolved; and that they are reinforced, fortified, undergirded, and nourished within by a new inflow of courage, faith, joy, peace, and hope. A rich worship experience is a living, thrilling, personal communion with God. Verbal forms seek to penetrate directly to the citadel of the soul and bring about such an experience. When that occurs in all its manifold meanings, visible forms are pushed out on the periphery of worship.

Manifestly all the many forms in which these types of materials may be expressed cannot and should not be utilized in any single service. Some method of choosing and arranging the materials must be sought. This is done when an order of service is planned. To the problem of devising such an order we now turn in the next chapter.

12

The Cultus and the Order of Service

A. Question of Fixed or Fluid Liturgy

A PERENNIAL worship problem is whether or not to adopt a fixed liturgy. Like so many other questions connected with worship that question can be answered properly only in the full light of New Testament Christianity of which the present-day Church is the successor and guardian. New Testament Christianity was Spirit-led, Spirit-filled Christianity. Jesus promised, "When he, the Spirit of truth, is come, he shall guide you into all the truth" (John 16:13), and, "Ye shall receive power, when the Holy Spirit is come upon you" (Acts 1:8). These promises were abundantly fulfilled in various unexpected ways in the New Testament Church. Under the promptings and guidance of the Holy Spirit early Christians continuously engaged in bold and dangerous enterprises. They reshaped or discarded old systems and created new ones better fitted for the new life they were experiencing in Christ. They inaugurated a missionary movement to take the gospel to the whole Gentile world, in spite of the fact that it went contrary to all their traditional customs and beliefs. They took a church-wide collection for the relief of the famine sufferers in Judea, thus originating organized Christian philanthropy on a large scale. They made so many changes of so many kinds that it was charged they were turning the world upside down (Acts 17:6).

They provoked bitter opposition by their innovations and were given such courage to face it boldly that they amazed both themselves and their opponents. They believed and unhesitatingly taught that men in

Christ are new creatures and that new men ought to invent new instruments, new forms, and new institutions and to try to build a new society in which to use them. There is no way to standardize the work of the Spirit of God or capture and freeze it in the forms of any age. He works "when and where and how he pleases." It is doubtful whether the order of worship can ever be fixed if Christians are true to their heritage. That worship must always be adapting itself to the changing, growing experiences of Spirit-led men. The essential spirit of evangelical Christianity was expressed by John Robinson to the pilgrims who were leaving Holland for America. He had chosen to remain in Holland with that portion of the group who either could not or thought it unwise to leave. His parting words to the group emigrating were:

I charge you before God and his blessed angels, to follow me no further than I have followed Christ; and if God should reveal anything to you by any other instrument of his, to be as ready to receive it as ever you were to receive any truth by my ministry; for I am confident the Lord hath more truth and light yet to break forth out of his Word. I bewail the condition of the reformed churches, who are come to a period in religion, and will go no further than the instruments of their reformation. The Lutherans cannot be drawn to go beyond what Luther says; for whatever part of God's will has been imparted and revealed to Calvin they will rather die than embrace it. And the Calvinists, as you see, stick where Calvin left them. This is a misery much to be lamented; for though Luther and Calvin were precious shining lights in their times, yet God did not reveal his whole will to them; and were they living now they would be as ready and willing to embrace further light as that which they had received. I beseech you to remember your church covenant, at least that part of it whereby you promise and covenant with God and with one another, to receive whatsoever light or truth shall be made known to you from the written Word of God.

He here points up one of the fundamental principles of Protestantism—namely, adaptation. We have observed many times in this study that the liturgies of the church were continuously undergoing changes. Christians of all ages and places not only have felt free to modify the liturgy but have felt obligated to do so that it might serve their needs.

As has also been emphasized, evangelical worship, to be true to its genius, should be organically related to practical life. The word "liturgy" literally means "public," or belonging to the people. In its largest sense therefore it means common worship, worship intended to help the worshipers find God and to live their daily lives under the sense of his presence. If it achieves this purpose, it must be in the vernacular of the people. That word in its restricted sense means the native language, or mother tongue, of the people. But in its wider meanings it includes the contemporary concepts, categories of thought, interests, and life situations of the people. If worship belongs to the people, not to an order of clergy, the people must be able to participate in it intelligently and actively. What is going on must have a maximum chance to penetrate into their minds and touch their lives in practical ways. Words lose their meanings. Languages and dialects constantly undergo changes. New ideas require new words for their expression and comprehension. Worship might as well be in a foreign tongue as in terminology that conveys no meanings to the participants. Worship, in short, must be relevant to the times if it is to be practical—and evangelical. This rules out complete, standardized, fixed formularies.

This does not mean that the use of familiar and traditional forms is entirely excluded, but only that they should not be continued after they have lost their significance and that the door should always be kept open for new forms fitted for changing times. It is often stated that there is a psychological law operating in worship that makes it impossible for worship materials and practices to attain their full effect until they become familiar, until they reach a considerable age and have the authority of tradition.[1] We are told that people are naturally conservative, that they "dislike alteration in established forms," that worship forms must have a "considerable degree of accepted uniformity" before they can be effective, that like music they must be time-honored and familiar before they speak to the inmost soul.[2] There can be no doubt of both the force and the value of traditions. No living liturgy can cut itself off from the past, nor should it try to do so.

But familiar forms have their distinct limitations and dangers. Forms that are continued merely because they are old and after they have lost their meaning degenerate into superstitions. Everyone who has had long experience in the conduct of public worship can testify that numerous people suffer in silence and numerous others quietly remain away from church, because of the failure of worship to "speak to their condition." They grow weary of the same forms used over and over, and say so. They thrill when new prayers, music, responses, yea, and

[1] See Pratt, The Religious Consciousness, ch. xiii.
[2] See Devan, op. cit., pp. 14-15, 91, 98.

the Scriptures in modern translations are used for the first time, because they speak to them in language they can understand, or as they say, "It gets down to where we live." If there is a psychological law working in favor of the familiar form, there is also one working to demand variety in forms and forms in language that is familiar.

The fact is that both the old and the new, the familiar and the unfamiliar, the novel and the customary, are essential to every living liturgy. Theoretically it ought to be possible to keep these in perfect balance. In actual practice it is impossible to do so. This is due in part to the inability of human beings to keep their minds in perfect balance and in part to their tendency to take the line of least resistance. It is always easier to continue the use of customary forms than to create new ones. If worship is to be kept a vital experience, it must be weighted in that direction. Deliberate efforts must be made to impress the leader and the worshipers with the primary importance of free, spontaneous expression. The core of worship should consist of those elements and forms that are designed to make and keep it evangelical, or else, as history teaches us, it inevitably tends in time to become lifeless formality. Eternal vigilance is the price of spiritual religion as well as of liberty.

B. Basic Needs to Be Satisfied

There is usually no problem of deciding upon the basic needs of worshipers to be provided for in a complete worship service. Different lists have been made by different people, not because of any disagreement as to the needs, but because the terms and groupings used have varied. One of the older lists is that of Willard L. Sperry, which contains: (1) praise, (2) penitence and the assurance of forgiveness, (3) thanksgiving, (4) petition, (5) intercession, (6) edification, (7) inspiration, (8) consecration, and (9) benediction.[3] A more recent list is that of Albert W. Palmer, who says, "There are . . . seven great moods or life situations to which worship may minister, namely (1) our need of common religious fellowship, (2) our sense of spiritual joy, (3) the quest for deepening insights, (4) the renewal of faith and vision, (5) our craving for comfort, (6) our need for confession and absolution and (7) our impulses toward dedication or re-dedication to God and to our tasks."[4] If these lists were compared in detail in connection with

[3] *Reality in Worship*, p. 277.
[4] *The Art of Conducting Public Worship*, p. 25

the comments of the authors, it would be discovered that they are different ways of saying substantially the same thing.

All that is necessary for our present purpose is a list explained very briefly so that it obviously covers what would generally be regarded as a comprehensive list of the needs of ordinary worshipers. The following list is suggested:

1. Vision of God: adoration, sense of his presence
2. Confession: humility, penitence, contrition, repentance
3. Forgiveness: relief, release, cleansing, assurance of pardon
4. Thanksgiving and praise
5. Joy: comfort, exaltation, and exultation
6. Fellowship: sense of common or corporate bonds
7. Instruction: illumination, insight
8. Dedication: sacrifice, offering
9. Call: ethical demands, inspiration, stimulation to action

These needs are met by the use of the materials described in the last chapter.

An initial difficulty arises from the fact that each of the major elements is capable of being used to evoke a wide variety of moods and of being used to satisfy a number of different—even contrasting—needs. Prayer, for example, may express adoration, thanksgiving, and praise to God; serve as a suitable channel for humility, confession, and repentance, and as an instrument of rededication; and through petition and intercession move out into the field of sympathy and service for one's fellow men. Similarly the several uses of the Scriptures can provide for adoration, thanksgiving and praise, pardon and forgiveness, comfort and joy, instruction and dedication. Likewise music is an instrument for the expression and creation of a wide variety of different moods. This is especially true of hymns, as can be discovered by checking the classified table of contents and the topical index of any church hymnal. Still again, the sermon potentially is capable of gathering together all the moods and needs of the entire service and weaving them into a final, dramatic expression and appeal. It is not possible therefore to use one element for one particular purpose only or to provoke a single mood desired. If this were possible, the task of building the order of service would be simplified greatly.

C. Sequence and Arrangement of Materials

Considerable thought has been given, especially in recent years, to the problem of arranging the material in the proper psychological sequences. Some thirty years ago Von Ogden Vogt and Sperry almost simultaneously but independently suggested that the order of service should be based on the sixth chapter of Isaiah. They found that the experience of Isaiah was psychologically speaking a typical, complete worship experience. Vogt lists and explains the constituent elements of this experience as:

1. Vision: attention to God which induces the experience.

2. Humility: littleness, self-abnegation, which is the first reaction of the worshiper to God.

3. Vitality: God comes into you, fills and possesses and enlarges you. Humiliation is changed to dignity, degradation into exaltation.

4. Illumination: under the influence of that new impulse life takes on new meaning. You see new heights. Old things pass away; all things become new.

5. Enlistment: You cannot contain this experience long. Quickly you feel a desire to engage in a new undertaking. You have a new purpose. You are gripped with a sense of dedication and consecration.

Vogt says: "This is the course and order of an experience of worship, an experience of the sense of God, . . . and something like the great experience of Isaiah is what the worship of the Church ought to help people to have." [5]

To Sperry the experience is a series of contrasting moods, which may best be described by thesis, antithesis, and synthesis, three philosophical terms in Hegel's philosophy. Isaiah first had a vision of the greatness and holiness of God (thesis). This inevitably made him feel by contrast his own unworthiness (antithesis). The conflict of these two ideas and emotions resolved themselves into a recovery of the sense of God and a rededication of the self (synthesis). This same pattern he finds in certain other lyrical and autobiographical passages in the Bible (for example, Pss. 42; 90; 139; John 1:1-14; I Cor. 13; II Cor. 6:6-18; Rev. 7:9-17), in certain selected hymns, and in the Anglican prayer-book service. This pattern "is not an arbitrary type of literary construction, it is simply the formal transcript of the spiritual life." Every worship service should definitely follow this order, in fact can follow no other.

[5] *Art and Religion*, ch. xv.

Hence every worship service has three main parts: (1) The attention of the worshipers is directed to one great attribute of God—his holiness, his eternity, his beauty, his peace, his strength, or his wisdom. (2) Then they turn their attention to themselves, where by contrast they are made aware of their own sinfulness, the brevity and transiency of human life, the squalor and ugliness of life about them, their lack of peace, their weakness, or their ignorance as the case may be. (3) Finally the worshipers turn again to God and in the last devotional period of the service find answers to their needs and are moved to rededicate themselves to the service of God.[6]

Clarence Seidenspinner groups all the needs and the materials to be used to meet them under three headings, which he calls the three movements of worship: (1) the adoration of God, (2) the communion with God, and (3) the dedication to God.[7] Maxwell also has three groupings under the headings: (1) the preparation of approach, (2) the Holy Scriptures, and (3) the oblation and fellowship of prayer.[8]

As interesting and suggestive as these analyses are, they must be used with caution. Their contribution to a better understanding and a better arrangement of the order of public worship is limited. This is due to a combination of several things. One is what was said above, that each of the elements is capable of being used for a variety of purposes. This makes it difficult and perhaps undesirable to place one element— for example, the scripture lesson, or the pastoral prayer, or the sermon— where it is supposed to contribute to only one main movement or mood of the service.

Again the leader of worship cannot, with any degree of success, control the effect of the particular prayer, scripture, or response on individual worshipers, nor guide the steps by which a particular effect is achieved. And it is a question whether it is good psychology to let the worshipers know by the headings and groupings of items in the printed order of service that such an attempt is being made. Still again, different minds have diverse notions of what constitutes a logical psychological sequence of moods and ideas. I once heard a sermon in which the preacher undertook in all seriousness to arrange the sequence of ideas in I Cor. 13 in a more logical manner than Paul had originally written them.

[6] Sperry, op. cit., pp. 282 ff., 299 ff.
[7] Form and Freedom in Worship, pp. 70 ff.
[8] Concerning Worship, pp. 23 ff.

It is therefore by no means certain the patterns set forth by Sperry, Vogt, and others are universal or even typical patterns.

For these reasons elaborately analyzed orders of service run the risk of being mechanical and unreal. Sperry seems to have had this in mind when he said, "The possible permutations and combinations of these several items are theoretically many. . . . We may safely say that the quest of novelty for novelty's sake in the revision of orders of worship offers little hope of better services. . . . We need have little interest in bizarre orders of worship." [9]

Fortunately it is not necessary to construct an order held together tightly by carefully preconceived psychological sequences in order to have a satisfactory service. That complicates an already difficult problem. There is a better procedure, and strange to say, it is suggested by Sperry in connection with his psychological study of the order just dealt with. He suggests that a more or less stable general outline of the conventional type become the skeleton for the order. Around this the completed order can be built by interspersing the other materials in whatever manner may be desired to lead the people through the successive stages of a satisfying worship experience. It is difficult to see how his scheme of a service divided into three parts, roughly corresponding to thesis, antithesis, and synthesis, can be accommodated to a conventional order, unless he really does not mean for it to apply strictly to the service as a whole, but rather to a series of contrasting moods which move along both together and in succession. That appears to be his meaning.

At any rate he is strongly of the opinion that the service should not be unified around one idea or mood or proceed on a single level. A single idea, if too intensely and intensively treated, he points out, puts a severe strain upon the worshipers, tends to grow monotonous and to tire the worshipers out. The unity of the service ought therefore to be like that of a symphony. "Symphonies habitually begin with affirmative, objective, allegro movements. They then lapse into middle movements which are meditative and perhaps minor, in largo or andante tempo. A final more rapid movement works out some reconciliation of the objective and subjective themes." [10] In a similar fashion a worship service should have sequence of movements, contrasting moods,

[9] *Op. cit.*, pp. 277-78.
[10] *Ibid.*, p. 280.

270

different states of feeling, until it reaches a climactic ending—and can be provided supposedly within the framework of the conventional order.

This general procedure was that used by the early Church. We have no way of knowing whether the early Church arranged their scheme of worship, to be referred to again shortly, according to a well-thought-out liturgical theory. On the other hand, it could be that they rejected all carefully devised schemes because after due experimentation they came to realize some of the unsatisfactory results from such schemes mentioned above. What we do know is that the method of constructing the order suggested by Sperry is precisely the method by which the ancient liturgy expanded. The basic outline, as has hitherto been emphasized, remained fairly constant through all the centuries; but additional elements were interspersed in it here and there to produce the elaborated rites, with their many variations, of the pre-Reformation days.

A similar procedure was suggested by Cyril C. Richardson of Union Theological Seminary in a workshop on worship in 1950 at Andover-Newton Theological Seminary. He divided the elements into two groups: (1) those "whose order in the service is more or less fixed because of their relationship to each other in a worship experience, and (2) those which are 'movable' because they may be incorporated in a service at various places. The two groups are not to be thought of as conflicting or mutually exclusive lists, but rather as lists which are to be joined together as believed best for any particular service." In my judgment this is a sound principle upon which to proceed. It avoids many of the difficulties inherent in an order that is too closely knit together. It provides for flexibility, variety, and adaptability to different purposes, and above all for the wide range and complexity of interests, moods, and needs of the people. It also makes possible psychological movements of the type suggested by Sperry and others, but leaves the reactions of the worshipers to go their own psychological way without any specific attempt at close direction and control.

The first step is to decide on the items to include in the basic general outline. Interestingly enough, most writers either begin or end with what turns out to be the traditional outline, referred to several times in this study as having remained relatively constant over the centuries. This may be traced to the first part of the medieval Mass (the liturgy of the Word) and through that to the synagogue service. Sperry begins with that outline as he understands it, listing the items as follows: (1) praise, (2) penitence and forgiveness, (3) "Psalter" and lesson, (4) pastoral prayers, (5) sermon—with hymns and anthems appropriately interspersed.[11] With reference to this ancient order Gregory Dix says:

> The original unchanging outline of the christian synaxis everywhere was as follows:—
> 1. Opening greeting by the officiant and reply of the church.
> 2. Lesson.
> 3. Psalmody.
> 4. Lesson (or Lessons, separated by Psalmody).
> 5. Sermon.
> 6. Dismissal of those who did not belong to the church.
> 7. Prayers.
> 8. Dismissal of the church.
> 9. On occasions a collection for the poor, the expenses of the church, etc.[12]

For his fixed basic outline Richardson offers a list that corresponds roughly to that of Dix. It is as follows: (1) recognition and adoration of God, (2) praise, (3) confession of sins and assurance of forgiveness, (4) illumination through the Word, (5) communion through prayer, including petition and intercession, (6) consecration of self, (7) conclusion of service. It is to be observed that the chief difference between the lists of Dix and Richardson and that of Sperry is that they place the prayers after instead of before the sermon.

The scholars cannot agree on the exact items and their sequence in the ancient list. That is of no great significance since an ancient list is not to be regarded as sacred and unchangeable. But it is interesting to discover that the *general* outline for public worship has remained *relatively* the same throughout the centuries from the time of the ancient synagogue service. When modern men start out *de novo* (anew) to construct an order of worship, they are likely to arrive at an order similar in general outline to the ancient order. This would seem to indicate that the ancient outline is natural, logical, and psychologically sound. One can adopt it with a feeling that he is on fairly solid ground.

I would suggest an outline that corresponds roughly to that of Sperry, with the following items: (1) adoration of God, (2) praise, (3) prayer of confession and promises of forgiveness, (4) responsive reading of the scripture, (5) the scripture lesson, (6) the pastoral prayer, (7) the

[11] *Ibid.*, p. 278.
[12] *Op. cit.*, p. 38. Used by permission of A. & C. Black, Ltd.

sermon, (8) the conclusion. This would leave for the more or less movable or variable elements such items as: the offering and the materials used in connection with it, the Lord's Prayer, the "Doxology," the *Gloria Patri*, the versicles and responses, the creed, the items to be used at the opening and closing of the service, the various types of prayers (other than the prayer of confession and the pastoral prayer), and the several kinds of music. These movable elements could be placed as desired according to the season, the special day, the contemporary situation, the needs of the people, and the theme and purpose of the minister.

Some such procedure would provide an order of service that could in all essential particulars conform to the principles of evangelical worship. It allows for both order and flexibility. It embodies the values that come from having a relatively fixed general order as a recurrent pattern, yet leaves the minister free to use it or modify it or move out in some other direction as in his judgment best serves the principle of edification (I Cor. 14:26). This places a heavy responsibility upon the minister but there is no way for this to be avoided if he functions as an evangelical minister.

D. Qualities of Good Outline

In spite of all that has hitherto been said about the undesirability of trying to work out a detailed, close-knit psychological outline, it must be said that the planning of the order of service does nevertheless involve "psychological understanding," "logical insight," and "aesthetic acumen," to use Seidenspinner's expressive terms, if that order is to have the proper qualities. The most important qualities to be sought are:

Unity. This has already been discussed to some extent. As has been said, this should not be the unity of a single idea. The needs of the people at any one service are too varied and complex to be met by the use of a single mood. The unity of the order is provided primarily by the mind of the leader. He chooses the type of materials to be used for his immediate purposes. He arranges them in such relation to one another that they are calculated to provide the contrasting moods sought. Each item or group of items thus supplements the others until the whole service arrives at a climactic focus and expression at the close—a climax which the minister planned from the beginning.

Alternation. This quality should be embodied in the contrasting moods already dealt with and also in contrasting movements of expression and silence and of standing and sitting. Special care should be taken that the people are not kept standing for too many items in succession and that they are asked to stand at intervals to give them a rest from sitting. But it is also to be remembered that alternating the movements of a congregation can easily be overdone and become a means of diversion as well as of exhaustion. An Episcopal minister warns his fellow ministers of the too frequent use of the *Gloria Patri,* which necessitates the people facing the altar. He says this can "degenerate into a sort of liturgical St. Vitus dance, a nervous twitching toward the east to cover up any and every imaginable pause." He goes on to speak of the "bad habit of subjecting the people to the following sequence of posture: stand for half a minute; kneel for the time it takes to recite the Lord's Prayer; stand again." [13] Ordinarily it is wise also to alternate the types of material used. That is, two different musical numbers, or two different items to be read, or two different prayers should not be used in succession. In effect alternation means simply making wise use of the psychology of rhythm.

Balance. A just proportion should be preserved between the several parts of the worship, such as reading, singing, praying, and preaching. Time, and its relation to the complexity and speed of modern life, and the attention curve, or attention limits of the people, must be taken into consideration in determining the length of the service as a whole, the number of items used, and the length of the several parts. The Westminster divines suggested the planning of the service so that "neither reading, singing, praying, preaching or any other ordinance be disproportionate one to the other; nor the whole rendered too short or too tedious . . . (and so as) to preserve a just proportion between the several parts of public worship." [14]

Simplicity. Care should be taken not to overcrowd the service with too many items, as was the case in medieval days, when practically all the known versicles and responses, including musical responses, and types of the same items were used in every service. Economy and restraint should be exercised at this point as well as in the matter of symbols. Better a few, appropriate, well-chosen items with dramatic appeal and that make

[13] *Episcopalians United,* a symposium, ed. Theodore P. Ferris, p. 98.
[14] *The Directory for the Worship of God,* III, 3; VII, 4.

quick, direct impressions than so much material that the worshipers are confused and their energies both dissipated and exhausted.

Movement. The service should flow smoothly step by step to its conclusion. Smoothness is secured primarily by the skillful use of incidental music and of sentences, ascriptions, and so on, which conclude one part of the service and introduce the next. These transitional devices are the glue that holds the several parts of the service together.

Climax. It is generally agreed that consecration or dedication should be the climactic mood of the service, but there are differences of opinion as to what materials are best suited to achieve it. The current notion, now popular in some quarters, is that this can best be brought about through the offering which follows the sermon and precedes the benediction. In Seidenspinner's plan, for example, the climactic movement of dedication to God is epitomized by the offering, because gifts of money, he believes, are the "outward and visible sign of the inward and personal dedication" of the worshipers. In most Protestant churches, however, the offering is placed shortly before the sermon and is often looked upon as a minor climax in the series of movements up to that point. A scriptural bidding, music, preferably an organ number, while the plates are being passed which provides a few moments for meditation, a bit of dramatic action in the return of the plates to the table while the people stand and join in the "Doxology" or some other response, and a concluding prayer easily constitute a single unit of the service, if so desired. The offering should be an act of worship. It is a symbol of the dedication of time and energies that produced the money offered. But it is a debatable question whether it suffices as a symbol of the dedication of the whole self, whether it is capable of engendering the emotions and thoughts appropriate for such a dedication, and whether it provides a worthy climax with which to conclude the service.

In his order Maxwell places the offering after the sermon, but follows that with the general prayer, composed of thanksgiving, self-dedication, intercession, and commemoration of the saints. This is followed by the Lord's Prayer, a hymn of praise, and the benediction. As indicated earlier, Dix insists that the prayers followed the sermon everywhere and always in the services of the early Christians and that this was undoubtedly a fixed tradition almost from the New Testament times. The tradition cannot with certainty be traced much—if any—earlier than the fourth century, by which time the emphasis was being placed upon the liturgy of the Upper Room rather than upon the liturgy of the Word. This may account for the fact that prayer rather than the sermon was the climax of the service when held without Communion. Whatever the explanation for the tradition and the reasons assigned for it, it can be argued with considerable justification that the general prayer or prayers are not a suitable climax for the worship service. They are lacking in the dramatic effect, emotional appeal, and persuasive power that ought to accompany the high point of the service.

In his order Sperry places the sermon at the close of the service but follows it with a concluding hymn, preferably one of service and action. The closing hymn, he says, marks the worshiper's return to his practical life in the world. He speaks of the custom of closing the service with a brief prayer and benediction immediately after the sermon as a "current heresy." This he regards as a psychological mistake and a grave lack of generosity on the part of the minister for not giving the people a final opportunity to express themselves in the service. There can be no doubt of the appropriateness of a concluding hymn of the right sort. It provides the medium for expressing and putting into temporary action, along with one's fellows, the emotions and inner decisions engendered by the service. The sermon may be followed by a hymn, but it is the sermon that should be regarded as the climax to the service. It not only is a suitable and effective climax, but gives complete unity to the whole service. It should recapitulate the various moods and movements of the service and draw everything together at the close. It is fitted to bring into play all the higher elements of human personality; it brings the worshipers face to face with God within the sacred precincts of their souls, focuses their minds and consciences upon the duty of decisions, and moves them to action. It is therefore an appropriate climax to the personal and spiritual worship of evangelical Christianity. The use of lengthy materials of any nature after the sermon constitutes an anticlimax. Without much delay the worshipers should be permitted to leave the house of worship under the influence of the sermon and to return to the practical world to wrestle with the problem of putting into effect any resolutions made.

E. Keeping Worship Evangelical

A central problem connected with planning worship is how to make it and keep it evangelical. It can never be worship in general; it must be worship of a particular type, cast in definite thought molds, framed in definite terminology. It is the duty of the leader of such worship to clothe the whole service in the language of evangelical Christianity. The word "language" refers not only to the meaning of the actual words spoken but to the meaning of action, symbols, and attitudes; all these must be evangelical in content. Evangelical worship should convey no hints that clergymen are priests or that they are of a different order from laymen. It should be kept free from all suggestions of magic, of intermediaries between God and the worshiper, of the veneration of sacred objects and places and people that borders on idolatry, and of all pagan superstitions. In short, it should be cast in the thought forms of Protestant theology.

Earlier I spoke of the care that should be exercised in the use of the term "altar." The use of the word "altar" and of all objects used to decorate altars, together with the terms denoting them, should be carefully avoided. The term "absolution" is definitely non-Protestant. It may also be questioned in all seriousness whether the term "assurance of pardon" is Protestant. A Protestant minister can offer the comforting promises of the Bible relating to the forgiveness of sins and can pray that sinners be delivered of the burden of them, but he has no authority to absolve anyone of sins nor to assure anyone that he has been pardoned. The word "saint" should not be in the ecclesiastical vocabulary of Protestantism. Only once is that word in the singular used in the New Testament, and then it is used in the distributive sense (Phil. 4:21). At no place in the New Testament is any man singled out and individually called "a saint" or "the saint." The term is always used in the plural to designate the whole group of Christian believers. All Christians are saints, but not one of them is ever to be thought of as superior to the others or to be given homage greater than the others. To teach otherwise is to go contrary to all that Jesus himself taught and exemplified concerning humble service and the ministry of self-forgetful service. To adhere strictly to Protestant terminology, the term "saint" should not be applied to the apostle Paul, to the writers of the four Gospels, and to other New Testament apostles; nor should Protestant churches be named in honor of a "saint." Because a halo indicates a saint, all paintings or other symbols containing figures with haloes should be eliminated from the building.

Music giving homage to the Virgin Mary or that sets forth other medieval ideas contrary to Protestant beliefs should not be used in evangelical worship. In a pamphlet describing the symbolism and art in a Protestant church I know of, there is an explanatory sentence reading, "The symbol attached to the *dossal*, just above the *altar*, is a reproduction of a *monstrance* that is used in the Roman Church on certain occasions. The medallion originally came from a French ecclesiastical hanging of around the seventeenth century." A monstrance is the elaborately ornamented vessel in which the consecrated host is exposed to receive the veneration of the worshipers. The carelessness and thoughtlessness in the use of such non-Protestant objects and terms are ominous for the future of evangelical Christianity.

The mention of these matters may sound like trivialities. But in the long perspective they are of tremendous importance. The corruption of Christianity by the adoption of pagan terms and practices was almost imperceptible at first. But the use of those terms so familiarized the Christian mind with pagan ideas that their full acceptance followed in due time. This can happen again. There is no way whatever to assure that Protestantism will survive unless it keeps its terminology "pure," unless it indoctrinates its followers with terms that convey its distinctive beliefs instead of carelessly and loosely using terms that are associated with beliefs contrary to its nature. As was said in connection with the study of symbols, the evangelical minister is the guardian of the precious values of spiritual Christianity handed down from the long past. By what he does and says, by the contents he pours into worship forms and procedures, he is determining whether those values shall be transmitted properly to future generations. What Paul said to Timothy needs to be heeded by modern evangelical ministers: "O Timothy, guard that which is committed unto thee," which translated literally means, "Guard the deposit" (I Timothy 6:20).

F. Teaching Evangelical Christians to Worship

Once again we find ourselves facing the fact that teaching evangelical Christians to worship has a specific meaning. Primarily it is not instructing people in the etiquette of worship procedure. Liturgical manners have a function to perform. There are graceful, orderly, dignified ways of doing things in connection with worship. Lack of uniformity in movements often causes confusion. But the minister can easily guide a congregation in all the necessary movements by a few suggestions to the organist and choir and to a few persons properly coached and strategically

278

situated in the congregation. The mood of the leader himself, his demeanor throughout the service, his composure, his dignified movements and orderly procedures, and the manner in which he himself worships—genuinely worships and enters feelingly and worshipfully into the various parts of the service—largely set the tone for the congregation. But elaborate rules regarded as fixed and unalterable, considered the *sine qua non* of worship, may defeat the purpose of evangelical worship for both the minister and the people.

The danger of overemphasizing the importance of rules is that they will become a substitute for the real worship itself. Speaking of a particular period of history of Harvard University, Van Wyck Brooks once said, "Decorum was a Harvard characteristic. . . . In time, it even became, with Irving Babbitt, one of the many Harvard religions." [15] When the meticulous observance of liturgical procedures becomes the chief end and aim of worship, when the worship is thought of as consisting primarily of the performance of traditional movements, then in effect the rules are worshiped instead of God. They have become idols. Furthermore rigidly adhering to elaborate rules tends to make worship stiff, stilted, and mechanical. It squeezes out individuality, initiative, spontaneity, and adaptability. The values of rules of etiquette for evangelical worship then have distinct limitations. They are definitely secondary to the major purpose of that worship.

The main function of Protestant worship is to teach the worshipers how to find God, each for himself, within his own soul. People genuinely worship when they participate in the use of the elements of worship, when, so to speak, they get on the inside of what is going on, and when what is going on gets on the inside of them. They worship when God, as interpreted in evangelical Christianity, penetrates their minds and hearts, when they personally experience God's presence and the impact of his ethical personality and claims upon them. An old mystic used to say that God must put his face against the windowpane of our lives. That is the only way he can come alive to any man. There are no proxies for the soul. No individual can borrow or buy a spiritual experience from another. No person can lend or sell or give his own experience to someone else. Each must have his own experience of God at firsthand. The task of the leader of worship then is clear: it is to teach the people how to enter genuinely and personally into all the worship procedures and to

[15] *The Flowering of New England,* p. 35 and footnote.

keep the pathway to God cleared of all obstructions and diversions, so that so far as he can control the situation, everything will aid and nothing prevent every person from finding God meaningfully for himself.

G. Responsibility of Evangelical Minister

Frankly this lays a heavy responsibility upon the evangelical minister as the planner and the leader of worship services. But there is no way to escape it if evangelical worship is to fulfill its purposes. All phases of worship need to be done "with a great deal of holy skill," to use Richard Baxter's expression about preaching. Worship cannot be made nor kept evangelical unless the minister is willing to do his work with "holy skill." Here, as elsewhere in human life, skill depends upon self-discipline, hard work, continuous devotion to the task. The skill can become "holy" only as a result of a great deal of humility, of fellowship with God, of consecrated imagination, and of reliance upon the guidance of the Holy Spirit.

Let no one suppose that a book of printed, fixed formularies will obviate the necessity of the "holy skill" on the part of the individual minister. Speaking to a group of ministers of the Episcopal Church, to whom the *Book of Common Prayer* is available, John W. Suter, dean of the Washington Cathedral, pleaded with them not to use the prayer book as a "piece of literature," without imagination, as serving the purpose of "letting the minister off with the smallest effort possible." He exhorted them to "use liturgical skill" and "ministerial creativeness" in the building of a living worship for a living church—not merely to read the service out of the book, but to utilize the materials of that book as something out of which to shape a service that fits the needs of people in the practical human situation in which they live. He deplores the "laziness which obeys all the rules and evades the opportunity for stabbing the congregation awake by the sharply pointed pertinence of a prayer here or a clause there designed for the particular day." "The act of composing a service in particular for a given day and hour," he reminds them, "is one which may easily be neglected, slighted, bungled, or otherwise mishandled," and says that the failure to understand this has cost the church—his liturgical church—"much in both influence and membership." Somewhat by way of summary he says, "Indeed the secret of

280

liturgical practice lies in the ability to combine a substructure of regular repetitious inflexibility with a superstructure of flexible variation." [16]

To a great extent every evangelical book of common worship—even those intended to be fixed formularies—can be used wisely only as a guide. A book can never substitute for the over-all creative leadership of the individual minister. Upon him rests the responsibility for making evangelical worship a vital, living experience.

[16] Ferris, *op. cit.*, pp. 83-84, 98.

Part III

Conclusion

13

Worship and the Future of Evangelical Christianity

A. Backward Trend of Protestant Worship

T HE purposes of the liturgical movement have been to make the setting more conducive to worship, to make the worship procedures and practices more orderly and dignified, and to enrich the service with varied forms and symbols. That is, it has sought to restore some of the values discarded by the radical reformers. These purposes have been achieved satisfactorily. Houses of worship have become more beautiful and more worshipful. Orders of service have become better balanced, more orderly and more dignified, and have been enriched with many new forms. Everything pertaining to worship appears more "churchly" and is done in a more "churchly" manner than in previous generations. Those who have been in close touch with what has been going on in Protestant churches for the last quarter of a century or longer know these things to be true and rejoice that they are so. Furthermore during all these years the architectural arrangement of sanctuaries and the worship practices of Protestant denominations have been slowly approximating uniformity. So the average worshipers of one denomination now may attend the services of other denominations and feel almost, if not altogether, at home. Thus worship has been bringing the denominations nearer together and helping to create a more ecumenical Protestantism.

But there is another and darker side to the picture. The liturgical movement has brought about results not so desirable, results that one likes to think were neither foreseen nor intended. One wishes it could be said that Protestants, launching out on their basic principle of adaptation, have been making daring and courageous experiments in creating more meaningful, more relevant worship in accordance with their own peculiar evangelical beliefs. But this cannot be truthfully said of the liturgical movement as a whole, although here and there some successful experiments have been made in developing a new and distinctive evangelical worship. But speaking in general, Protestants have been busy reproducing medieval worship instead of producing a more significant worship on the basis of their own peculiar beliefs. Wittingly or unwittingly, Protestant worship has been facing backward instead of forward.

The evidence supporting this view has already been given in this study, but may be summarized briefly at this point. The Communion table has been transformed into an altar, and with it practices and ideas repudiated by the reformers have been restored. Altar guilds have been organized and are being given detailed instructions in the use of the various articles and terms that traditionally go with altars. Protestant churches are printing pamphlets to explain the architectural arrangement and furnishings of sanctuaries that are replete with such terms as reredos, altar hanging, dossal, retable, gradine, credence table, mensa, prie-dieu (prayer bench), ciborium, office lights, frontlet, frontal, superfrontal, pall, altar vases, altar candles, altar candelabra, and altar crosses. This is not enriching Protestant worship but returning it to medieval worship.

Now and then someone remarks about the "creeping" sacerdotalism in Protestant worship. It would be more appropriate to call it "sweeping" sacerdotalism. The altar is elevated high above the nave and the pulpit, and the area in which it is placed is separated sharply from the other parts of the sanctuary and treated as a holy place to be entered only by the minister when performing his priestly functions. Sacrificial and sacerdotal ideas and terms are coming back into usage. Ministers are donning vestments ornamented with symbols and insignia like those traditionally worn by priests. The medieval sacramental system is gradually being revived. The sacrament of the Lord's Supper occupies the central place in worship, above the other functions of the minister. The terms "priest" and "priestly" are now almost as frequently used as the term "minister." This is not an extension of Protestant worship, but a return to a set of ideas discarded early in the history of Protestantism.

Medieval symbolism in all its forms and in great profusion is being utilized in Protestant sanctuaries. A well-known Protestant church has printed a pamphlet explaining the symbolism of the sanctuary, which reveals that practically every symbol known to have been used by the medieval Church has been incorporated somewhere in the building. So far as can be ascertained from the printed description, an aggregate of 150 to 175 symbols have been used in this single sanctuary. Monograms, coats of arms, inscriptions, crosses, and objects of various kinds may be seen in the floors, ceilings, walls, windows, ornamental hangings, and light fixtures, and are carved on the furniture and woodwork, some of them recurring as many as five or six times in different places. Allegorical meanings of numbers from one to eight are utilized in various ways. There are more than ten different forms of the cross. There are several large flags elaborately decorated with the same symbols found elsewhere and with metaphorical meanings that require a number of pages to explain. In the windows there are a score or more of human figures, some of them life-sized; ten or more saints, biblical and secular; many biblical scenes depicted in great detail with scores of objects in them. This over-crowding of the sanctuary with medieval symbols is typical of many Protestant churches that have been constructed in recent years. It is beginning to approach the excessive decoration of places of worship which was the custom in medieval times.

The pulpit has been subordinated to the table, and preaching has become of secondary importance in many churches. Preaching is not only disparaged, minimized, and neglected, but actually despised, by some. A ministerial candidate is reported to have said, "I consider preaching as a necessary evil. I shall do as much of it as my position demands in order to qualify for the other more important tasks on which my heart is set. But I could well wish to avoid preaching almost entirely." [1] It would be tragic if this attitude were to become typical of any great number of Protestant ministerial students. The number of theological students preparing for the preaching ministry is slowly decreasing, and some are actually rebelling at the necessity of having to learn a discipline they neither hope to use nor think worth using in the Protestant ministry. Many older ministers reflect the same feeling in both public and private utterances and openly show their distaste of what they consider the irk-

[1] Quoted by Miller, "Words or a Deed," in *Interpretation*, April, 1952.

some and unnecessary task of preparing and delivering sermons. This parallels the manner in which preaching fell into complete disfavor and disuse in the medieval Church.

Orders of service are being elaborated and lengthened by the excessive use of versicles, responses, and prayers of all types, so that modern orders of service are gradually approaching in length and complexity those of medieval times. Just as some Protestant churches have undertaken to utilize in a single sanctuary every known medieval symbol, others seem to feel the urge to utilize in a single service every known medieval variable. The use of Latin terms in worship is increasing so rapidly that ere long a glossary will be needed to define them for the average worshiper. Medieval music, with theological content contrary to Protestant doctrines, is growing in popularity. In the last fifty years books of forms have appeared, officially or unofficially, in practically every sizable Protestant denomination in the English-speaking world; and in some of the denominations the ministers are required to use them as fixed forms. The church year has come back into usage in some denominations, together with the lectionary, the seasons, fixed festivals and movable festivals, and liturgical colors for the same, paralleling those of the medieval Church which were so largely discarded by the Reformers.

The liturgical movement is not leading Protestants out into new areas, putting Protestant principles to work in the improvement of worship, adapting worship to the needs of modern folk, so much as it is bypassing the Reformation and endeavoring to restore Christian worship to its ancient priestly type. The determining factor in the choice of most of the materials used in Protestant worship is whether or not they are ancient, not whether or not they best fit the nature of evangelical Christianity or whether they are calculated to perpetuate that Christianity. In short, the liturgical movement has started Protestant worship on the road back to medievalism.

B. SOME EXPLANATIONS FOR TREND

The explanations and justifications offered for these practices and procedures are even more disheartening than the facts themselves. For one thing it is claimed that the Protestant Reformation, like all spiritual reformations in religion, has spent its force. Thus far in the history of prophetic religion reformations in worship have not succeeded in holding gains made. We traced the course of the successive prophetic reformations of the Old Testament times and found that their results, so far as worship was concerned, were not permanent. After every reform movement, regardless of its purposes and force, the priestly system of the Temple remained intact, in fact emerged stronger as the result of what might loosely be called a counter reformation. Jesus and the Christian movement he inaugurated finally developed for his prophetic religion a worship system completely detached from the sacrificial system of the Temple and that was congruous with its nature and its needs. Yet within a few centuries—probably as few as two and no more than four—thereafter Christian worship had become a semipriestly system which was incompatible in many respects with its original principles and beliefs. For a thousand years the Christian cultus was more like the ancient priestly system of the Hebrews than like New Testament worship. In time the abuses and corruptions of that system became so glaring that a reformation became necessary to put Christian worship back on its original course. It can be said that in spite of all their limitations, failures, and faults the leaders of the Protestant Reformation did succeed to a large degree in their efforts to accomplish this. So it may be legitimately claimed that Protestantism became the successor of New Testament Christianity. More than four hundred years have passed since the beginning of the Reformation, and all the signs point to the fact that once more Christian worship is rapidly being transformed into a priestly cultus.

Thus as history goes, reformations in worship are short-lived. The prophets provoke them, and then inevitably by a natural process in the history of man's upward climb the priests take over again. That process is said to result from the weakness of human nature, the weakness of prophetic religion, and the perennial appeal of priestly religion. One generation is unmoved by the high ideals of previous generations or lacks appreciation of their significance, so what once were noble aspirations are ignored, neglected, forgotten, and simply die for lack of support. Or it is said, prophetic religion lacks sustaining power over the hearts of men. The enthusiasm and zeal engendered cool perceptibly in transmission from generation to generation, slowly subside, and then stagnate. Or again, it is claimed that prophetic religion is psychologically incomplete. The high purposes of reformers are to high, too severe, too puritanic, too extreme. The people crave and require what priestly religion offers. That religion contains an authentic spiritual need. Hence for one

289

reason or another worship sooner or later reverts again to some form of priestcraft. It appears impossible to keep the two types in perfect balance. A few centuries pass during which weaknesses appear or abuses develop necessitating another reformation. So one gives way to the other in recurring cycles. Thus the cyclic, or rhythmical, alternation of prophetic and priestly worship have followed one another in as yet an unbroken series. According to this theory Protestant worship is now taking its inevitable backward swing. The prophetic movement we call the Reformation has spent its force, and we are now at another turning point in the history of Christianity when the prophet must again give way to the priest.

This somewhat pessimistic outlook shall be referred to again later. Suffice it to say here that the facts do not warrant such a semifatalistic view of Protestantism or of history. No inexorable law is at work in history making it inevitable that the door be closed on evangelical worship.

Another explanation of the backward swing is that hinted at immediately above, namely, that human nature is unable to bear the responsibilities of a purely moral and spiritual worship. It is too high and too exacting for the great masses of the people. This was why the prophetic movements of the Old Testament failed to wean the people away from the Temple system. It also explains why Christianity ultimately developed a priestly type of worship and why Protestantism now is so fast adopting the forms, practices, and concepts of priestly worship.

Paul Tillich presents this thesis in his book *The Protestant Era*. One who reads his books must constantly remind himself that though Tillich openly professes Protestantism, he is actually Roman Catholic in much of his basic thinking. For this reason it is often very difficult to follow the thread of his arguments. In this instance his argument starts with the position that the "traditional form of the Protestant attitude cannot outlast the period of mass disintegration" which is the prevailing mood of our era. Disintegrated masses "do not want to decide things for themselves. . . . They are longing for a leader, for symbols, for ideas which would be beyond all criticism." They crave bishops, priests, and monarchs with a "sacramental authority which cannot be taken away by arguments and which is independent of the intellectual and moral qualities of its carriers. . . . Masses that are disintegrated need symbols that are immediately understandable without the mediation of intellect. They need sacred objectivities beyond the subjective quality of a preacher." Since "very few such objectivities remain in the Protestant churches," since Protestant education has "dissolved the religious mystery more and more," and as a result "more and more individuals became unable to endure the tremendous responsibility of permanently having to decide in intellectual and moral issues, . . . Protestantism as a church for the masses can continue to exist only if it succeeds in undergoing a fundamental change." That is, it must find its own way of using symbols and all those things called "sacred objectivities," as does the Roman Catholic Church, if it is to survive in this era.[2]

Let the reader ponder over that a moment and then ask himself where such a position leads to. If the common people must worship "without the mediation of intellect," we are already well on our way back to paganism. If ordinary folk are not capable of assuming the responsibility of thinking things through for themselves, exercising their moral judgment and making decisions of their own in worship, then they are not capable of doing so in government and democracy must give way to some form of dictatorship. Are we to conclude that God's effort to develop mature, responsible personalities is doomed to failure? If so, Protestantism might as well proceed at once to return to the Roman Catholic Church and submit to the pope.

No one has seen this more clearly and stated it more dramatically and forcefully than Fyodor Dostoevsky in his notable story of "The Grand Inquisitor." He imagines Jesus returning to earth and pictures him surrounded by the people before the great cathedral at Seville. There he is found by the Grand Inquisitor, the head of the Inquisition, who orders Jesus arrested and thrown in prison. That night he visits Jesus in his cell and says:

Thou hast no right to add anything to what Thou hadst said of old. . . All has been given by Thee to the Pope, and all, therefore, is still in the Pope's hands, and there is no need for Thee to come now at all. . . . Instead of taking possession of men's freedom, Thou didst increase it, and burdened the spiritual kingdom of mankind with its sufferings forever. Thou didst desire man's free love, that he should follow Thee freely, enticed and taken captive by Thee. In place of rigid ancient law, man must hereafter with free heart decide for himself what is good and what is evil, having only Thy image before him as his guide. . . For fifteen centuries we have been wrestling

[2] Ch. xv, pp. 222-33.

with Thy freedom. . . Man is weighted down with the fearful burden of free choice. . . He is tormented by no greater anxiety than to find someone to whom he can hand over his gift of freedom. . . Men have brought their freedom to us and laid it at our feet. . . We are ready to endure the freedom which they have found so dreadful and to rule over them. . . We . . . persuade them that they will only become free when they renounce their freedom and submit to us. . . They . . . submit to us gladly and cheerfully. The most painful secrets of their conscience all, all they will bring to us and we . . . have an answer for all. They . . . are glad to believe our answer, for it . . . saves them the great anxiety and terrible agony they endure at present in making a free decision for themselves. . . Tomorrow Thou shalt see that obedient flock who at a sign from me will hasten to heap up the hot cinders about the pile on which I shall burn Thee for coming to hinder us. [He waited for Jesus to speak. But Jesus said not a word.] Then suddenly He approached the old man in silence and softly kissed him on his bloodless aged lips. That was all His answer. The old man shuddered. His lips moved. He went to the door, opened it, and said to Him: "Go, and come no more . . . . come not at all, never, never!" And he let Him out into the dark alleys of the town. The Prisoner went away.[3]

In effect, and this the novelist saw clearly, when men admit they are "unable to endure the tremendous responsibility of permanently having to decide in intellectual and moral issues," they are saying to Christ, "Go, and come no more." When men refuse to carry the responsibility of free worship, when they try to worship "without the mediation of intellect," they reject Christ and surrender the freedom he brought to them as their divine right.

Still another explanation is that just as free worship is too high for the people, so it places upon the Protestant minister a responsibility no individual can be expected to carry. "Admittedly," says Devan, "the 'free' service puts a tax on the minister that no man can adequately bear. Perhaps it is for this very reason that the vast majority of Christians throughout history have so willingly accepted the use of liturgy in worship leaving the individuality of the minister to appear in his preaching and his pastoral care and other forms of leadership." [4] So a book of forms is provided for the minister as a sort of liturgical crutch to lean on. It is far better, so the argument runs, to have printed prayers than carelessly worded extemporaneous prayers. The average minister cannot be ex-

---

[3] Condensed from *The Brothers Karamazov*, Bk. V, ch. v, "The Grand Inquisitor."

[4] *Op. cit.*, p. 93. Used by permission of Mrs. Winifrede R. Devan.

pected to plan an order of service free from his own caprices or to choose, or mayhap compose, other worship forms without expressing his individual prejudices or perhaps "riding his own pet hobby." So his work is done for him and placed in his hands in book form. This makes for dignity and uniformity and guards against careless informality itself becoming a fixed form.

Every minister who has had to carry the responsibility of worship for a period of years appreciates the force of these arguments and understands the risk and pitfalls of "free" worship. But he also realizes the temptations and dangers to his own soul, to the quality of his public ministry as a leader of worship, and to the contemporaneousness of the worship itself, involved in fixed liturgies and forms. And it should be said quite frankly that there is no reason whatever for entrusting preaching, pastoral care, and other forms of leadership to Protestant ministers who cannot be entrusted with worship. It is no more difficult to become an expert in leading Protestants in worship than to become an expert in other Protestant ministerial functions. If Protestant ministers are not qualified to be ministers in the full Protestant sense or are unwilling to qualify themselves by proper training and discipline, then Protestantism might as well be abandoned for a form of religion that is easier and less exacting.

C. What Can Be Done About It?

What can be done about the situation depends primarily upon whether evangelical Christians wish to do something about it. The worst thing that can be done is to sit idly by while events take their course. God's rulership over the affairs of men is predicated upon their active, instead of their passive, participation in the history of which they are a part. If they desire to do something about it, the first important step is to look the facts squarely in the face. Someone reading of the death of Stephen in the book of Acts and noting that it resulted from telling his hearers the truth wrote on the margin of an old manuscript, "For they could not look the truth in the eye." Can modern Christians look squarely in the eye the truth about what is happening to worship? If they can and will do so, one of the first things that will confront them is the necessity of making up their minds what kind of worship they really want and what direction they want it to take. We are deceiving ourselves if we think a perfect balance can be maintained between formal and free worship.

Worship is always more of one than of the other type and must be designedly so. A choice must be made where the emphasis is to be laid, and that choice determines whether the worship is to be predominantly one type or the other. If Christians intend that worship shall be spiritual, they must exercise a good deal of active control over it to make sure it will move in that direction. If they are willing to take these fundamental attitudes toward the present situation, they can then go on to do a great deal about it.

First, they can set to work to make and keep worship evangelical. If Christians embark upon the determination to make and keep worship evangelical, they will need on the one hand to eliminate some things and on the other to embody certain other things. That is, the task will require at the same time both a negative and a positive procedure. Both procedures have been dealt with in detail in the course of this study and now need only be listed with brief comments by way of summary.

1. With the same courage and determination manifested by the early reformers, modern Protestants should eliminate altars from their worship and also all the ideas, objects, and practices associated with altars.

2. They should eliminate from their interpretation of the Lord's Supper all suggestions that it is a propitiatory sacrifice; all ideas of magic, of superstition, and of the semiphysical presence of Christ; and all conceptions bordering on sacerdotalism. Likewise they should make it and keep it what it was in the New Testament times and what the reformers made it—a fellowship of believers.

3. With courage and the exercise of much restraint they should reduce the visible symbols in their places of worship to a reasonable number, and these should be chosen because of their ability to convey distinctive evangelical doctrines.

4. They should rigidly adhere to the use of terms and procedures that are in harmony with their basic beliefs. This means expurgating from their worship vocabulary all words and expressions that convey medieval theology which Protestants no longer accept.

5. Discriminating thought should be given to building houses of worship specifically for evangelical worship. There is no reason why houses of worship should not at the same time be worshipful and harmonize with evangelical beliefs. Such houses need not be barren, cold, severe, and unartistic if they are properly planned by building committees who are exercising adequately the functions of their office.

294

6. Similarly much thought should be given to constructing evangelical orders of worship. Free worship does not necessarily imply disorderly worship or worship detached from the traditions and forms of the past. Such worship should and can fulfill all the psychological needs of common worship and do so in a decent and orderly manner.

7. Above everything else let attention be centered upon something spiritually significant happening in the souls of the worshipers. The chief weakness of Protestant worship in recent decades has been at this point. Because nothing vital and meaningful has occurred within their hearts, people have longingly looked to outward symbols for the satisfactions they are missing. If the sermon is of the right quality, if evangelical fervor pervades the whole service, if consciences are stirred, if wills are provoked to action, if worshipers find forgiveness for their sins and food for the manifold needs of the inner man, and if they are vividly aware of the presence and power of the Spirit of God in their hearts, they will be satisfied and will come again and again without having either the desire or the need to overcrowd their worship with sensible forms.

Second, modern Protestants can be depended upon to be evangelical if they are given the proper worship leadership. It is seriously to be questioned whether the common people in any age have ever deliberately demanded a priestly system of worship on the ground that spiritual religion was too high for them. That worship has been foisted upon them by their leaders whose faith was bankrupt. The ancient prophets took the priests and the false prophets to task for misleading the people. Jesus chastised the leaders of religion for laying "heavy burdens and grievous to be borne" on the shoulders of the people, for blindly leading the people astray (Matt. 23:4 ff.). The liturgical movement of our day is not a "grass-roots" movement. Generally speaking and except in periods when the people resort to revolutionary methods to right abuses imposed upon them for centuries by their leaders, the masses of the people accept the type of worship devised for them by their leaders. They expect those leaders to be experts, follow them with implicit confidence, and are not aware until generations pass that they have been misled. It is an escape mechanism as old as the days of Aaron, when leaders who themselves are responsible for the pagan worship of the people plead, when faced with it, "The people demanded it." Let the leaders really lead the people! If common people are indoctrined, trained, trusted, and given the right examples, they will not forsake their faith no matter how exacting it is.

295

To believe otherwise is to distrust their educability and to negate God's effort, culminating in the gospel of Jesus, to bring the race to spiritual maturity and to develop his children into responsible persons.

It is to be remembered that the common people heard Jesus gladly and followed him in great multitudes because he spoke to them in their own language and made religion easily comprehensible and practicable. It was the common people who organized themselves into antisacerdotal, lay-led groups who became the "evangelical undertow" that prepared the way for the Protestant Reformation. Numerous cults now exist in our generation, most of which separated from a Protestantism whose worship had become unsatisfactory. They are finding in the simple, free, spontaneous worship of their own groups what they failed to find in the denomination from which they separated. Their number will increase, and in future years they may well become the evangelical, antisacerdotal, lay-led groups who will prepare the way for another reformation to restore Christian worship to its original simplicity—unless Protestants become aware of the direction in which their worship is moving. Marcus Bach, who has made a study of many of these groups, warns Protestants that their rise in such large numbers and the satisfactions the people find in them mean something important—even ominous—for Protestants. He tells of a Catholic priest who said to a Protestant minister that "he was glad that Protestantism is coming back to an emphasis on the liturgy, 'It will be just so much easier when we take over.' " [5] The ordinary folk want simple, direct worship, not a complex, intricate system of priestly worship which does not fit their needs. And they have a right to it.

Let us grant for the moment, however, that the common people are not even yet—after some two thousand years of Christian history—fitted to bear the responsibilities of "free" worship. That does not justify the abandonment of that worship for a worship less in harmony with the principles of our evangelical Christianity. In the early days when our forefathers were striving diligently to establish a government of and for and by free people, many distrusted the common people and said they were not capable of governing themselves. To this Thomas Jefferson replied, "I know of no safe depository of the ultimate powers of society but the people themselves; and if we think them not enlightened enough

[5] Report to Protestants, p. 233.

to exercise their control with wholesome discretion, the remedy is not to take it from them but to inform their discretion by education." If people are too immature psychologically or mentally for high religion, the remedy is not to take it from them but to fit them to become mature enough to carry its responsibilities. H. A. Overstreet says that if a culture is what it ought to be, it will be "conducive to . . . [the] psychological growth" of the people who live in it. If it is authoritarian, if it does the thinking for the people, it will set a "premium on the prolongation of immaturity," invite the individual "to remain immature," and offer him rewards "to perpetuate his psychological childhood." [6] Protestantism puts a premium on individual initiative and responsibility. By its very nature it is obligated to maintain a worship culture designed to stimulate worshipers to think and act for themselves, a culture that is conducive to their growth toward mature Christians.

Third, ministers can be evangelical ministers. The preference shown by some Protestant leaders for priestly worship and the lack of discriminating thinking involved in the reasons given for that preference are painfully disturbing. For example, Protestant worship is severely criticised for its emotionalism, but the emotionalism of priestly worship goes unnoticed. The problem of emotion is not obviated by the simple procedure of exchanging Protestant worship for priestly worship. In the former, emotions are attached to singing and preaching; in the latter, they are attached to color, to rituals, to holy objects, to movements of the priest while he is performing a miracle at the altar. In the one case the emotions may be attached to a preacher and in the other case to a priest, but in both cases they are attached to a mere man. Emotions are always dangerous; they run the risk of getting out of control and leading to fanatical excesses in both types of worship. They cannot be eliminated from worship. But they can be attached to the right things, directed to socially desirable ends, and put under the control of informed minds and disciplined wills.

Again, priestly worship is praised as being more satisfactory, as having more power to attract and hold the people, than Protestant worship. Crowds of people in attendance at Roman Catholic Mass are cited as proof of this. Specifically it is stated that Roman Catholic churches attract the attendance of people because they are so beautiful. People do not attend Roman Catholic services because of the beauty of the sanc-

---

[6] *The Mature Mind,* pp. 119-21.

tuary but because they believe that in the dramatic miracle of the Mass Christ becomes visibly, physically, and locally present. They build expensive and highly decorated sanctuaries and utilize all the skills and refinements of liturgical art, not primarily to attract worshipers but to make a beautiful and worthy dwelling place for the physically present Christ. Roman Catholics go to their churches alone not to meditate and pray as Protestants do, but to pray *in the presence of the host,* the body of Christ, on the altar. Prayers offered there are more meritorious and give them added claim for themselves and their loved ones upon the Treasury of Merit in heaven controlled by the priests.[7]

Anyone who presumes to judge the power of the Mass by the number of people who attend it is viewing it superficially. The power of Roman Catholic worship is not in the worship as such but in the whole theological structure of Romanism surrounding it. Attendance at Mass is required and secured by priests who claim authority to control the affairs of people and of their loved ones in this world and their destinies in the next. The priest at the altar claims the power not only to perform a miracle and dispense the grace resulting from it, but to forgive sins or withhold that forgiveness, to release from purgatory and save from hell, in Christ's name to speak authoritatively on matters of faith and morals, and to control an infinite Treasury of Merit accumulated in heaven. It is a combination of fear, of blind acceptance of infallible truth and authority, and of whatever personal satisfactions of security and assurance result from everything associated with the whole Roman Catholic system in the minds of the worshipers that gives that worship power over the faithful. To suppose its power can be secured or produced without accepting the theology that surrounds it is gratuitous thinking. Attendance at Protestant worship is purely voluntary. Its power depends not upon what happens on an altar, nor upon the authority over the worshiper and his loved ones possessed by the minister, but upon what happens to him inside. But when that happens, it is of great significance; and where it happens regularly to worshipers, there they will be found in large numbers.

Still again, those ministers who convince themselves that a revival of liturgical worship will put new life into the Protestant churches are

---

[7] John F. Sullivan, *The Externals of the Catholic Church,* pp. 377 ff. for an official description of this treasury and pp. 259 ff. for the special indulgences gained by "those who piously recite a third part of the rosary in the presence of the Blessed Sacrament publicly exposed or even reserved in the tabernacle

surely engaging in wishful thinking. When and where in history has Christianity been spiritually revived by more formal worship? The reverse has rather been the case: increased emphasis upon formality in worship has in time made spiritual revivals necessary. The revival of liturgical worship has followed, but never produced, spiritual revivals. The very appearance of increased interest in formal worship is often an indication that spiritual religion is on the wane. Spiritual revivals have been singularly indifferent to formal worship, places of worship, and the like. They have frequently taken place out in the open, wholly apart from all organized religion. If the Protestant churches are revived, it will be because of a resurgence of the fervor, passion, and spontaneous spiritual life, accompanied and partially produced by prophetic preaching, which characterized evangelical Christianity in New Testament times. Protestants had better view Christianity with a long-range perspective and listen to what the centuries have to say to the years.

When one observes the excessive zeal of many Protestant ministers for priestly worship, it is difficult to escape the feeling that this is a form of compensation for a deep-seated prejudice against the faith they profess or for the loss of enthusiasm for that faith. Many ministers have surrendered some of the basic doctrines of their faith. They have lost their evangelical fervor. They have no feeling of urgency about securing conversions. They distrust the emotionalism of even the sanest form of evangelism. They have no significant preaching ministry and consider preaching of secondary importance. They dislike both pastoral and administrative responsibilities. So they succumb to the allurements of decorated vestments, insignia, ritualism, symbolism, pomp and display, dramatic action, and other features of priestly worship. The fascination they find there becomes a form of compensatory psychological satisfaction for the loss of evangelical passion elsewhere. In short, they give the impression of being "tired evangelicals." Having grown weary with the known weakness of their own ministry, they turn to the imagined strength of priestcraft. Having grown discouraged with small returns from their own labors, they adopt what they suppose will promise larger and quicker returns. It is similar to what happens when people become disheartened with the results of democracy and embrace the communistic creed, imagining it contains no weaknesses but only promise of sure results. They take the easy way out. They are unwilling to pay the price of freedom. Wherever ministers have a significant evangelical ministry as leaders of worship, people come in great numbers and keep on coming because they find nourishment for their souls. Let evangelical ministers be evangelical!

D. Conclusion

Once more evangelical Christianity has come to a turning point in its history. The decision as to the direction it will go in the next few centuries rests with its guardians. That direction will be determined chiefly by the type of cultus maintained. The system of worship is the major factor in stamping the character and shaping the form of that Christianity. It is the main medium for inculcating and the principal instrument for transmitting that faith. If people are to become and remain evangelical Christians, they must live and move and have their being in a religious milieu saturated with the tenets of their faith. The spiritual atmosphere they breathe must be permeated with its spirit. They must never be allowed to forget its principles. They must be indoctrinated with its traditions. The surroundings, materials, and procedures of worship must embody and proclaim, yea, radiate its beliefs. Week by week through the worship services presided over by its ministers Protestantism must hand down the great tradition it has received from the past. Evangelical Christianity does not belong to this generation to do with as it pleases; it was purchased for all humanity at a price—a heavy price to God and to many generations of faithful souls who were determined that free religion should not perish from the earth. Protestantism is the custodian of evangelical Christianity, and by virtue of their responsibilities, primarily as leaders of worship, its ministers are its chief stewards.

No inexorable law of necessity is at work transforming Protestant worship again into a priestly cultus, but it will be so transformed unless its ministers are willing to pay the price of the leadership entrusted to them. If they lose confidence in the importance and significance of their faith and in the ability of men, redeemed by the grace of God, to live by it; if they give up because going is hard and retreat because the odds are against them and the results scant; if they submit fatalistically and pessimistically to what appears to be the end of a cycle, then Protestantism will revert to some form of priestly paganism. And some day many years hence another costly, agonizing reformation will be necessary to restore it once again to its original course.

The possibilities of the present situation are doubly significant because when Protestantism goes into eclipse, the Western, democratic culture closely associated with it and for which it is partly, if not largely, responsible will also go into eclipse; and the political and social gains of many centuries will be lost for generations to come. To contribute to such a backward movement by indifference, inertia, discouragement, loose and careless thinking, or lack of vigilance is to betray a great trust and to fail God.

"It is required of stewards that they be found trustworthy." (I Cor. 4:2 R.S.V.)

INDEX

Absolution
  in reformers, 141
  John Wesley's prayer of, 151
  nonevangelical, 277
  opposed by Puritans, 136
Academic hood in worship, 239-40
Accomplishments of liturgical revival, 285
Acoustics in worship, 229
Act of Supremacy, 133
Action in worship
  in Lord's Supper, 212
  overdone, 274
  possibly the only historical standard for worship, 161-62
  pre-Reformation Church, 108-9
  sacramental, 193-96
  in service, 233
Adaptation, a principle of Protestantism, 147, 264
Adoration, prayer of, 244-45
Advantages of table-centered sanctuary, 227
Agape
  in the days of Pliny, 88
  in New Testament worship, 78-80, 84
Agnus Dei, 134, 200
Albigenses, 120
Alexandria, rites of, 99
Allegory in worship, 109, 110, 117, 223
Alleluia, 107
Altar
  abolished by reformers, 142
  discarded by New Testament Church, 67
  and evangelical worship, 229-30
  incongruous with evangelical worship, 277, 294
  in modern Roman Catholic arrangement, 231
  restored in liturgical revival, 157, 286
  restored in medieval Church, 105, 110
Altar cloth, 233
Altar guilds, 157, 158, 233, 286
Alternation in worship, 273-74

Amalarius of Metz, 109
Ambo (pulpit), 103
Amen, peoples'
  in modern worship, 236
  in New Testament worship, 73, 74
  in second century A.D., 89
Amice, 117
Amos, 19, 20
Anabaptists, 137, 154
Anamnesis, 106, 132, 159, 205
Anaphora, 92
Announcements, 261-62
Ante-Communion service, 134, 139, 141
Antioch, rites of, 98
Antisacerdotal sects, 120
Apocrypha, lections from, 131
Apologists, the, 94
Apostles' Creed, 261
Apostolic Constitutions, 99-100
Apostolic Tradition, 90
Appeal of Roman Catholic worship, 297-98
Appeal of symbolism, 219-20, 237
Appreciation range in worship music, 254
Apse, 103, 113, 226, 229
Architects and arrangement of sanctuary, 231
Architectural arrangement of sanctuary, 224-32
Aristotle, 222
Arrow prayers, 246
Art
  in churches of U.S.A., 155
  in early worship, 102
  in evangelical worship, 234
  in liturgical revival, 157
Articles of Religion, Anglican
  body of Christ, 189-90
  definition of true church, 207
  objective sacrifice, 200
Articles used in early worship, 103
Augustine, 92, 143, 200
Auricular confession, 136, 137, 141

303

316

318